# The Turk
# Who Loved Apples

∾

And Other Tales of
Losing My Way Around the World

## Matt Gross

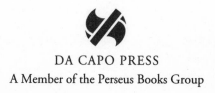

DA CAPO PRESS
A Member of the Perseus Books Group

Designed by Cynthia Young

Library of Congress Cataloging-in-Publication Data
Gross, Matt.
   The Turk who loved apples : and other tales of losing my way
around the world / Matt Gross.
      p. cm.
   Includes index.
   ISBN 978-0-306-82115-8 (pbk.) — ISBN 978-0-306-82202-5 (e-book)
   1. Travel writing.   2. Voyages and travels.   I. Title.
G151.G77 2013
910.4—dc23

                                  2012047129

Published by Da Capo Press
A Member of the Perseus Books Group
www.dacapopress.com

Da Capo Press books are available at special discounts for bulk purchases in the U.S. by corporations, institutions, and other organizations. For more information, please contact the Special Markets Department at the Perseus Books Group, 2300 Chestnut Street, Suite 200, Philadelphia, PA 19103, or call (800) 810-4145, ext. 5000, or e-mail special.markets@perseusbooks.com.

10 9 8 7 6 5 4 3 2 1

*For Jean,*
*who has been patient*

# Contents

~

# Acknowledgments

This book took a while to come together, and it wouldn't have happened without the efforts of a number of people whose support and enthusiasm continue to surprise me. My editors at the *New York Times*—Stuart, Mary, Denny, Danielle, Suzanne, Laura, and Dan, among many others—gave me unimaginable freedom to travel the world and write about what I discovered. Other editors—Jim and Dana at *Saveur*, Jen and Julia at *Afar*—likewise listened to my ideas and, astoundingly, allowed me to pursue my obsessions wherever they took me. Together, the assignments they gave me produced most of the raw material of this narrative.

Shaping that material into an actual book was a process that began with my agent, Nat Jacks at Inkwell Management, and evolved over many discussions (and drinks) with my friends and fellow travelers Mary Ellen Hitt, Justin Barrera, and Peter Jon Lindberg. When the proposal reached Da Capo Press, Jonathan Crowe and John Radziewicz were not only excited about its prospects but, after they'd acquired it, both encouraging and demanding throughout the editing process. Insightful notes from my friends Mai Hoang and Jeff Booth also helped the manuscript evolve into its final form.

Throughout the years, I've also been able to rely on many friends, both at home and abroad: Duj, Andrew, Nader, Jaipal, Ian, Park,

Wah-Ming, Christine, Seth, Other Seth, Farley, Ted, Nathan, Bonanos, Vincent, Andy, Todd, Tessa, Justin, Yotam, Horia, Lauren, Ben, Greg, Bradley, Julia, Egil, Erik, Hanh, Tuyen, Chris and Kenny, Kirk, Robert, Vince, Bonnie, Niki, Regis, Patricia, Miss Thanh, Dylan, Howard, and X-Quang, to name just a few. Thanks for putting up with me when I was around and not resenting me when I vanished into overseas silence for months (or years) at a stretch.

My family, obviously, gets a lot of credit for molding me as a traveler and for giving me a reason—several reasons, in fact—to keep coming home. And I must also paraphrase my father: my daughters, Sasha and Sandy, did nothing to aid the writing of this book; in fact, they delayed its completion. But it was for them that I wrote it in the first place.

Finally, I need to thank all of the strangers who, despite not knowing me from Adam, offered help and the hand of friendship when I needed them most. You give me, and everyone, a reason to keep exploring.

~

# Introduction

In early 2005, after I'd finished an assignment for the *New York Times* in northern Thailand, I took a weekend trip to Myanmar. Myanmar, or Burma, as it's also known, was under exceedingly tight military rule back then, but Americans could, for reasons I didn't try to understand, cross the border without a prearranged visa, provided they stayed less than fourteen days and did not travel beyond eastern Shan State. Since I had just a couple of days free, and wanted only to see the unusual and fascinating hill tribes of the Golden Triangle, the famously lawless opium-and-gun-smuggling region, these were not onerous restrictions.

My friend Bonnie Yoon, a graphic designer who was visiting me from Los Angeles, and I arrived at the border post of Mae Sai just before 4 p.m. and began the process of changing countries. The Thai border guards stamped our passports good-bye with little ado, and we crossed a small bridge over a river and into Myanmar. At the entry point, an immigration officer, a polite young Burmese woman whose cheeks were dusted with yellow sunblocking powder made from the *thanaka* root, approached us and offered to help us through the process. First, she led us to a photo booth, where we paid several dollars to have our pictures taken. Then she brought us to an immigration kiosk, where another officer, a broad man in a pressed white shirt and embroidered sarong, handed us visa applications and the woman glued our pictures into what she described as "internal travel documents"—single sheets of rough purple construction paper, printed with a form in Burmese and folded in half, like a first-grader's art project. These we'd use in place of our own U.S. passports, which, she informed us, the authorities would gladly hold for us here at the border until we returned.

"Is that okay?" she asked expectantly.

Bonnie and I looked at each other. Leaving our passports here did not seem like the wisest course of action, particularly in a country where journalists, foreigners as well as locals, were commonly arrested, deported, or worse. On the entry application, I'd written "video game consultant" as my occupation, and while I didn't expect we'd get busted, keeping at least some official identification on my person seemed like a good idea, just in case.

"Actually," I told the woman, "I think we'd like to keep our passports with us, if that's okay with you. We'd feel safer that way."

"Oh, no," she said, "that's not possible." She shook her head, looking down and smiling apologetically. Then she looked back up. "Is that okay?"

It was, we decided, okay. Was the Burmese *government* really going to steal *our* passports? We accepted our purple travel documents and entered Myanmar.

The difference between the two countries was instantly obvious. The Thai side of the border had hummed with energy and commerce, the signs electrified, the automobiles new and shiny, the streets well-paved. Here, in the town of Tachileik, it was as if we'd stepped back in time a couple of decades. The concrete was cracking, and the light-bulbs were feeble. Frankenstein cars, assembled from whatever parts were available, rumbled slowly down the streets. The only common-ality between the two sides was the goods we saw for sale in markets or being loaded onto trucks: international-brand shampoos, diapers, soaps, melamine dishes, bottles of Johnny Walker Black and Red, acrylic blankets, and rice cookers. This was a border post, and goods passed through as often as people.

The gates of the town, we were told, were about to close, and we wouldn't have time to travel onward until the morning, so Bonnie and I found a hotel for the night and set out to explore Tachileik. Tachileik turned out to be a very small town. A few old brick buildings in disrepair offered hints of the British colonial era, but architecturally Tachileik was dumpy—all concrete structures assembled without regard to aesthetics, as if everyone had arrived in a hurry and with little intention of sticking around. And why would they? It was a border town; it existed only because the border existed, and the diplomatic machinery of the border required certain support services: mechanics, food vendors, a market, hotels, a Buddhist temple or two, and somewhere to drink and sing karaoke.

Just after 6 p.m., night began to fall, as it does at virtually the same time every day in the tropics, and in the dark Bonnie and I began hunting around for somewhere to eat. On a street whose overgrown empty lots hinted at the wilderness that lay just outside the limits of town, we spotted a couple of bars, open-air platforms whose low tables were forested with tall glass bottles of Myanmar Beer. We hustled over and ordered two bottles, along with a tomato salad, its bright red slices scattered with fried shallots and briny dried shrimp. As we clinked glasses and started planning the next day, we noticed a man sitting at another table. He was tall and thin and dark-skinned, with a long straight nose, and his posture, his demeanor, and his outfit—loose white tracksuit, white baseball cap—made him look out of place among the other Burmese guys at his table. He couldn't be Burmese too, could he? Australian, I figured, or Singaporean.

The man noticed us watching him, nodded hello, and came over to join us. In perfect English, he introduced himself: "Slim—like Slim Shady," he said. He smiled, and Bonnie and I knew: He liked Eminem; ergo we liked him. Over the course of a few more beers, we learned more of Slim's life. A physics graduate at Mandalay University, he'd been unable to find work in his hometown because, he said, jobs went to ethnic Burmese, while he, a Muslim with Indian roots, was denied. And so he'd moved his wife and young child out here, to the forgotten end of a forgotten country, where he hoped to work as a tour guide. He spoke English and good French, and Western tourists such as ourselves occasionally passed through.

For a moment or two, I wondered if Slim was actually an intelligence agent, a member of Burma's legions of secret police come to check up on us foreigners. His story, though touching, seemed improbable. Who decided to become a tour guide by moving to one of the least-touristed corners of the country? Or was that just canny planning?

In the medieval dark of the Tachileik night, the stars were easily visible above, and as I looked at them I realized I didn't care if Slim was monitoring us. We were having such a nice time, Bonnie and I had no ill intentions, I wasn't even planning on writing about this side trip. Nothing could go wrong. Indeed, everything was right with the world. There we were: Slim, a Burmese-Indian Muslim; Bonnie, a Korean-American Christian; and myself, an American Jew—bonding over beers in the Golden Triangle. This was how it was supposed to be—this moment, however brief, was why I traveled. I was happy, and I told Bonnie and Slim why.

We all laughed and raised our glasses and drank, and then Slim said, "Hey, do you guys like Pink Floyd? How about the Scorpions?"

At the time, I was already a fairly well-traveled person. I'd made my way to Mexico, India, Western Europe, all over the United States, and through much of East Asia. But I was about to begin a period of intensive travel that would put those experiences to shame. The *New York Times* assignment that had me in northern Thailand was one of my very first, and over the next seven years that paper, and magazines such as *Saveur* and *Afar*, would send me to more than fifty countries, from the great capitals of Europe and the megacities of Asia to Turkish apple orchards and flyspeck Caribbean islands. I would spend months on the road at a time, and create hundreds of articles, dozens of videos, and enough digital photos to bring several overpriced computers to a crawl.

That weekend in Burma marked a turning point for me in another way, however. It was so short, so sweet, so weird, and so perfect—and it had all taken place so far from any location of significance. Tachileik was the middle of nowhere, a town overlooked by everyone but those required to spend the night (or their lives), and yet there was Slim, and there we were. The connection, the moment, could happen, even there.

Until then, my travels had shrunk the world. I had crossed continents by every conveyance imaginable and was developing not only some mastery of the practicalities of travel but also, more important, a fundamental ease in the role of traveler, a sense that the discomforts and awkwardness of exploring the world were worthwhile because I was, at last, doing was what I was supposed to be doing.

Now, though, the world was starting to appear bigger than ever, a massively expanding network of tiny points where anything at all could happen, and within each point another infinite web of possibilities. Indeed, the very next day, as Bonnie and I took a group taxi north to the city of Kengtung, we stopped halfway, at a minuscule village whose one restaurant served, alongside some decent curries and stir-fries, incredible tomato-based salsas spiked with unfamiliar herbs and familiarly pungent fish sauce—a Mexican condiment by way of Southeast Asia. If Tachileik was the middle of nowhere, this was nowhere's very edge, and yet here too were treasures.

Over the course of my subsequent travels, the world grew and grew. I found fascinating halfway points between two larger points, and then halfway points between those halfway points. Big cities ballooned as I focused on neighborhoods and then subneighborhoods and then single blocks. Highways splintered into fractal root systems of possibility. It seemed I would never be able to claim the entire world, and yet I kept trying.

As far as I traveled, and as many breakthrough moments as I experienced in some of the most and least renowned locales on Earth, I could never get entirely out of my own head. I may have learned how to snag cheap plane tickets, how to cross borders on foot, how to show up in a strange land and find a welcoming bed, a fine meal, and eager new friends, but I was still plagued by the same anxieties: that I didn't know what I was doing, that I was going to fall ill, that I was spending far more than I could afford, that I would succumb to loneliness and never really penetrate or understand the places I was being paid to penetrate and understand. These anxieties weren't entirely imaginary. I had evidence of my failures—nights spent in crummy motels or in the way back of my station wagon, memories of three-day stretches in which I hardly spoke, a collection of perforated foil packets of antibiotics.

This is not to say I wasn't enjoying myself. Every time I boarded a long-haul flight, I marveled at the opportunity I'd been given to roam the world on someone else's dime. On those trips, I found close friends, discovered new foods, and stumbled into unfathomably joyous experiences—the time a clan of mountain goats surrounded me at midnight in the mountains of Montana, the gentle way a carful of Chinese railroad passengers took care of me on a forty-eight-hour trip from Urumqi to Beijing.

Still, the sad side of travel continued to occupy me, in part because it always seemed to lurk so close beneath the surface. One minute I could be sipping espresso with a Carthaginian playboy and the next I'd be friendless and adrift. (Vice versa, too.)

But the real reason, I think, was that mastering the psychic challenges of travel felt more important than mastering the practical challenges. As I tried to convey in "The Frugal Traveler," the *New York Times* column I wrote from 2006 to 2010, anyone could learn to travel both well and on a budget. There were Web sites to make use of, smart tricks and tips to employ, and an open attitude to adopt.

You didn't need to be a well-known "*New York Times* travel writer" to do this stuff, and indeed I traveled anonymously, and wrote as an Everyman, to prove it.

That approach, however, often left out the intangibles, for which there are no universal solutions. I could teach anyone how to minimize credit card surcharges overseas, or how pick up enough Indonesian to roam around Java for a week, but could I offer a one-size-fits-all cure for loneliness? Or explain how to confront, ethically and emotionally, the reality of Third World poverty? No matter how deeply you understand the vagaries of booking cheap flights—on a Tuesday afternoon, or via a foreign carrier's home-country Web site, or whatever—you may still be saddled with inexplicable feelings of depression and inadequacy when you venture out into the world. No need to feel guilty about those persistent problems, though. They're simply the Advanced Placement test for frequent travelers—they mean you're graduating to the next level.

*The Turk Who Loved Apples*, then, chronicles my ongoing attempts to come to terms with those psychic challenges. I've tried to arrange the chapters in an order that represents what many travelers go through. We begin with ignorance and naïveté—the biggest stumbling blocks for the novice—then delve into the twin issues of eating well and getting sick, the similarly paired problems of being alone and making friends, and then traveling frugally and turning a profit from travel. Ethical dilemmas are followed by the quirks of getting lost, and the ultimate, unavoidable horror of traveling with family. After addressing the eternal debate of tourist versus traveler, I finish with one of the heaviest burdens: homecoming.

Throughout, I refer back frequently to the postcollegiate year I spent in Ho Chi Minh City, Vietnam. Though that trip took place long ago, in 1996 and 1997, it was my first major solo adventure abroad and brought me face to face with the epiphanies and anxieties I would encounter again and again for decades to come. Whenever

I am lonely, or ill, or guilt-ridden, I think back to the model that year provided me. It doesn't always give me answers, but it does remind me that I survived once before and can do so again.

That year abroad provides a backbone for the book as its various themed chapters leap around, from country to country, from my childhood to my most recent experiences. This is, I've discovered, one of the inevitable consequences of a lifetime of travel—that one's constant dislocation in space produces a parallel dislocation in time. An ill breeze in Brooklyn recalls to me with instantaneous effect the streets of Saigon, and a bar of music overheard in a Taipei bar puts me in a Volvo crossing the Texas desert. I trade messages with Facebook friends I haven't seen in person in years and make plans to see others far from their homes—in eastern Java, in Mongolia. Wherever I happen to be at this moment, I can close my eyes and imagine myself a million other places.

If your life has not been filled with constant travel, these sorts of jumps may be disconcerting—a kind of narrative jetlag, I suppose. For me, at this point in my traveling life, it's become normal, and I know I'm not entirely alone. When my travel-writer friends and I gather over drinks, our conversation is always filled with lines like "That reminds me of when I was in Osaka . . . " or "Oh, just like in Bogotà!" Yes, it's insufferable to outsiders, I'll be the first to admit, but for us the world has opened up, and to act like we don't notice the deep connections between disparate points on the globe would be to pretend we've learned nothing at all.

Another, more important phenomenon I've learned in assembling these nearly thirty years of travel anecdotes is that they tell the tale of a very independent traveler—one who almost never outsourced the planning and execution of his adventures to travel agents, tour companies, concierges, or friends and family. In many ways, I was an independent traveler by default. At first I didn't have the money to depend on outsider help, and by the time I had the money, it was my duty to readers to deal with everything myself, so that they might learn from my example.

Still, those practical factors were always secondary. From an early age, I've simply wanted to do things myself. Whether I was spending hours on Lego projects in my room or taking independent study courses in high school and college, I've always been more comfortable figuring the world out on my own, and enjoying the private rush of triumph that comes from knowing I alone was responsible for my success. Or something like that: I never set out to be independent, and until recently wasn't self-aware enough to identify that as one of my character traits.

Of course, no one is born independent, nor is independence an absolute value, immutable once it's achieved. This book is a chronicle of my ongoing progress toward independence, each minor step forward a tentative one, each victory shaky, liable to be overturned at the next foreign challenge. By the end of my story, you should be able to see how far I've come—and how that's also not, maybe, really very far at all. When you go around the world, you wind up back where you started.

Now that I recognize my own independent streak, I can see, too, how it's aided me as a traveler. Because when you travel, things will go wrong: baggage will disappear, your guts will betray you, and you will find yourself alone in a poor, strange land where you don't speak the language. The illusion of control that you set out with, fueled by a fevered studying of guidebooks, planning of itineraries, and e-mailing of friends of friends (of friends), will evaporate, leaving you with no one to rely on but you. Money and experience can insulate you from calamity, but never perfectly; when it comes down to it, you are responsible for your own happiness. Are you ready for that kind of responsibility? I wasn't always—but I am now, I think.

Which is why I cannot present this book as some kind of elaborate instruction manual for becoming a good traveler yourself. No, this is simply how and why I did what I did, related in what I hope is an entertaining and dramatic format. For me to claim you should make similar choices would be worse than presumptuous—after all, you are not me—it would be dangerous. If anything, I want you, too, to become an independent traveler, to think and act for yourself wherever you might be, without the aid of guidebooks and the kinds of newspaper and magazine articles I write for a living. I want you to experience and understand the miserable things that can happen when you travel, to learn how to deal with them, and, like Sisyphus, to transcend them, to find joy in the crushing inevitability not so much of failure but of near-failure. I want you to leave home and return with stories to tell, not of disasters dealt with the way Matt Gross would have but of how you improvised your own solutions. *The Turk Who Loved Apples* should be the last guidebook you'll ever need. And if things actually work out that way, then, well, as Kemal Görgün, our eponymous apple farmer, would say: WOW.

Chapter 1

# Schrödinger's Boarding Pass

Perpetually Unprepared—
and Totally Comfortable with That—
I Set Off for Vietnam, Tunisia, and Beyond

O ne night in early August, about a week after my twenty-second birthday, I drove head-on into a pickup truck on Maryland's eastern shore. I'd been coming down from Washington, D.C., to Chincoteague, Virginia, to meet my parents for a brief beach vacation; my girlfriend, Tammy, was in the passenger seat. It had been raining hard, with heavy traffic, but then, near the town of Salisbury, the showers stopped and the road cleared. I relaxed—too soon. The unfamiliar highway curved, I hit the brakes, and my lilac Plymouth Acclaim skidded across the lane and directly into the oncoming pickup. Bang.

An instant later the street was silent. Tammy and I looked at each other; neither of us was hurt. Nor was the driver of the pickup, just then clambering out of his vehicle. Soon, a police car arrived on the scene. The officer told us we were the third accident at that spot that night. Then he brought us to the station, where I called my mother at the bed-and-breakfast in Chincoteague to come get us.

While we waited, I took a photo of Tammy, looking miserable and exhausted in the yellow lamplight. And then a serene calm settled over me. Understandable, I think, for someone who'd just survived a potentially disastrous wreck, but my happiness was more a sense of relief—relief that the car was totaled.

Because from the moment I'd acquired the vehicle, it had been the source of constant troubles. The Acclaim had come into my possession only because my maternal grandmother, who'd owned it previously, had died three months earlier. She'd lived in Wilmington, Delaware, and I, finishing up college in nearby Baltimore, was carless, so without much ado, the Plymouth became mine.

But not for long. Less than a week after I'd driven it back to Baltimore, it vanished off the street one night. A theft, I figured, particularly since Grandma Rosalie had outfitted the car with a newfangled cellular phone. A few days later the police found the car wrapped around a lamppost—*sans* cell, of course—and promptly notified my late grandmother by mail. Only when I called to check in did they direct me to an impound lot.

In addition to being strangely technologically prescient, Grandma Rosalie had also arranged zero-deductible insurance for the car, so it cost nothing to put the car in the shop, where after another couple of weeks it emerged almost as good as new. (Which, for a lilac Acclaim, was not really so good.) The car chugged along in relative health for another two months, until one day in Washington—where I was spending five weeks learning how to teach English as a foreign language—I discovered it wouldn't go more than about thirty-five miles per hour. The transmission was shot. Worse, by then insurance wouldn't cover it.

One week and roughly $600 later, I picked up the Plymouth from yet another garage, threw my bags and books in the trunk, and headed for Baltimore to fetch Tammy and enjoy a nice vacation with my folks.

Bang.

This series of calamities would signify nothing—the all-too-short life and death of a generic American sedan—were it not for my post-Chincoteague plans. That is, less than a week after the crash, I was supposed to be moving to Ho Chi Minh City, Vietnam.

The year was 1996. I'd just graduated from college with a degree in creative writing, an expensive certification of my unsuitability for work. Unsure of what to do next, I'd fixated on Vietnam, which had recently reestablished diplomatic ties with its old enemy the United States. It would be my future, my destiny, my salvation. I would go there and . . . do something. I wasn't sure what. I had some vague ideas about mastering the Vietnamese language and joining the Communist Party (less an ideological goal than a route to power and influence). Also, I was going to write big, important, best-selling novels in English at the same time.

But mostly, I really liked Vietnamese food, and figured that if I was going to live abroad, it should be somewhere I really liked the food.

In other words, in the months leading up to a life-changing move, the Fates seemed to be delivering me a series of dire, travel-related warnings, the kinds of omens that, in a bad movie, would foreshadow the protagonist's travel-related demise. Had I been able to take a step back from my life and observe the events with a more analytical (and possibly more paranoid) attitude, I might have delayed, canceled, or at least worried more about what awaited me in the former Saigon.

Instead, I was oblivious, as I had been for much of my life, to the reality that things could go awry, and in ways that could do me physical or psychological damage. Like Chauncey Gardiner in *Being There,* I moved through the world unaware of looming danger and potential disaster.

In preparing for the move to Vietnam, for example, I had done the minimum of research. There was that teacher-training course in Washington, which I'd taken more because I didn't have the first clue about teaching English than because I thought having a certificate might help me find a job. Even so, that was general preparation—it had nothing to do with Ho Chi Minh City as a specific and unique destination.

In those days, the Internet was of little use to travelers. This was before TripAdvisor, before Travelocity and Expedia, before blogs, before—if you can conceive of such a thing—Google. I hadn't posted about my plans in any online forums. I had never seen a map of Ho Chi Minh City. I didn't know where I was going to live, or whether Le Thi Thanh, an acquaintance of a friend of my father, would show up to greet me at the airport, or whether the teaching job that Ms. Thanh had written me about (by actual international airmail) would materialize.

Instead, I'd been supplementing my preexisting knowledge of Vietnam—which came entirely from movies and TV—with books. Not serious histories of the war by writers like Stanley Karnow or Philip Caputo, which might have given me some perspective on the matter, but contemporary Vietnamese novels in translation: *Novel Without a Name,* by Duong Thu Huong, and *The Sorrow of War*, by Bao Ninh. Both were interesting, but their focus on the war era left me cold. That is, I knew the war, or at least the pop-culture version of the war, and I understood how deeply it had consumed my parents' generation. But what all the war stories left out was Vietnam itself. What was this country? What kinds of lives did Vietnamese people live? How did they think and act? And now, more than twenty years after the war had ended, what had the place become?

I decided to find out not by reading journalistic accounts (such books hadn't yet been written) or guidebooks (I don't remember ever even looking for one) but by delving into even earlier Vietnamese literature. One book I read on the plane from Washington to Paris to Ho Chi Minh City was a piece of literary reportage from 1920s French Indochina, by a Vietnamese journalist who'd worked undercover driving a cyclo, the tricycle pedicabs that plied the streets of Saigon. It was, I believe, entitled *I Am a Cyclo Driver*. It did not tell me much about present-day Vietnam, but it did give me a foundation for discussing labor issues and racism under the French colonial government.

I did, however, have one true guidebook in my possession—though not, unfortunately, one by Lonely Planet, which I would later learn dominated the Southeast Asia guidebook world. No, mine—which I believe my mother bought me as a birthday gift—was a lesser guidebook, with lots of general historical and cultural information but no details about, say, acquiring a long-term tourist or business visa, opening a bank account, finding work, learning the language—all those survival-related things that, as the jet neared its destination, I suddenly realized I was going to have to do. I flipped back and forth through the guidebook with mounting anxiety, until at last I looked at the publisher's information page.

The book, I noticed, had been published in Slovenia. That did not seem to be a good sign. Thanks, Mom.

Fourteen years later, nothing had changed—and everything had changed. After dozens of trips abroad, to sixty countries on five continents, having produced hundreds of newspaper and magazine stories, I was once again setting off on an adventure, utterly ill-informed—possibly even less informed than I'd been when I flew off to Vietnam. Because this time, as I waited for the A train to Kennedy Airport in the bowels of a Brooklyn subway station, I did not even know my precise destination. All I knew, on this Saturday in June of 2010, was that an Air France plane ticket had been purchased for me, and that I needed to get to JFK on this particular day and at roughly this time.

Knowing nothing more was the whole point. This journey to wherever was sponsored by *Afar*, a then-new travel magazine, based in California, that had assigned me a "Spin the Globe" story, in which the editors select a destination at random (supposedly by spinning a globe in their offices) and, without revealing it, buy the writer a plane ticket. Of course, certain details had to be worked out in advance—when I'd be available, whether I'd need a visa or vaccinations, what the weather would be like—but the fact remained: I would be going off into the wild blue yonder, with no idea whatsoever of what awaited me. I was as excited as I'd ever been.

Still, if I wanted a clue, I had one right at my feet. On the damp platform sat the black leather weekend bag I'd bought in the late 1990s, and inside, atop four days' worth of warm-weather clothes, was a small package wrapped in brown paper. My wife, Jean Liu— whom the *Afar* editors had provided vital data like my departure time and destination—had put it there. "It's a hint about where you're going," she'd said.

I wanted that hint, and badly, but just as badly I wanted to wait. The longer the mystery remained, the more I cherished it. Because who now truly gets sent off into the void? I was on the cusp of adventure—an adventure whose appeal lay almost entirely in my lack of knowledge of what the adventure would be. Right this second I was in a filthy Brooklyn subway station, but in a few hours I might be in Paris, or Dakar, or Dushanbe. Who in this borough, in this city, in this country, could say the same with equal (un)certainty?

Not knowing was key. Surely, there were thousands of people about to do crazy things in crazy places all over the globe. But how many had planned nothing at all? Who among the brave was willing to give up total control, to set forth blindly into unknown lands?

You had to be particularly brave to do this, I thought. So many hundreds of thousands of Americans stay home, refuse to travel, precisely because of a lack of knowledge—because they don't have time to fully plan trips, because they don't know their options, because they are afraid to confront the near-certainty that when they leave the confines of their homes, *something will happen*, something that could shake their fundamental understanding of the world and their place in it. Me, I wanted to be shaken, to be the ultimate blank slate on which the world would leave its marks.

And yet I also desperately wanted to know where I was going. At some point soon, of course, I would find out—like when I checked in at the Air France counter of Terminal 1. And at that point, I feared, my dreams would collapse. Just knowing I was flying Air France was dangerous; that meant, most likely, I was bound for the Caribbean, Canada, North Africa, or France itself. And perhaps it would turn out I already knew someone in the destination, or that it would be a country or city I'd read about extensively—maybe even written about without ever having visited. After traveling for decades and working in journalism for years, there were many such places. Even if it was somewhere brand new and unfamiliar, simply knowing the location might be a disappointment. *Moldova, seriously?* On that plane bound for somewhere, I'd be just another passenger who knew where he was supposed to disembark, and what he might do when he got there.

At last, the A train arrived, and I boarded. My journey was beginning. I'd been patient long enough. I might as well open the package and reveal my hint. I untied the twine and shuffled off the brown paper.

Inside was a hardcover copy of *Fodor's Tunisia*—from 1973, the year before I was born. Jean and I had found it at a used-book store maybe a decade earlier, and without ever reading it I'd fantasized about someday using it to explore the country. Someday was apparently today.

As I started to flip through the book, I felt ambivalence build up inside me. First, there was a warmth, the delight of finally getting to visit a land I'd held in my imagination ever since, at the age of around three, I saw *Star Wars*, whose desert planet opening scenes had been filmed near the Tunisian town of Tataouine. And I appreciated the serendipity of simply having this guidebook in my possession, as if I'd secretly planned this very trip a decade in advance. Plus, there was the sweetness of Jean's having packed it in my bags. *I married well*, I thought.

At the same time, I could sense my travel writer's instincts—honed over countless professional trips for the *New York Times* and other publications—kicking in. At JFK, I knew, as soon as I'd passed through security I'd go online, scanning CouchSurfing.org and A Small World, a theoretically exclusive social network, for contacts. I'd hit Facebook and Twitter and let my friends and followers know where I was headed; maybe they'd have advice. Hadn't my old coworker Marie-France lived in Tunis as a child? She'd get a direct e-mail. And hadn't Jean herself once visited Tunis and flirted with a local guy from whom she'd later received postcards? Did she still have the postcards? Could I track down the man who'd once tried to woo her? Now, that would be a story!

And that was just my strategy for filling in the things I *didn't* already know. What I did already know was that Tunisia was a relatively small, comparatively secular Muslim Arab country, its beach towns popular with European vacationers, its government stable thanks to the police-state tactics (e.g., jailing bloggers) of its longtime president, Zine El Abidine Ben Ali. People there would speak French better than me, not to mention Arabic. I could search the markets for *harissa*, a spice-enriched chili paste, I could see how Tunisian *merguez*, a lamb sausage, stacked up against its Moroccan and Algerian counterparts, which I'd eaten elsewhere, and I'd absolutely have to try *brik*, a deep-fried packet of phyllo dough stuffed with shredded tuna, spices, and egg. Oh, and orange juice—lots and lots of fresh-squeezed orange juice.

By this point, the A train was maybe halfway to the airport, and I'd already mentally mapped out the next several days. I hadn't wanted to, honestly. I'd hoped to maintain that blissful feeling of not-knowing for as long as possible, but as long as possible wasn't very long at all. And now I had this guidebook, too, which would no doubt reveal to me even more secrets of Tunisia, the family taverns of bygone days, the tenth-generation artisans still weaving cottons and carving wood in sea-cliff caves. Why even bother going now?

Except that as I read deeper into the book, I realized something else: *Fodor's* was useless. Parts of it discussed Tunisian history, both recent and ancient, which I knew somewhat, while the rest dealt with "culture," from Carthaginian art ("very little remains") to contemporary carpet makers. Compared with guidebooks of today, which include copious listings of where to eat and sleep and what to do to keep yourself occupied, *Fodor's Tunisia* was sketchy. In the listings of "moderate" hotels, four hotels appeared, none of them with any identifying details or description other than address. Restaurants tended toward the touristic ("many tempting specialties . . . oriental dancers tempting too"). One section, however, was fanatically detailed—a two-page walk-through of every funerary stela and Roman sarcophagus worth seeing in the Bardo Museum, Tunisia's national repository of relics from antiquity. But somehow all that highly specific information felt tedious and unnecessary; who needs a guidebook *in* a museum?

This was, in a way, disappointing. I'd hoped I could use the book to track down some of the older businesses in Tunisia, or to uncover forgotten attractions, but in the span of 261 pages, *Fodor's Tunisia* didn't really get into such things. Instead, it was a gloss, a manual not for intrepid wanderers (as I imagined myself to be) but for those voyagers of the 1970s who'd float through the Maghreb in the care of a travel agent's time-honed itinerary.

Which meant there would remain at least some holes in my pre-arrival knowledge—and thank goodness. Because for a long time now, such holes had become harder and harder to find, or to create. As the *New York Times'* "Frugal Traveler" columnist from 2006 to 2010, I'd had to become an expert at researching every aspect of my trips. I'd mastered Google, and could, with a few clicks, dig up brand-new boutique hotels in Puerto Rico and little-known bed-and-breakfasts in far-flung corners of New Mexico. Through Facebook and CouchSurfing and A Small World, I reached out to strangers from Bucharest to Chennai, ensuring myself friendly local guides to strange, new cultures. I scoured food blogs and Chowhound.com and eGullet.org so I'd know what to put in my mouth in Seoul and Budapest. I set up bank accounts and credit cards to maximize frequent-flier miles and minimize fees. I figured out how to store high-resolution Google maps on my iPhone so that I could reference them abroad without incurring roaming charges.

For one Frugal Traveler column, I wrote about my system for getting the best possible deals on airfares. It was, I thought, a highly rational system, consisting of a dozen steps—or maybe twenty—that spanned the gamut of airline Web sites and third-party online travel agents and fare forecasters and seat recommenders (which is better, SeatGuru.com or SeatExpert.com?), and I didn't even get around to discussing the whole business of international-flight consolidators.

Perhaps predictably, this column got a lot of responses: 217 people wrote in, many of them thanking me for the advice and some offering their own tips. Others, however, were more critical. One compared my method to "herding cats"; another said it made her head spin. Someone called "Buddy" from Houston, Texas, wrote, "So, you spent how many hours and saved how much for all that effort? Exactly how much is your time worth to you?"

As it happens, this was a question I'd already begun to ask myself, in a slightly different form: What was the point of all this preparation?

It's not that I was utterly dissatisfied with how I was traveling. I never felt like I'd *over*-researched a trip, to the point where I was merely executing a set of pre-planned maneuvers through Paris or Bratislava. There were always moments of randomness, spontaneity, and serendipity. There was the bistro owner on the French Riviera who offered me a free meal if I'd send him video footage of his restaurant. There was the afternoon I walked into a Slovakian village, my feet blistered, my legs collapsing, and met a family who invited me in for fresh-baked pastries, homemade wine, and a place to spend the night, out of the rain and safe from the Gypsies. Once, in the Gulf Islands of British Columbia, I was walking down a rocky beach when I somehow caught the attention of a quartet of hip locals in their early twenties; within minutes, we'd all stripped off our clothes and were skinny-dipping in the freezing surf. Although they later told me this was the "nudie beach," I could find no reference to it on the Internet. You try it—Google "nudie beach" and see what you come up with.

These episodes made me wonder if I needed the research part at all—they happened so naturally and beautifully they overshadowed the quotidian parts of the trip: checking into hotels, taking buses or trains from one spot to another, dutifully seeing sites considered historically or culturally important. More frustrating, when I'd sit down to write my articles, I'd find that including the quotidian stuff— which publications generally require, since they're in the business of telling readers how to travel—left little room for the serendipitous moments that made the trips special to me.

But if you're going to be a professional travel writer, you can't exactly stop researching your destinations or give up advising readers on how to travel. The business doesn't work that way. You don't call up an editor, tell them you want to go to Morocco or Ireland for a couple of weeks, and have them cut you a big check. And you don't generally head off on your own dime to one of these places, hoping you'll be able to turn your adventures into a salable story afterward. That's how you go broke.

No, if you want to go to, say, Tokyo, first you come up with an angle: some subset of activities or specific thematic bent. For example, ramen. Hugely popular in America, both the inexpensive, dried, college-food form and the fresh, high-end New York restaurant style, ramen is, in Japan, a full-blown cultural phenomenon. There are ramen magazines, ramen TV shows, ramen bloggers, a ramen museum, and five thousand ramen shops in Tokyo alone. So: seeing and understanding Tokyo by trying to make sense of its ramen shops and ramen aficionados—Tokyo through a noodly lens—that's the angle.

Then you figure out what the story will cost to report—or really, how you can do it as cheaply as possible, since magazine and newspaper budgets are always tight—and when you can do it, and the editor has to see if it conflicts with any other stories in the pipeline, and then, finally, the editor says yes, and you sign a contract that specifies how much you can spend and how little you'll be paid—and then off you go to Tokyo!

More or less, that's how I got myself there in December 2009, and—after scouring Web postings and corralling Tokyo's ramen bloggers—I spent a week eating four bowls of ramen a day: pork bone ramen, miso ramen, cheese ramen. That was a pretty damn delicious trip. And I couldn't have done it, either the on-the-ground reporting or the actual writing of the story, without intense preparation.

But the hell with intense preparation! Maybe I was just getting old, but I seemed to remember a time, long before I became a travel writer, when I not only didn't prepare but couldn't prepare, when I didn't have the tools to plan ahead because those tools hadn't been invented yet. And yet those adventures seemed more real to me, more all-encompassing, more life-changing, more objectively important. I looked back on them nostalgically, knowing they'd made me the traveler I am today even though they seemed to have happened to an entirely different person. In short, I found myself facing questions that all travelers face, but now on a deeper, more existential level: How did I get from where I started to here? And how do I get back there again?

My first memory of travel is a simple one: I am four years old, or maybe five or six, sitting in the backseat of the family station wagon, looking out the window. It is raining, and fairly hard, too. Hard enough that the raindrops defy gravity, streaking up and rolling across the window just slowly enough that I can follow their progress—trace their wobbly trails—until they dead-end in the slat of vertical rubber. Then I drag my gaze back to find a new droplet.

Where are we Grosses going? In my memory, it's always to my paternal grandparents' house, in Bridgeport, Connecticut, about a two-hour trip from our home in Amherst, Massachusetts. Two hours is a long time for a little kid, made longer by the abstractedness of the journey. What are Amherst and Bridgeport? How are they connected geographically? The fact is, I don't know, and I don't know enough to even ask the questions. There are steps I remember are necessary to take. We will cross the Connecticut River via the Coolidge Bridge. At some point, we will drive down something called the Merritt Parkway. Finally, we will turn onto Dixon Street, whose Waspy name always seems so proper and stately that it's almost a joke that people called Gross live there.

And that's it: the road, the rain, the minor details that drizzled into my consciousness, the sense that we would begin one place and end at another, and that if I were relatively patient, I would be rewarded with hugs and gifts from my grandmother. Beyond that, I knew—and expected—nothing. This was how journeys went. You started out at one place, and ended in another, and spent most of the time in between in a state of semi-boredom that constantly threatened to veer into fidgety, unrealistic anticipation of imminent delight.

That was how my perception of travel began, and for a very long time it remained unchanged. When my father, a historian specializing in Revolutionary War–era Concord, Massachusetts, first took me abroad—to Denmark and England at the age of almost-eight—I had no map or guidebook to prepare me, just a sense that, somewhere on the other side of the Atlantic, a paradise of Lego bricks and unseen *Dr. Who* episodes awaited me. And perhaps that was all I needed, for nothing of importance that took place on that adventure could have been predicted in a book.

And it was an important trip, maybe the most important of my life. The Matt Gross who arrived in Copenhagen one afternoon in the summer of 1982 was a strange, nearly feral creature: messy curly hair neither tamed nor touched by brush or comb; tough dungarees with grass stains at the knee; blue eyes huge and unblinking, like an alien. And, always at his side, a crocheted yellow polyester blanket, softened by years of love, that provided a sense of security, particularly when paired with a thumb in the mouth. Picture Linus from *Peanuts*, crossed with Pig-Pen.

The first thing this Matt did, upon arriving in his hotel room, was look out the window and spot the glowing red neon sign of a bookstore. *Books!* This was a treat. He hadn't really known where to start exploring, or what to do in the days before he and his father would make the trip to Legoland, in Billund (wherever that was), but now here was a bookstore. He could read, and pretty well, too: *Encyclopedia Brown*, *Dr. Who* novelizations, Tolkien. No surprise for the child of an editor and a history professor, really. So when he saw the bookstore, he leapt with excitement to show his father.

Only, there was a problem. A tricky problem that Dad didn't know precisely how to explain, or rather, he knew how but wasn't sure Matt would understand. And so he just said it.

"Matt, that's an *adult* bookstore."

Did Matt understand? He did, somehow. It had something to do with sex, whatever that was, with a world that he'd sensed existed but that had been, until now, beyond him. Well, it was still beyond him, but here, on his first day in Denmark, it was closer. He could see it, he could be told where it was, and though he was denied entry, this one step, this knowledge was enough. He'd inched closer. He laughed, I imagine, and his father laughed with him. It was funny, that he could understand even though he didn't really understand. And besides, he'd brought other books to read anyway.

From there, the revelations and significant moments began to flow, seemingly at a rate of one per day. At Tivoli Gardens, the grand amusement park at the center of Copenhagen, Matt attempted to eat a fast-food burger from a kiosk—but rejected it as disgusting, inedible. His father, unbelieving, cajoled the tearful boy to finish until, at last, he himself bit into the foul gray thing. Into the trash it went; they dined on french fries instead. For the first time he could remember, Matt had been right about something in the grown-up realm: taste. And soon he was learning more. At Legoland, he had his initial plate of the heretofore exotic spaghetti bolognese, and liked it, enough that the dish became his mainstay, the food by which he could judge a restaurant, and on which he could rely in the absence of compelling alternatives. He was moving forward.

Although at times, it did not feel like moving forward. After a few days in Denmark, Matt and his father departed, by train and ferry, for England. It was an unbelievable journey—the train actually drove *onto the ferry*, Matt was stunned to learn—and despite the rocky seas and attendant nausea, he managed to play Centipede in the ferry lounge well enough to win a free game, another breakthrough. Once in England, however, Matt made a horrifying discovery: his blanket had vanished. Had he left it in Copenhagen? At Legoland? On the train? The only thing certain was that it was gone. But Matt did not cry, as he had over the Tivoli Gardens burger. Tears were of no use anymore, and besides, he was almost eight.

In the years since, I've often wondered about the disappearance of my blanket. It seems almost too perfect, in the context of this overly symbolic growing-up tale, that the most visible symbol of my babyhood—that frayed, ultrasoft blanket whose Cheerio-sized ringlets I can, thirty years later, still imagine against my bearded cheek—would go missing. My father, I've long suspected, must have removed it from our luggage, but whenever I've cornered him, he's pleaded innocent. I guess I have to believe him.

The point is that you can never really know what's going to happen when you travel. Or at least I never did, not when I set out on my heavy blue BMX bicycle to roam the hills of Amherst; not when, partly at my behest, my dad took a new teaching job at William & Mary and moved us all to Williamsburg, Virginia, in whose high school I was the only Jew, and a Yankee, and a skateboarder back when skateboarding was anything but cool; not when I chose to study math at Johns Hopkins, having visited the campus for a day and been so impressed by the focus with which students walked from quad to quad that I forgot that laziness and improvisation, not intensity and labor, were my natural modes of being. I was, for so much of my early life, either uninformed or ill-informed.

And I didn't care. The risk was what motivated me, though for a long time I couldn't have articulated that. The possibility of failure—of getting lost, hurt, ostracized—made the eventual successes that much sweeter, although again, this was an unconscious process. I'd hate for anyone to think I was some preternatural daredevil courting death, or humiliation, willy-nilly. No, I was the opposite—so unaware of what awaited me on the other side that it was only once I'd discovered what dangers lurked that I realized how lucky I'd been to survive them. That discovery, however, often came too late—or sometimes never.

Which is how I arrived in Vietnam: twenty-two, clueless, and lucky. From the air, Vietnam seemed instantly different from anywhere I'd been before. It wasn't the rice paddies or farming villages—images I recognized from movies and TV—but the trees. As the Air France jet coasted in toward a landing at Tan Son Nhat Airport, the trees looked tight and nubby, gnarled like broccoli florets, a shorter, denser carpet of foliage than I'd ever seen elsewhere. I don't know why this struck me so strongly. I'd never particularly cared about trees before. But the maples and birches and pines of North America had insinuated themselves so deeply into my consciousness that every other kind of tree cover would instantly signify not just difference or newness but indelible foreignness.

This hadn't been in my Slovenian guidebook: the very *trees* will look different. Nor had anything else, from the Pepsi logos enveloping the shuttle buses that greeted the plane on the tarmac to the MTV playing on video screens throughout the terminal. These, at least, were easier to integrate into my consciousness—because *of course* this communist country making its first steps toward Western-style capitalism would immediately latch onto pop culture and fast food. I could stand back and safely reflect on the irony. I knew that pose.

Not so with the trees, or with the reality of Vietnam once I left the airport. Le Thi Thanh, a petite literature professor at Ho Chi Minh City Open University, a kind of community college, met me at the gate with Phuoc, one of her students, and we hustled into a taxi for the thirty-minute drive into the city. What I felt, in addition to the rainy-season heat and humidity, was the nearly overwhelming closeness. The streets were narrow, jammed with motorbikes and bicycles that darted and wove around the cars and pedestrians and each other, a writhing sea of transportation bound by rows of numberless concrete shop houses, all four meters wide, with businesses on their ground floors ("Product Consumption Store" was the English name of one) and living quarters above. Tangled skeins of electrical wiring hung between poles. A smell I eventually concluded was overripe fruit and exhaust filtered through the taxi's windows. The Vietnamese words printed on signs and billboards may have used a modified Latin alphabet, but I couldn't read a thing, and could barely muster a chuckle at phrases that should have had me cackling (e.g., "Mỹ Dung"). The city was loud—every motorbike honked constantly—and dirty, and while I was appalled by what I saw, I could also feel an unfamiliar energy pulsing through the streets, an activity so furious and ambitious it both invigorated and frightened me, so much so that Ms. Thanh, Phuoc, and I barely spoke on the drive.

And then we arrived. The Lucy Hotel, just off Pham Ngu Lao Street at the edge of the backpacker quarter, looked not much different from its neighbors: narrow, seven stories tall, the sidewalk its driveway. It was, Ms. Thanh explained, what was known as a mini-hotel, a residential building that catered to both tourists and long-term visitors; the neighborhood was full of them. Yet even from the outside, the Lucy betrayed subtle signs of sophistication. Its concrete façade looked freshly painted, and a movable white picket fence separated the entrance from the terra-cotta-tiled parking area. A door opened for me. I walked in.

Inside was cool and spacious. Tiled floor. High ceilings. Water trickled in a fountain somewhere. A willowy teenage girl practiced piano, the notes echoing gently off the walls. I sat down in a lounge chair, its frame cast iron, its pillows fresh and soft and linen-white, and was handed water by a thin, kind, middle-aged woman who spoke excellent French. Maybe I was exhausted from the long journey, but I couldn't quite believe where in this New Vietnam I'd wound up—an oasis of peace and order. A somewhat illusory one, I would later learn, but for the moment that illusion was enough.

My room lay at the very top of the building, a thirteen-by-thirteen-foot square with a queen-size bed, a writing desk, an electric fan, a spacious bathroom (no hot water, alas, but it was 90 degrees outside), a large closet, and windows overlooking the sprawl of Saigon, as everybody seemed to call it—a ragged field of ochre buildings and TV antennas in which, if I looked carefully, I could pick out the aging, still-elegant curves of a French-colonial building or the bright fresh layers of paint on a Buddhist temple. The room was not exactly chic, but it had been put together by someone with an eye for aesthetics: Everything was either black or white—no garish colors, harsh fabrics, or plastic kitsch. Even better, I had maid service, provided by Thuy and Duyen, two impossibly sweet-faced girls from the countryside who, giggling shyly, would scoop my sweaty clothes off the floor and wash them every day.

The rent was $300 a month.

As I sat there in my new home, watching thick cumulus clouds hover disconcertingly low over the city, I . . . What did I do? This is one of those frustrating places where the intervening years have left my memory blank. Did I realize I'd bumbled into a situation where I was dangerously out of my depth? Or did I think I'd lucked out? I feel fairly confident in saying I wasn't scared or depressed—at least not yet; those emotions leave too deep a scar to fade so easily.

And so I must not have thought anything at all. I was in that weird jetlagged state that encompasses both total exhaustion and total alertness, and I had certain things to deal with, like asking Ms. Thanh when I'd start teaching at the Open University, arranging to take Vietnamese classes somewhere, finding my way around the neighborhood, and, most immediately, getting something to eat. I walked down the seven flights of stairs and out into the streets.

Pham Ngu Lao was a mess. Along one side of the street, where in the 1960s and '70s the city's railroad terminal once stood, was a vast shantytown of improvised tin-roofed shacks selling bootleg Vietnamese pop CDs and filthy-looking noodle soups. The proper buildings on the other side—mostly mini-hotels and other four-meter-wide concrete structures—were better, but not by much, primarily because the sidewalk, such as it was, was half rubble, and the half that wasn't rubble was overrun with minivans, Honda mopeds, street vendors, and small, panting, short-haired dogs with prominent nipples. As I picked my way down the block, cyclos—the very vehicles I'd been reading about in ancient journalism!—began to follow me in the road.

"Cyclo, you!" the lanky drivers called out. "Cyclo! Cyclo you!"

"I'm walking," I said firmly, as much to myself as to them. They did not give up.

That evening, I ate a mild, coconut-milk-based curry with shrimp—a dish I knew was not very Vietnamese at a restaurant I knew was not very Vietnamese, but then again I didn't really know where to go. I had no map and had given up on my guidebook and hadn't yet realized that Lonely Planet existed or that bootleg editions of its "Southeast Asia on a Shoestring" guide were being sold all around me. After dinner, I walked a little farther down Pham Ngu Lao until I found the Saigon Café, a dumpy corner bar whose folding tables were covered with tall bottles of beer, whose chairs were occupied by white expatriates, frazzled by heat and booze. I sat down and ordered a beer. I was in Saigon, at last.

There is no perfect arc I can draw between then and now. I only know that, for the next year, my ignorance both hindered and protected me, allowing me to make mistakes but not realize them until later, when it was far too late for sharp stabs of pain and humiliation. Over that year, however, the ignorance faded, and by the time I returned to America I was a savvier traveler, comfortable with the idea of blind adventure.

Or was I? Hadn't I always been comfortable with this? Throughout high school, I'd driven across Virginia with my skateboarder friends in search of new places to practice our pastime. Afternoons and weekends, we'd roam without maps from Surrey to Washington, D.C., following up on rumors of dry drainage ditches or backyard half-pipes, eating Taco Bell and sleeping on couches, and not once do I remember ever feeling any hesitation, any sense that things might go wrong in a dreadful and permanent way. And luckily for me, nothing did go wrong except for a speeding ticket and the disappointed looks on my parents' faces when I returned home, late for dinner, the Toyota's gas tank nearly empty. Perhaps something should have happened, something to teach my teenage brain a lesson about the risks a human being faces in the world. Instead, I got lucky and stayed lucky.

Deciding to go to Vietnam was little different from deciding to sneak off to Washington without informing my parents. One moment I was wondering if I should do it, and the next I knew that simply by wondering I'd already made the choice. From that point on, I can't remember ever hesitating about a destination, either in the occasional travels of my twenties or the professional trips of my thirties. Cambodia at a time of political instability? Okay—there's a film festival to cover. The Zapatista villages of Chiapas, Mexico? Sure, I can fake my way inside. A walk from Vienna to Budapest, a horseback excursion into the mountains of Kyrgyzstan, a mapless drive across dismal Ireland—why not?

Of course, none of these was particularly dangerous. I have been to no war zones, and I have merely breezed through the wilderness. And yet I think such adventures might give pause to many travelers: *Is this really something I can do with no special knowledge or training?* I don't want to make myself sound too special, but that question makes no sense. That's because I already know the answer, which is "Well, I guess I'm going to find out, even if I don't speak Kyrgyz and haven't ridden a horse since that one time at summer camp when I was fourteen."

Perhaps this is a failure of imagination. If it's boredom (with regular life) that impels me to travel widely and strangely, then boredom, I assume, will also hold sway over my wanderings. Not that my adventures themselves will be boring, but that whatever drama ensues will be muted: I will not die, or otherwise destroy my life, and any troubles I confront will be of the psychological and emotional variety, which I think—I hope—I can handle.

This assumption has, on occasion, come very close to being disastrously wrong.

One day in July 2006, I rode off on horseback into the foothills of the Tian Shan Mountains of Kyrgyzstan, accompanied by Bakut, the middle-aged proprietor of the yurt camp south of Lake Issyk-Kul where I'd spent the previous night. That morning, there'd been one minor hitch—Bakut had showed up two hours late with the horses, after getting lost in what he called "the badlands"—but I was optimistic. The horses were small and seemed easy to control.

"Pull left, go left," Bakut showed me. "Pull right, go right. Pull back, stop. Go forward, say 'Chut!'"

"Chut!" I said, and the horse stepped forward. I could handle this.

The landscape we trotted through was stark and dry, with scrub grass and patches of lavender sprouting from the sandy earth. There were big snowcapped mountains we could barely see beyond the ridge we were slowly ascending. The sky was a hard, blank blue. I felt I could ride forever.

About an hour in, however, I remembered I'd left my hat, my sunglasses, and my bottle of water back at the yurt, and although Bakut had assured me we'd find natural springs in the mountains, the fact that we were riding through an arid sandstone canyon suggested otherwise. I kept my mouth shut, though, and put my faith in Bakut. How could this gold-toothed seminomad lead us astray?

Soon, he'd proved his knowledge: we reached a broad green plateau covered with tall grass for our horses to graze. While they ate, Bakut and I relaxed in the shade of some bushes, and he asked me what I did for work. I wasn't quite sure how to answer. This trip was part of a three-month around-the-world Frugal Traveler jaunt, and I'd grown accustomed to deflecting questions about my employer. Tell people in the hospitality field you work for the *New York Times*, and their attitude instantly changes. They become friendlier, more involved; they make sure you have whatever you need, and often won't let you pay for it. But I wanted to be a normal traveler, and so I kept it a secret.

Here in the mountains of Kyrgyzstan, however, these secrets seemed silly. The other day in Bishkek, the capital, I'd met a young, educated Kyrgyz guy who'd never even heard of the *Times*. Surely gold-toothed Bakut was no more worldly.

"Journalist," I said, pronouncing the word in the French-Russian way, the *j* a *zh*.

"Oh?" Bakut said with a glinty smile. "*New York Times?*"

"Ha ha ha! I wish!"

That was the end of that conversation. We remounted our horses and covered more ground, taking in the enormity of the view, across the lake to yet more mountains. The sun glinted on the steel domes of far-off mosques. The sense of space was boundless—the opposite of Vietnam, where all was dense and humid.

As the day wore on, I was growing thirsty, and we'd still not found any water. Worse, we'd left behind the grassy areas and moved into a zone of rough red cliffs, like something out of an old Western. This, Bakut decided, was where we would descend, and as the narrow non-path grew slippery with sand, we dismounted and led the horses by the reins. But even then, the horses balked, and we found ourselves perched precariously, a sheer drop below, an unclimbable hill above, and the horses refusing to negotiate the way down.

"Chut!" Bakut yelled as he yanked the first horse's bridle. "Chut!" he yelled, leaning back with all his weight over the edge of the cliff. "Chut!" he yelled, then paused and, chuckling, turned to me and said, knowingly, "Extreme."

Meanwhile, I sat on the hill with my head in my hands, trying to envision a way this could end happily. It was difficult. I was on the verge of freaking out, as one might expect. But with nothing to do but watch Bakut teeter on the precipice, my imagination took hold. With the hot afternoon sun blazing, I saw the horse slip, taking Bakut with him over the cliff edge, one last "Chut!" echoing through the canyons as they fell. And what then? It almost seemed like this would make things easier for me—I'd just tie up my horse, descend on foot, locate Bakut's mangled body, and return to the yurt camp for help. It was horrible to envision, but at least it would let me do something, move forward, instead of just waiting here, puzzling out horrible eventualities precisely because I knew I would soon have to write about this very adventure for the *Times* and needed to make it sound dramatic.

Which it was. Tired, thirsty, ill-equipped to handle the situation, I was worried. But not so worried that I would do something rash, like try to help Bakut pull the horses down or storm off on my own. Instead, I remembered Siddhartha's proclamation—"I can think, I can wait, I can fast"—and did likewise here, in the foothills of the Tian Shan, a mere thousand miles north of the Buddha's birthplace. Honestly, I'd always liked waiting and watching and thinking, maybe even more than I liked doing and moving and talking. Waiting and watching and thinking was how I'd not only survived innumerable intercontinental flights and interminable bus rides but come to enjoy them, look forward to them. Those interstitial moments allowed me a rare freedom—freedom from the need to act and interact, as I'd had to at home and would have to once I arrived, as well as freedom to imagine the future, to revel in its glorious potential: Who knew what would happen on the far side of Customs? In the raki bars of Istanbul? On the slopes of Cerro Catedral? Around the hot pots of Chongqing? Not I—but I could let my mind run wild, unconstrained by reality. None of these fantasies—in equal parts tragic and heroic— would likely come true, but in contemplating the extremes I'd prepare myself for the easier to cope with realities, like being stuck with stubborn horses and no water on a sandstone mountain far from home.

If there was a difference between my blind adventure in Vietnam and my blind adventure in Kyrgyzstan, it was this: in neither case did I know what I was getting into, but my absolute innocence in the first had in the latter been tempered into mere ignorance. The distinction between the two actually came into my mind in my first months in Vietnam. Among the many books I'd lugged with me was *The Sot-Weed Factor* by John Barth, which follows the late-seventeenth-century adventures of a poet, Ebenezer Cooke, as he travels around colonial Maryland, guarding both his innocence and his virginity (the same thing, kind of). The novel continually returns to the problem of innocence and ignorance, as in this exchange between Ebenezer and his former tutor, Sir Henry Burlingame:

> Burlingame showed more irritation by the minute. "What is the difference 'twixt innocence and ignorance, pray, save that the one is Latin and the other Greek? In substance they are the same: innocence is ignorance."
>
> "By which you mean," Ebenezer retorted at once, "that innocence of the world is ignorance oft; no man can quarrel with that. Yet the surest thing about Justice, Truth, and Beauty is that they live not in the world, but as transcendent entities, noumenal and pure. Tis everywhere remarked how children oft perceive the truth at once, where their elders have been led astray by sophistication. What doth this evidence, if not that innocence hath eyes to see what experience cannot?"

Ebenezer is, of course, a fool who overvalues his unworldliness. And when I read his story, in my hot little room atop the Lucy Hotel, I was equally the fool for failing to see how it applied to me. Or—and let's be generous here—I was perhaps slightly less of a fool, for Barth's musings on innocence and ignorance resonated with me. It made sense, as Barth (through Ebenezer) explains, that Adam and Eve were punished not for violating God's laws but for being innocent of sin in the first place; it's only when one knows and understands sin that one can consciously choose to commit or abstain from it. In other words, you have to lose your innocence to begin to come to terms with your ignorance. Unfortunately, innocence, unlike virginity, is not lost in a flash, nor ever fully expunged.

One night in late 2007, I even tried, somewhat tipsily, to make this argument to a couple of strangers I met on a boardwalk on the island of St. Martin—who were not at all amused to hear their beloved Adam and Eve described as "ignorant," a word that in the Caribbean implies not lack of knowledge but roughness, anger, internalized stupidity. In the English-speaking Caribbean, you do not call someone ignorant lightly—it's a fighting word—and once I'd realized this I quickly backed down and apologized. An innocent mistake, right?

Or perhaps just lingering ignorance, for I really should have known better—this had all actually happened before, in the fall of 2006, a few months after I survived Kyrgyzstan. I'd gone on assignment with my friend Michael Park to Jost Van Dyke, a tiny island in the British Virgin Islands, and within minutes of arriving, we'd settled into a rickety beachside bar for a late lunch, a beer, and a cup or two of local rum. As happens in the Caribbean, we soon wound up participating in a bar-wide argument—they called it a "discussion"—that ranged from who was worse, Saddam Hussein or Idi Amin ("Idi Amin ate children," I declared), to one man's rant about, as Michael later put it, "how violence against all white people was justified because of the area's history of institutionalized anti-black racism or something."

I don't recall the precise details of Michael's response to this, but apparently it included the word *ignorant*. The gentleman's response was predictable—or would have been predictable, had Michael or I known what we were doing. He was angry—rum-drunk and fighting angry—and things might have escalated to actual fisticuffs had not someone stepped in and calmed things down on both sides. (Michael, too, has temper issues.)

That peacemaker, oddly enough, was me. Why don't I remember this—what I did, what I said? Why is that not as vivid to me as the mistakes I made? Why do the memories of failure, pain, and humiliation nag with undying ferocity, while the successes—my successes, the moments when I performed admirably—fade into oblivion?

I can only imagine that this is some self-preservation protocol, a subconscious subroutine that reminds me how fallible I am, on the off-chance that overconfidence—or even mere confidence—will bring about my end. I am probably not quite as ignorant as I claim here to be, but I will never allow myself to think otherwise. At most, I will acknowledge a kind of Rumsfeldian progress: I have left the land of the unknown unknown and entered the realm of the known unknown. I do not know what I am doing, or what will happen next, and accepting those limitations has brought me incredible, unexpected joy.

In Kyrgyzstan, the horse budged, and Bakut and I descended the slopes into an apricot grove fed by a natural spring, where we lounged in the shady grasses, ate almost-ripe fruit, and slaked our daylong thirst.

On the flight to Tunisia via Paris, I breathed the clean air of an Airbus A380, drank red wine from little bottles, and stretched my legs as much as I could.

At the Saigon Café, I poured my bottle of beer into a glass filled with a fast-melting chunk of questionable ice, and wondered what might happen tomorrow.

## Chapter 2

# *A Model Organism*

In Which, Craving Culinary Adventure,
I Eat My Way Across the World and Figure Out
How to Handle the Consequences

Giardia, blight of my life, fire of my loins. My germ, my joke. Gee-arr-dee-ah: the tips of my toes taking a trip of three steps to the toilet, to squat, to squirm, on the pot. Gee? Arr. Dee! Aaaahhhh . . .

Ho Chi Minh City had never been a particularly quiet place. In the first half of the twentieth century, Saigon—as it was then known—was the bustling business heart of French colonial Indochina. In the 1960s and '70s, it was the hard-partying base of the American-supported South Vietnamese government. And by the time I'd arrived, the city was buzzing harder than ever, aswirl with new motorbikes, construction crews, and tourists gawking at how this nominally communist stronghold of seven million was transforming itself into a capitalist powerhouse.

The only time Ho Chi Minh City ever seemed to calm down was just after noon, when everyone was either eating lunch or post-prandially napping through the midday heat. For an hour or two, you could hear electric fans chopping at the still air, you could flip through today's *Viet Nam News* or last week's *Time* magazine, you could breathe and relax and think. This respite from the perpetual chaos is probably the only reason that one day, two weeks after I landed in Vietnam, as I sat awaiting my own lunch at a downtown restaurant, I noticed the man with the gun.

He was across the street, emerging from one storefront into the brilliant clarity of the sunshine. He was Vietnamese, and maybe in his thirties or early forties. He wore sunglasses. And at his side, in one of his hands, he held an Uzi—or what I, who knew submachine guns only from movies and music, recognized as an Uzi. Then he disappeared into the next storefront. If the street had been full of 100cc Honda bikes, as it had been an hour earlier, I would've missed him entirely.

It was a very odd sight, especially in a country as tightly controlled as Vietnam, and I wanted to ask someone—anyone—about it. Was the man a gangster? A cop? This was a mystery that needed solving.

Then my food arrived. I hadn't known quite what to order, but something on the menu caught my attention: *lươn nướng mía*. A variation on *chạo tôm nướng*, the popular dish of shrimp paste wrapped around sugarcane and grilled over charcoal, this was made instead with freshwater eel—held in place with a chive tied into a bow—and as I bit in, I fell in love. The eel was rich and oily, caramelized from the charcoal heat, infused with garlic, fish sauce, and the raw sweetness of the cane. And the cane itself, when I gnawed it, released a burst of sugary juice tinged with the meaty slick of the eel.

This, I knew, was what I couldn't get back at Chez Trinh, the only Vietnamese restaurant in Williamsburg. This was why I'd picked up stakes and moved to Vietnam—for the food. The eel, in fact, was so great that I wanted to tell strangers about it, to turn to my neighbors and tell them—in English if they were tourists, in pidgin Vietnamese if not—that it justified everything.

But I had no neighbors. I was alone in this restaurant—alone and confused. After all, this seemed to be a quality spot; the eel was proof of that. So where was everyone? Or, really, what was I doing wrong?

It was a question I asked myself often in those first months in Vietnam. I'd told everyone I'd moved there for its cuisine—the grilled meats, the startling herbs and crunchy vegetables, and, of course, *phở*, the aromatic beef noodle soup that is the national dish. And it was true I liked Vietnamese food. But liking a cuisine is not the same thing as understanding how to eat it—how to order it, and where, and when, and why. And I understood none of it. I'd eat *phở* for lunch, for example, usually going to the famous (and overrated and overpriced) Pho Hoa Pasteur for a bowl and a few small, sweet bananas as dessert. But when I'd tell the students in my English classes about my lunches, they'd look at me quizzically. To them, *phở* was breakfast, not a major midday meal.

I'd protest, noting that plenty of Vietnamese people were at Pho Hoa Pasteur. And then my students would backtrack. Oh, sure, they'd say, you can eat any Vietnamese food anytime you want. *Không sao*—no problem.

But it was a problem, clearly. And I knew the roots of it. At a Vietnamese restaurant in America, like Chez Trinh, all kinds of foods would be served together—noodles, soups, stir-fry, spring rolls. But in Vietnam, restaurants would often be devoted to a single dish or set of dishes. Pho Hoa Pasteur sold *phở*, and no other noodle soups— no *hủ tiếu mi*, no *bún riêu*, no *bánh canh*. If I wanted *gỏi cuốn*—known in English as summer rolls, they're rice-paper packets stuffed with thin rice noodles, veggies, herbs, and pork or shrimp—I could get them, and other combinations of rice noodles, veggies, herbs, and pork or shrimp, at a hole-in-the-wall behind the grandiose Ben Thanh Market.

Adapting to this was harder than I'd expected. Knowing only a small subset of Vietnamese dishes, and speaking only a few words of Vietnamese, I didn't even know what to commit myself to at one of these single-specialty restaurants. And though I knew I should just blindly walk in, point to whatever I saw on other tables, and enjoy the result, fear and shyness kept me at bay. Is there anything more alienating than not knowing how to eat?

And "knowing how to eat" was a big deal. That was actually how the question was phrased in Vietnamese: *Anh biết ăn cá không?* meant "Can you eat fish?" but translated as "Do you know [how] to eat fish?" It was hard for me to escape the implication: Maybe I *don't* know how to eat fish, or anything else, for that matter.

Which is not to say I wasn't eating, or eating well. One night, I found my way to a restaurant that served nothing but *cua,* or crab: *chả giò cua* (fried crab spring rolls), *miến cua* (glass noodles stir-fried with crab), and *cua lột chiên* (deep-fried soft-shell crab, served with lettuce and herbs), a revelation to this young man who'd grown up not far from Virginia's crab lands. And even the second-rate *phở* at Pho Hoa Pasteur was light-years better than what I'd had in America.

Still, however, I felt flummoxed at mealtimes, and too often wound up eating at the foreign restaurants in the backpacker and tourist districts. They were all surprisingly good: fresh tomatoes and basil made for excellent Italian, a devoted expatriate clientele demanded serious Japanese, and a century of French colonialism meant pâté, red wine, and onion soup were vernacular dishes. But put together, they all reminded me of my ongoing failure to penetrate Vietnamese culture.

Which still might not have been so bad—had I not been constantly sick as well. My guts had begun to rebel a few days after I arrived in Vietnam, during a trip to the Cu Chi Tunnels, where Viet Cong guerrillas hid underground during the war. The journey took forty-five minutes on the back of a motorbike, and at first I mistook my intestinal rumblings for vibrations from the rough road out of town. But once I arrived and started to clamber awkwardly through the tunnels, like any other less-than-limber Westerner, I knew something was wrong. Only through sheer sphincteric fortitude did I forge on: I saw the underground hospital and the underground mess hall, and I was properly amazed that human beings had spent so much time—years, in some cases—down here, going about the day-to-day processes of their lives in the bowels of the earth. They ate, slept, plotted strategy, survived shelling, set booby-traps, and even, as I remember it, watched movies underground, until one day the war was over and they emerged, flowing en masse into the sunlight. The release, I imagined, must have been wonderful. For the ride home to the Lucy, I took a taxi, not a moped.

Returning to my home toilet was not enough, however. For days my guts cramped up, I belched unceasingly, and my diarrhea—well, let's just say I had diarrhea. Finally, I'd had enough. Through the English-language newspapers, I located a Dutch doctor who diagnosed my troubles instantly: I had giardiasis.

Now, before I'd left the States, I'd taken some health precautions: vaccinations for typhoid, Hep A, Japanese encephalitis. On a Virginia doctor's advice, I'd even started taking Lariam, a malaria prophylactic also known as mefloquine. (Neither of us understood there were no malarial swamps in Saigon.) But none of those had protected me from the shrimp curry I'd eaten that first night in Saigon. Or the *phở* I'd been eating daily. Or the ground-pork omelette at the cute little Thai restaurant around the corner. Or the tap water I used to brush my teeth. Or the fat chunks of ice in my beer—ice that had been produced in sterile factory conditions, then zipped across town on the back of a motorbike, protected from the grit and dust only by a filthy damp piece of canvas. Or the fact that I used to bite my nails unthinkingly.

Any and all of which could have installed in my gut the protozoan parasite known as *Giardia lamblia*. A single-celled creature that is one of the most primitive organisms on the planet, it lives in the intestinal tracts of both humans and animals, and passes from host to host through water contaminated with feces. Under a microscope, the flagellated anaerobe looks like a pair of buttocks with five legs and a cape. And its macro effects were precisely what I'd experienced, give or take a bit of vomiting.

In my case, the only strange factor was that I'd gotten sick so quickly: According to the Centers for Disease Control, it takes one to two weeks for giardiasis symptoms to emerge. But I didn't care what Atlanta had to say—if the Dutchman said he could cure my giardiasis, I was willing to believe him. He prescribed a five-day course of the antibiotic metronidazole. I bought the metronidazole. I took the metronidazole. And voilà! I was better.

For a little while.

Within days, the diarrhea was back. I took more drugs, it went away. Then it came back again. For at least the first half of the year I spent in Vietnam, I had the shits.

This wasn't quite as bad as it sounds. After all, there's nothing travelers in Third World countries love more than discussing their bowels. The subject was an icebreaker at scuzzy cafés, and if you couldn't top your tablemates' tales of gastrointestinal woe, then it was like you were excluded from the club of real travelers. You hadn't earned your stripes, even if those stripes were skid marks.

In more genteel establishments, outside the backpacker hangouts, digestion was a topic, too, but eased into via coded language. "So, how's your health?" "Do you eat street food?" "Do you brush your teeth with tap water or bottled?"

These were tentative forays, designed to identify those like-minded masochists who reveled in their suffering. If the right response was given, then we could get down to business, describing foul squat toilets in the Mekong Delta, or a frantic search for Imodium in the Central Highlands. I'll spare you the florid descriptions of exactly what emerged from whose rear end, and how, but trust me, they were rarely pretty.

But as much as gastrointestinal distress enabled us to communicate, I quickly got bored by these conversations. They were always the same: sad tales, misguided notions of health and hygiene, often tinged with racism—this idea that natives could and would eat anything, no matter how filthy, because their stomachs had been born into it. Which was totally ridiculous if you ever talked to any so-called natives, or watched young kids squatting uncomfortably at the edge of the sidewalk. In communist Vietnam, diarrhea was democratic.

Pretty soon, despite my own struggles with my guts, I began to shrug off those coded openings. The experience of diarrhea had a discouraging sameness, and I almost never heard any variations on the theme: tourist eats something, gets sick, complains, gets better, complains.

And besides, no one's symptoms really seemed to match mine, because while I had diarrhea, I would also get . . . constipated. Yes, I would race to the bathroom, sit (or squat), and then nothing. Until later, perhaps, maybe, if I was lucky. My god, what frustration! Why couldn't my body make up its mind?

Desperate, I eventually returned to the Dutch doctor, where I happened to mention for the first time that I was also taking Lariam, the anti-malarial medication. Immediately, he whipped out the *Physician's Desk Reference*, the thick black encyclopedia of commercially available drugs. He flipped through to Lariam, turned the book around, and directed me to the section marked "Side Effects."

Nausea, vomiting, diarrhea—and constipation. Hm. Dizziness. Sleepiness, insomnia. Anxiety, nervousness, light-headedness. Ah. Nightmares, hallucinations, psychotic episodes. Well.

I hadn't experienced all of these, but taking a potentially anxiety-provoking drug when you've just moved to a new country where you don't speak the language, don't know anyone, and aren't sure what you're supposed to be doing seemed like a bad idea. I quit Lariam, and the intestinal problems went away . . . for a while.

Then they returned, and vanished, and returned again, a low-grade torture that wore on me mentally. Sometimes I would take more drugs, but usually I'd just try to tough it out. I remember one particularly sleepless, wretched night where that telltale gurgle in my lower abdomen would just not stop. I'd get out of my bed, in my un-air-conditioned room on the top floor of the Lucy Hotel, and stumble into the bathroom, and . . . nothing. Then I'd stumble back to bed until 20 minutes later the gurgle would return.

I did everything possible to relax myself, from breathing deeply to taking a shower (a lukewarm one, as I didn't have hot water) to, at one low, desperate point, masturbating. (FYI: Didn't work.) Some-how, though, I forgot that rich, intensely caffeinated Vietnamese iced coffee could be ordered from the street and brought to my room—a delicious laxative I never partook of in those hours of need.

Too toilet-bound to go out at night, I'd turn in early—and lie there, sleepless, listening to the churn in my bowels, wishing I could cure this blight with a single pill, but also knowing that if only I could hang on, keep my shit together (so to speak), I'd get better, become my old, robust self again, and get back to the important business of living and eating.

And I did.

But as I traveled farther and farther afield over the next twenty-five years, my health failed again and again, although, to be sure, this didn't always happen. Many—most—trips have involved no sickness at all, but when they did, I never became the guy, sidelined by Montezuma's revenge, who ruins everyone else's good time. I was never hospitalized. I never cut the voyage short. I put up with it, as all travelers must at one time or another. We get sick—the rigors and discomforts and adjustments inherent in the experience of travel pretty much guarantee that some microscopic bug will eventually overcome our immune systems and wreak havoc. And it's how we deal with the horrors of our own haywire bodies that toughens us as travelers, even as it weakens us as human beings.

More than once, it's been the flu, the symbol of international contagion, that struck me down. For example, on New Year's Eve 1999, when a group of friends and I traveled to Cambodia to watch ten thousand chanting monks welcome the new millennium in the sandstone temples of Angkor Wat. Or anyway, that's what they did. I spent the night sweating and shivering in my hotel room, while my pals were busy partying until dawn with Malaysian princesses.

But I've also had colds—the kind that simply rob you of energy and will without actually being severe—and allergy attacks and bug bites (including a yucky chigger infestation), not to mention the occasional extraordinarily close call. Near the end of my year in Vietnam, I visited the beach town of Nha Trang, where I spent a day scuba diving and snorkeling with no sunscreeen and little drinking water. By the time I returned to my hotel, I had a neck-to-ankle sunburn, a 103-degree fever, and a case of dehydration so severe my hotel called in a Vietnamese doctor to help. As I watched him fiddle with the I.V. saline drip, panic struck: Letting a Vietnamese doctor put a needle in you was the last thing the guidebooks said you should do! (By then I'd discovered guidebooks.) In delirium-addled French—my only means of communication with the doctor—I pleaded with him to make sure the needle was clean and that the tube had no air bubbles. He nodded and told me not to worry—he'd trained in Paris.

Reader, I lived! And throughout the next few weeks, when every crinkle of my lobstered back raked my nerve endings, I remember thinking—as I would think each time I caught the flu, or when my feet blistered as I walked from Vienna to Budapest, or when in Minneapolis bolts of pain shot through my skull during a stress-induced bout of shingles soon after my daughter was born—that there was only one consolation: *at least I don't have giardiasis.*

Because *Giardia lamblia* never gave up its pursuit. In 2003, its visit left me pale and weak, perched on tiptoes over a railroad car's toilet in a New Delhi train station, and four years later it had me vomiting all night into another Indian toilet, outside Darjeeling, in the Himalayas. Giardia intruded on a vacation with my wife as we drove from Mexico City down to Oaxaca and up the Pacific coast; while Jean ate tongue tacos at highway rest stops and backstroked in Acapulco swimming pools, I lay in pools of cold sweat, subsisting on Gatorade. And then, each morning, *I* would be the one to drive us to the next town, racing over dry roads and crushing lizards and curb-like speed bumps under the wheels of our rental car, wondering what was real and what I'd just imagined in my bacterial haze. Twice, giardia even ambushed me *before* my journeys began, one time striking the night before a flight to Switzerland, another appearing out of nowhere two days before a road trip to Maine. Once, in Kenya's Rift Valley, giardia kindly waited until my last day there before enveloping me in its ungentle flagella.

Throughout all of this misery, I always had an easy out: I could change how I eat—i.e., eat safely. No more fresh fruits or lettuce rinsed in tap water. No undercooked meats. No eating with my hands. No hole-in-the-wall restaurants. No street food.

No way.

For one, this would be capitulation. See, it wasn't the diarrhea I hated about giardia (though I wouldn't exactly say I enjoyed it), nor the lack of energy, nor the gaseous eruptions above and below. No, what drove me mad was the loss of appetite. During bouts of giardiasis, food disgusted me absolutely, and little would pass my lips but flavored water until the bug gave up or I'd taken a course of antibiotics. For many people, I imagine, not eating is just one more hardship to be endured, but for me it was catastrophic. To take away my appetite was to take away my identity.

Almost since I can remember, I've defined myself by my enjoyment of food. This came about gradually. When I was a kid, my parents ensured we ate well—not just home-cooked dinners with all of us at the table but actual culinary ambition. In the early 1980s, my mother was rolling her own pasta, cutting it on a beautiful Italian steel machine, and hanging it to dry in the pantry. My father, while not our family's most consistent chef, could be relied upon to produce, once a year, a ricotta-rich, sausage-stuffed lasagne (which I'd eat cold for breakfast the next day). Indian, Chinese, Thai, Mexican—this was what we went out for, and we went out a lot.

My first deeper encounter with food was in seventh grade, when I took Home Ec, learned to chop, boil, and bake, and earned a minor reputation as "Matt the Vac" for my Hoover-like ability to make food disappear. In high school, the massive ham-roast-beef-salami-swiss sandwiches I packed for lunch drew attention from my friends, and my fancy root beer in brown glass bottles drew attention from wary administrators. At the time, this was not the self-conscious showing-off of my tastes, it was just how we Grosses ate, although I was beginning to understand that not everyone shared my culinary passion. One night, friends sleeping over at my place turned their noses up at the dish of curried lamb meatballs I'd dug out of the fridge. It didn't make sense to me. How could they not like this stuff?

Which is not to say I liked everything myself. I still had issues with "gooshy" foods like yogurt; mayonnaise I avoided because a character in Judy Blume's *Superfudge* hated it; and for reasons I can no longer fathom I rejected the South's pulled pork. Apparently, it didn't fit with my New England–bred notions of what barbecue should be (i.e., ribs), and so for the three years I lived in Williamsburg, I ate none—a decision I regret even now, two decades later.

But then I went off to college, where something happened: coffee. It's no revelation that college students fuel their late-night study sessions with the world's second most popular caffeinated beverage, but I was slow to try it. At the Gross household, the smell of morning coffee trickling through a Chemex had been a constant, and yet I couldn't bear to taste it. That roasty warm pleasant aroma—how could it be so bitter and harsh on the palate? But one midnight in my freshman dorm a neighbor offered to make me a cup—instant French vanilla, I think—and I managed to drink the whole thing down.

It wasn't easy. I wasn't sure I liked this stuff, but I knew I wanted to like it. I knew I *needed* to like it. Coffee was part of the adult world, a ritual everyone else seemed engaged in, and I wanted to be a part of that, too. So, over the next six months, I drank coffee whenever it was offered to me. Usually, it was instant—this was long before the Starbucks revolution—but I gulped it down anyway. With enough time and repetition, I thought, I would grow to like the taste.

In my sophomore year, however, I had a revelation that has since come to govern my entire approach to food. It was late at night, and I was drinking bad coffee in a friend's dorm suite when it hit me: *If I didn't like a particular food, it wasn't necessarily the food's fault—it was my own failing.* Coffee is what coffee is, and I would have to learn to appreciate that, as I would have to learn not to wish that yogurt was stiffer or that Carolina barbecue were more rib-centric. Those things would never change, but my palate, and how I consciously processed the sensations coming from my mouth, could. And would. And did.

Nearly raw beef at a Japanese backpacker restaurant in Phnom Penh. Horsemeat sashimi in Kyoto and donkey stew in Venice. Tennessee cicadas in butter and garlic, Oaxacan grasshoppers with chili and lime, Cambodian deep-fried spiders. Half a roasted lamb's head in Tunis, curried goat brains in Rangoon. Spaghetti in an ice-cream cone in Seoul. Still-writhing octopus tentacles that suckered to my face in Seoul. Rocky Mountain oysters in Oshkosh, Nebraska. Pickled crabs in Koreatown. Stinky tofu in Taipei. Pig-blood "popsicles" in Taipei. Pig intestines, of varying levels of funk, in Taipei. (Goose intestines, too.) Grilled kangaroo. Grilled porcupine. Stir-fried mango leaves in the Golden Triangle. Chili-drowned rabbit heads—which I tore apart with plastic-gloved hands—in Chengdu. Tofu with pig brains in Chengdu. Fish pastes and shrimp pastes everywhere. Hearts, stomach linings, kidneys, esophagi, everywhere. Chicken feet, duck tongues, pig ears, everywhere and often. Congealed blood—everywhere.

Yeah, that's about it. Those are the strange things—the bizarre foods, as I guess we have to call them, thanks to Andrew Zimmern— that I've eaten since 1996. (None of them, as far as I know, has made me ill.) Some people, perhaps, will read the list with horror. Others, I'm sure, with smirking superiority: *What, no grubs, no dog, no poop?* But for me, as I sit here at my desk trying to recall all the odd bits I've put in my mouth over the years, I feel quite neutral. Certainly, I've enjoyed these dishes, and would eat most of them again without hesitation. (I would, however, seek fresher spiders, less gristly porcupine, more gently fried Rocky Mountain oysters.) But eating strange things was never my explicit goal. Rather, it was a logical consequence of my approach to food.

That is, on a very basic level, I liked eating, and my capacity for delight in the presence of new flavors and textures grew with each adventuresome bite, from the multilayered richness of a truffle-studded cow-sheep-goat cheese in Washington, D.C., to the sweet acid tang of a yellow passion fruit I scooped from the fecund forest floor of Kauai. Even in our food-mad culture, it's hard to explain the deep appeal of eating well, since pleasure itself is so hard-wired and individual. Why do we like things? Because we like them!

For whatever reason, food *worked* for me, and on me, and that sophomore-year epiphany—that not liking a food was my failing, not the food's—launched an instant shift that broadened my palate beyond what I'd expected. Now I knew I could and would eat and enjoy anything.

Or almost anything. A few days into my Vietnam sojourn, Le Thi Thanh, the only person I knew in this country of seventy-five million people, invited me to lunch at her home, around the corner from the Open University where I hoped to soon begin teaching. Ms. Thanh's apartment was neither tiny nor spacious, maybe four cool, blue-painted rooms on the ground floor of a not especially di-lapidated concrete building, and the tables and shelves were piled high with books and papers in English and Vietnamese. In one corner was a small shrine, with bowls of fruit and lit candles clustered around black-and-white photos of her ancestors.

To eat, Ms. Thanh, her husband, her niece, and I sat on the floor, thin rattan mats beneath us and crisp newspapers spread out as a tablecloth. I crossed my legs awkwardly and felt the bulges of my ankles rubbing against the hard tiles below. I was not comfortable, but I tried not to show it.

Many dishes came out of the narrow kitchen, brought by the niece, but only two have stuck in my memory: a small clay pot con-taining a slab of fish braised gently in peppery caramelized fish sauce; and a half-hatched egg, or *hột vịt lộn*.

Now, I'd heard of half-hatched eggs before and had been curious to try one. The idea is simple, if gruesome. A duck egg is fertilized and its embryo allowed to develop for a few weeks. Then, usually, the egg is hard-boiled, and the mix of egg white and semi-developed duck is scooped out with a spoon. This was, I'd heard, a popular snack for kids on their way to school.

What appeared before me on Ms. Thanh's floor was not what I'd expected. Rather than being hard-boiled, the egg had been fried, so that the duck fetus was splayed out amid a yellow scramble, like a suicide-by-skyscraper in a spreading pool of blood. The duck was dis-tinctly duckish—nearly fully formed, with a bulbous head and thin black feathers now floating free of its shiny, pale skin. As much as I loved eggs, and as much as I loved duck, this was not going to be easy.

I cannot tell you how it tasted. I know that I either received, or scooped myself, some egg with some duck limb, and that I nibbled as best I could at its cartilaginous bits, and I remember being surprised at how easily the feathers went down. But as for flavor and texture? They escaped me, and I concentrated instead on the other parts of the meal—the rice, the fish, the jasmine tea—though I was terrified that Ms. Thanh would notice and think me a coward or, worse, unsophisticated.

Naturally, she and her family took no notice whatsoever, complimenting me instead on my skilled way with chopsticks, and Ms. Thanh began telling me about her life: troubles during the war years, naturally enough, followed by her college studies first in French (not her favorite), then in English. Literature was her focus, and *Gone with the Wind* in particular, for how it related to the experience of people in Vietnam: North vs. South, the disappearance of an older way of life, and the tricky intersection of love, obligation, and economics. She'd visited America before, on faculty trips, and would eventually go on to get her Ph.D. in English from UMass–Amherst, with Margaret Mitchell's novel the focus of her dissertation.

So much of what she told me at that lunch I've since forgotten, and I feel terrible about it, for Ms. Thanh would show incredible concern for me over the years. It wasn't just the introduction to the Lucy Hotel or the teaching job that eventually materialized, but the way she asked after me, like a teacher worried about a bright, naïve pupil: Was I healthy? Was I staying away from the dangerous motorbike taxis?

I can't quite explain why she cared so much, since at that first lunch I'm sure I came off deluded and self-obsessed. Back then, I didn't really know how to relate to people, to get them to talk, except perhaps by showing them how completely vulnerable and accepting I was. Did Ms. Thanh see this? Or was she simply amazed that this unsavvy American was trying to start a life for himself in Vietnam, to the extent that he'd nibble scrambled duck fetus without showing his distaste?

There's a lot to be said, I think, for repression. No one at the lunch needed to know how uncomfortable, confused, and lost I felt—least of all me. Instead, I muddled through, willing myself to enjoy, or maybe appreciate, the meal and the company, and I think that counted for something. I may not have been at ease, but by exuding enthusiasm, sometimes honest, sometimes feigned, I put my hosts at ease, enough that they were willing to confide in me. And this is why in the ensuing years giardia would drive me so insane. By killing my appetite entirely, it left me unable even to fake being myself, to connect with the people and places I'd traveled so far to see.

It's such a tiny thing, isn't it? Ms. Thanh and her family served something unusual (for me), I calmly ate it (or tried to), and we got on with the process of getting to know one another. Yet eating the unfamiliar challenges people in ways they often aren't ready for. As Andrew Zimmern often points out on his show, what's normal to eat in one place is a cultural affront elsewhere. Violating food taboos hits us at deep levels—this is what we mean by disgust, not some innate biological response. By overcoming disgust, I tried to show I was making an effort—perhaps a pitiful, transparent effort, but an effort nonetheless—at fitting in to a new culture.

Still, it took another few months before I really began to fit in to the Vietnamese eating world. That was when I moved from my sixth-floor room at the Lucy Hotel to another on the fifth floor. The new room was larger and air-conditioned, with a weird bas-relief mural of ants climbing on vines across one wall, but I took it for the simple reason that it had a patio, lined with terra-cotta tiles, dotted with plants, and ideal for alfresco lunches.

But what to bring home for lunch? Ham-and-brie sandwiches from the French bakery? Or Thai ground pork with holy basil, served over rice with a fried egg on top? On a stroll around my neighborhood one day, I spotted a man grilling pork chops outside a *cơm bình dân*, an institution whose name translates as "the people's food," a very communist ideal. *Cơm bình dân* are everywhere in Vietnam. For less than a dollar, you can have a plate of rice and a serving of, say, pork belly braised in fish sauce and sugar, *rau muống* (water spinach) stir-fried with garlic, or a soup of bitter melon stuffed with pork and mushrooms. *Cơm bình dân* were pretty much fueling Vietnam's economic boom.

But they'd never appealed to me. Maybe these little storefronts, with their folding tables, plastic chairs, and worn silverwear, looked too grotty, especially given my ongoing battles with giardiasis. Maybe the premade dishes, sitting in the humid open air, turned me off. Maybe I needed to read a proper menu—to perceive my meals first linguistically, and only then with my palate. Indeed, some of my earliest restaurant memories are of menus, of scanning them with my parents for amusing typos, of matching transliterated phrases to ingredients. The words were essential gateways; without them, my tongue was useless.

Or maybe I was just afraid. My palate could handle a challenge, my psyche—fragile from failure—couldn't.

When I smelled the *sườn nướng,* or pork chops, however, everything changed. Marinated in garlic, sugar, fish sauce, and shallots, they gave off an intense aroma of fat and caramelization, one I couldn't turn away from. So I ordered takeout—*sườn nướng* on a mound of rice, with *rau muống* and sliced cucumbers—and carried the styrofoam box to my fifth-floor oasis. There I ate a perfect, and perfectly simple, meal in utter bliss.

The *cơm bình dân* around the corner became my standby, a go-to spot for good, unpretentious food to bring home. Usually, I'd get the *sườn nướng,* but sometimes I'd change it up. The shop also had squid, stuffed with pork and braised until soft, as well as crispy-fried fish. And you could get a fried egg on anything.

Eating on my patio was nice, but more and more I began to eat at the *cơm bình dân*'s flimsy tables, and noticing how other customers ate—with chopsticks, with fork and spoon, or with a combination of the two. I studied the way they prepared dipping sauces, either by filling dishes with blackly pungent fish sauce and a few shreds of red chilies, or by pouring *nước chấm,* a mix of fish sauce, water, lime juice, and sugar, from the plastic pitchers placed on each table. (I'd thought it was iced tea—whoops!) People ate without much ceremony. This was good cooking, but just as importantly, it was a refueling stop. As I watched and copied them, day after day, at the corner *cơm bình dân* and at others around the city, I didn't even realize that, at last, for the first time, I was eating like a regular person.

Nor did I realize that mastering this one meal would have collateral effects. That is, now that I'd locked down lunch, I could eat however I wanted the rest of the time. No longer did I have to feel guilty about not having *phở* for breakfast; a few hours after my strong morning coffee and fresh croissants—delicious legacies of French colonialism—I'd be feasting on cheap pork chops.

And with that lunch literally under my belt, I could experiment at dinner, whether that meant testing dosas at the southern Indian restaurant that had just opened downtown, partying in the Siberian Hunting Lodge room of the overwrought Russian restaurant, or eating braised snails and grilled mussels with coconut cream on the oil-slicked floor of a converted auto garage near the Saigon River. Whether these meals turned out delicious or dull, authentic or artificial, I knew that the next day around noon I'd be eating a people's lunch.

There was, however, one casualty of my newfound cultural adeptness. Now that I better understood lunch, the restaurant that served sugarcane eel no longer fit into my new eating life. In that year I spent in Vietnam, I never returned. The *lươn nướng mía*, so fixed in my memory, seems like a heat-induced hallucination, almost as illusory as the man with the Uzi. Except it was real, as real as the charcoal smoke and caramelizing pork vapor that still billow forth from the *cơm bình dân* on Bui Vien Street, on a thousand other streets throughout Saigon, and wherever regular folks gather to eat.

In late 2011, I was working in my office in Brooklyn when I received some interesting news. Hugo Luján, a fifty-year-old Argentine medical researcher and editor of the book *Giardia: A Model Organism*, was perfecting a vaccine for giardiasis.

"Yeah, we are close, very close," Dr. Luján told me from Buenos Aires when I called. "In fact, we have a vaccine that is now—it has been tested not only in laboratory animals but also in dogs, and cats, and bovine, which are the animals more close to humans that can be infected by giardia. And our vaccine is, in fact, the first one that is completely effective against any parasite."

The problem with developing a giardia vaccine, Dr. Luján explained, is something called antigen variation. Giardia, he said, may look like a primitive creature, but it functions in quite a complex way. When a giardia cell attaches to the lining of your intestine, it does so using a specific protein code on its surface. Taking antibiotics essentially disrupts that code so that the bacteria can't get a grip and is flushed away. But giardia doesn't have just one code, Dr. Luján said, it has roughly two hundred of them. His innovation was to puzzle out every single possible code.

"From this organism we collected, we purified the two hundred variants, and that is the formulation of our vaccine," he said. "So this is the first time in which antigen variation had been disrupted in any organism, and if we can vaccinate with all the possible variants, you are protected then. You won't need a treatment that has side effects."

I wasn't entirely sure how to react. For fifteen years I'd suffered the affections of this awful protozoan. I'd learned to recognize its symptoms and to handle the physical and psychological discomfort. Sometimes I merely persevered, other times I sought medication, usually Cipro (recommended by my physician in New York), but sometimes metronidazole or its cousin tinidazole. Four or five days of treatment, and I'd be better. In 2005, I'd even discovered a fast-track treatment: A 2,000-milligram megadose of Fasigyn, a brand-name version of tinidazole, would—I was assured by a Cambodia-based friend who'd been sicker than I ever had—eradicate giardiasis within twenty-four hours. He was not wrong: Ever since, at the first signs of giardiasis (some unusual gas, a proto-diarrhetic loosening), I've downed those pills, avoided alcohol, and woken up cured.

More important, giardia had taught me that the delight of eating came with risks, that no market taco or icy lemonade was entirely safe, but that the risks were worth the delight—always. A giardia vaccine, however, would mean a life of eating without consequences, and that felt far too easy. I liked the fact that I'd gotten sick and gotten better, that I'd survived my mistakes and emerged, if not more cautious, then at least humbler. I was a human being, and I had my weaknesses. And because I had weaknesses, I had a life worth living.

Besides, can you imagine a world of giardia-vaccinated travelers? How would they bond if they had no toilet tales to tell?

A giardia-free world is, however, a ways off. The vaccine is still only approved for veterinary use, and while Dr. Luján said a big pharmaceutical company wants to run human clinical trials, the deal was still in the works. Only the U.S. Navy, he said, had asked for his vaccine.

In thirty years of studying giardia, I asked, had Dr. Luján ever had giardiasis?

No, he said, adding that he'd take the vaccine now if he could.

So would I, I thought—without hesitation.


"*Zimmer frei*," read the hand-painted sign in front of the tidy modern house at the edge of Altenbrak, in the Harz Mountains of central Germany. I'd just emerged from an overgrown trail, having hiked twelve miles from the town of Thale, and the sun was starting to set behind the wooded hills. I recalled the old legends about the Harz—that witches fly around the peak of the 3,747-foot Brocken, and that a creature called the Brocken Spectre roams the misty forests—and in the growing dark they seemed all too plausible. I needed a place to stay.

And right there was the *zimmer frei*, the institution I'd been counting on. Throughout touristed zones of rural Germany, I knew, homeowners with rooms to rent would put up such signs—"room available," they say—to lure in wanderers such as myself, desperate for a bed but unwilling to pay the thirty euros or more for a pension or a proper hotel. And as the Frugal Traveler for the *New York Times*, saving money was my raison d'être.

I walked up to the front door, set down my backpack, and rang the doorbell. Nothing. Some lights were on inside, I could see, so I rang again. And again. Finally, a woman opened the door. She was older, large-ish, and thoroughly confused to see me.

"*Zimmer . . . frei*?" I asked.

Her expression changed to one of understanding. "Nein," she said in a neutral tone, and closed the door.

Fine, fine. I hoisted my twenty-five-pound bag and walked deeper into town. After twelve miles that day, what was another five hundred meters? If I couldn't keep my energy up at the end of a trek, I'd never get through the forty-odd miles I'd planned for the rest of the week, following in the footsteps of Goethe and Heine to the top of the Brocken. The walk so far had been perfect, starting out on well-trod paths, branching off on old logging roads, passing through tiny villages of dark-wood vacation homes. I loved the solitude, the jaunty pace of my feet on the ground, the slow accretion of mileage. Slowly but surely, I was making progress—and burning off enough calories that I could eat whatever I liked.

And that first night, once I'd checked into the Zum Harzer Jodlermeister pension and restaurant (I bargained them down from forty-five to thirty-five euros), I indulged indeed: schnitzel, noodles in mushroom cream sauce, apple strudel, vanilla ice cream, and a big pilsner. In bed by 10 p.m., I slept like the dead.

For four days, I ate big German breakfasts—rolls and cold cuts and cheeses and butter and jam, hard-boiled eggs, maybe some yogurt, buckets of weak coffee—and set off early in the general direction of the Brocken. I'd tramp for hours, sometimes through small, populated towns, more often through places that were no longer quite as wild as they'd once been. The logging routes led into patches of regrown forest, and more than once I found myself backtracking around lakes and over streams. The way forward was never obvious, and I covered more ground than I should have.

Though I never knew exactly where I was going to be, at lunchtime I always managed to pass through a town or village, where I'd pick up a hearty, rustic lunch of bread, cheese, ham, and maybe an apple. Once, at a traditional charcoal-making plant, I got a bottle of schwarzbier, a kind of black lager, and another day, just east of the former East Germany–West Germany border, I happened on Kukki's Erbsensuppe, a roadside stand selling bowls of thick split-pea soup with bacon that had opened just after reunification. Eating like this was perfect; when food was fuel I didn't have to think long or hard about what I was devouring, as I would for a story in, say, Paris or San Francisco, but it didn't hurt that it was all delicious.

Of everything I ate in the mountains, nothing was as gratifying as the wild raspberries and blueberries that grew alongside the paths. Whenever I'd spot the bright red or pale blue fruits, I'd hurry over and quickly strip them from their bushes, shoving great handfuls into my mouth. Each one was like a sharp pinprick of sweet flavor, intense and pure, and as far as I could tell this great buffet stretched across the region. As I popped berry after berry, I remembered childhood summers in Amherst, where my brother, my sister, and I would pluck blackberries from the backyard and sit on the porch consuming them, our fingers and lips stained dark with juice. Free fruit, unplanted by human hands, had always seemed to me one of nature's greatest gifts, and by my efforts I hoped to become worthy of her generosity.

A few days later, however, when my Harz Mountains story appeared on the *New York Times* Web site, I found a disturbing notice in the comments section. "I know all those raspberry and blueberry bushes throughout the forest look tempting, but most Germans wouldn't dare to eat them," wrote someone named Robyn. "The reason being the *fuchsbandwurm* a type of parasite that the foxes leave in the forest, contaminating all those lovely, free berries."

*Fuchsbandwurm*? I turned to Google and Wikipedia: The "fox tapeworm" (*Echinococcus multilocularis*) is a parasite carried in the intestines of foxes, and often dogs, in China, Siberia, Alaska, and central and southwestern Germany. The foxes, which eat berries, can contaminate the plants they touch, and when humans contract the disease, it attacks the liver like a cancer. It is, says Wikipedia, "highly lethal." Treatment is surgery followed by various forms of chemotherapy, but complete cures appear to be rare. Worse, the parasite has a long incubation period—ten or even twenty years—and is difficult to diagnose.

Even now, years after that hike across the Harz, my heart beats faster and my stomach turns as I contemplate what may befall me in another six to sixteen years. Worms may dissolve my liver, and there may be no hope. Of course, Louis Morledge, my travel doctor in New York, tells me not to worry; my liver tests have been fine so far. And I did generally—but not exclusively—eat berries from at least waist height, where foxes' fur wouldn't brush. And Klaus Brehm, a *fuchsbandwurm* specialist at the University of Würzburg, has reportedly said the idea "that one could get the fox tapeworm from berries belongs in the realm of legends." And my friend Christoph Geissler, another German doctor I met randomly on a shared taxi in Israel, giddily confessed to eating wild berries all the time, everywhere, regardless of the *fuchsbandwurm* risk. And, and, and . . .

And yet I feel terror. At least with giardia, I came to know my tormentor, to understand its causes and symptoms and cures, and to make a kind of peace with it. With the fox tapeworm, there can be no such rapprochement. If I have it, I will kill it—or it will kill me. And if the latter comes to pass, I will have no hand to blame but my own. But I hope, in those fucking miserable final moments a couple of decades from now (maybe), the berries—and everything else—will have been worth it.

~

## Chapter 3

# *Wandering Stars*

### In Which I Deal with the
### Inevitability of Loneliness and
### the Complicated Joys of Making Friends

"A re these edible?" I asked, pointing at one of the clusters of pink-purple berries I'd spotted along the trails leading through the woods of South Pender Island.

"Sure!" said Cassady Buchanan, a Pender native I'd known for approximately one hour. He plucked a few berries and ate them, and I did likewise. They were a little sweet, a little tart. Not bad. No match, of course, for the blackberries that grew in florid bushes along sunny roads here in the Gulf Islands, a sparsely settled archipelago just west of Vancouver, British Columbia. But I was happy to have discovered a new fruit, and even happier to have a new and knowledgeable friend.

I'd found Cassady by chance at Beaumont Marine Park, a secluded waterfront campground reachable only by boat or by two-mile hike through forested hills. There he was sitting at a picnic table, smoking a hand-rolled cigarette while his dog, a German shepherd mix named Haze, ate from a dish. I was carrying a camera on a tripod, and it caught his notice. We started talking and struck up a quick friendship.

Thirty-five years old, Cassady wore faded jeans, a black *Wicked* T-shirt, a floppy jungle hat, and wraparound shades. His goatee was bushy, his thick eyebrows deviously arched. After nine years of working on the mainland, he and Haze had just returned by Zodiac boat to Pender, where his family had lived for generations.

"My family, they're selling the place down at the end of the road there," he said, "so I'm just camping around and having fun. It's nice here. Well, you live in the city for so long and you see so much, it's really, really bad."

I could see what he meant, I guess. Pender and the other Gulf Islands were stunning, wild outposts of trees and rocks and water and light, with a touch of sophistication. On Galiano Island, I'd gone skinny-dipping with locals, scooped fresh oysters from the intertidal shallows, and slept in a cozy French-run bed-and-breakfast. Here on Pender, with the late-afternoon sun rippling golden across the water, I could imagine staying in just this hard-to-reach spot forever. Or at least never returning to the city.

"I'm gonna have a whiskey and a Coke," Cassady said. "It's Saturday." As he spoke more about the island—"You gotta go back about twenty years, and then it really was remote. But now it's a tourist trap. People saw it and went, *Wo-ow!*"—he came off as sharp and experienced. He spoke of finding fossils ("a piece of sandstone with a whole clam in it") and donating them to the University of Victoria, and he told me the woods were dotted with Indian caves.

Cassady also seemed a touch paranoid and a braggart—he called himself a horticulturalist, a Hungarian prince, a descendant of President James Buchanan (a lifelong bachelor, it should be noted). He claimed never to have been photographed, and he seethed at the Pender authorities, who were transforming the place into a yuppie (or as he put it, "yippie") shithole, with no regard for locals like himself. This was his island. He'd built its roads. It belonged to him in some intangible way. "Ha!" he'd add at the end of every sentence.

I listened to him intently—it didn't matter to me what was true or false, or that he'd nearly emptied his bottle of whiskey. Cassady was a local, a quirky character with inside intelligence and stories to tell, and he seemed to reflect my interest in him. I didn't look like a New Yorker, he said, and he kept asking about what I was doing hitchhiking around the islands. Finally, I felt comfortable enough to admit I was writing for the *New York Times*. Usually, I kept such things secret, so that people wouldn't act different around me, but Cassady had been so open already that it didn't seem right to hide it from him. He was a civilian, not an hotelier. In any case, he didn't react strongly to the news—he took it in stride. He felt like a friend.

On the ferry over from Galiano, I'd heard about a house party that night, and invited Cassady to join me. He tied up Haze and gave him some water, and off we marched back through the woods, stopping to sample those berries and explore one of the nearby caves. We returned to the more developed part of Pender early, and took a rest in my campground—a boring place I would've avoided if I'd known about Beaumont Marine Park—while I cooked a quick dinner of rice with sausage and dried mushrooms on my portable stove.

Not quite realizing what I was getting us into, I also uncorked a bottle of local red wine I'd bought in town. And as we ate and drank, I could now see that Cassady was really blitzed. When I added salt to my rice, he sneered, saying it was terrible for you. I wanted to explain about the relationship between salt and flavor, but I kept my mouth shut, opening it only to drink my own wine as fast as possible, so Cassady wouldn't get worse.

Finally, we left the campground and, in the dark, started walking up the island's smoothly paved main road toward the party, whose hosts Cassady said he knew. I was dreading our arrival: Was he really friends with them? Or would we find ourselves in an even more awkward situation?

The awkward situation found us. Halfway to the party, bright lights appeared behind us—bright lights that turned suddenly blue and red. A police cruiser. The cop, tall, blond, and clean-cut, got out and asked us for identification. Cassady had none.

"Where are you from?" the officer asked him.

"Right here," he said proudly. "I built that road! Where are you from, ha?"

He ignored Cassady's question and said, "You were weaving all over the road." It was true. Cassady couldn't walk straight, and it was partly my fault. "Have you two been drinking?"

"No!" Cassady said, sounding insulted. He turned to me, his eyes pleading for backup. He looked scared—his swaggering confidence drained.

I couldn't lie, but I couldn't indict Cassady, either. "I drank some wine with dinner," I said.

"Who are you?" the officer asked me. "What are you doing here?"

I gave him the short version: on vacation, island-hopping, camping. No mention of the *Times*. Easier that way.

"Okay, you can go on," he said to me, handing back my driver's license. I wasn't drunk. "Stick to the side of the road."

"I'm not leaving without him," I said, although all I really wanted was to leave without him. Cassady was beginning to be a burden, but I couldn't treat him like one, even if it meant getting arrested alongside him. "I'm not leaving without my friend."

"Fine," said the cop. "You stand there." He placed me in front of his car, with its high beams directly in my face, then led Cassady behind the vehicle. I couldn't see or hear a damn thing.

I stood there, imagining the worst: Cassady locked up, Cassady beaten up, his triumphant return home to Pender wrecked because he'd happened to run into me, a charming enabler with a video camera. And I wished, for a moment, that none of it had happened, that I could have just gone on my way, a lone traveler neither seeking nor needing companionship. But that, I knew, was a fantasy.

Ever since I can remember, I've been good at making friends, usually without consciously trying to. As a little kid, of course, I was willing to be friends with anyone who liked *Star Wars* figures or Legos; that was enough for me. But at the same time, my family was also moving about, from Amherst to Brighton, England, back to Amherst, down to Williamsburg. And so I was, perhaps slightly more often than most children, the new kid, always introducing myself in a fresh environment and trying to find other people who played *Ultima* on the Apple II or wanted to stay up all night watching horror movies and eating Domino's pizza. Lots of people, I bet, look back on their childhoods and see themselves at the center of multiple, ostensibly antagonistic groups—jocks and nerds, rebels and preps, blacks and whites, and Latinos and Asians. This, too, was me, though not because I specifically positioned myself between them but because I didn't care all that much who my friends were. As long as there was a single point of commonality, we could get along. I didn't ask much: Be available to hang out. Laugh at stuff. Don't beat me up. (I was short, nerdy, and accustomed to harassment.) Yup, that was about it.

The unforeseen consequence of this is that while I made friends easily, I also had a lot of crappy friends—kids who might have shared my nominal interests, like skateboarding, but who too often took advantage of my craving for companionship (and my access to the family car). Some of those high school friendships ended in acrimonious breakups, and one of them in an actual fistfight (if you can call my getting punched once in the jaw a "fight"). Meanwhile, I spent less time with certain friends who were kinder people but less enthused about skateboarding, more into playing guitar.

Over the years, I've come to realize that these sorts of friendships are normal for kids. Stuck in the same classroom, the same high school, the same small town, your choices are limited, superficial, not really choices at all. Circumstances force you into friendships that, given the options of a wide world, you might otherwise never have forged. If you're lucky, the friendships can last, maturing as the friends themselves mature. But they don't have to, and that's okay.

The wider world, however, presents its own challenges.

If you are alone in a strange new place, where you don't speak the language, don't know anyone, and aren't sure why you're there to begin with, the last album you want to listen to, over and over and over again, is *Dummy*, by the English trip-hop group Portishead. With its slow, rumbling beats, oddly looped samples, and psychedelic instrumentation (heavy on theremin, supplemented by orchestral strings), Portishead's music evokes a world of isolation, longing, regret, and misery—all of it made unutterably sweet by the spooky-sexy voice of Beth Gibbons.

"Please, could you stay awhile, to share my grief," she pleads on "Wandering Star." "For it's such a lovely day to have to always feel this way." On "Strangers," she asks, "Did you realize no one can see inside your view? Did you realize for why this sight belongs to you?" And at the end of "It Could Be Sweet," as the bass line thrums quietly on and the electronic keyboard repeats a tranquil melody, Gibbons lets out a final, nearly inaudible sigh that seems to express both the bliss of desire and a certain variety of resignation, the understanding that desire may never be fulfilled but that the desire itself is enough, and maybe, in the end, more delicious than its fulfillment.

For months, Portishead's music echoed in my top-floor room at the Lucy Hotel, matching, assuaging, and amplifying my own deep loneliness. I owned not more than six CDs—quirky mid-'90s bands such as Cibo Matto and Stereolab—which I played on a boom box purchased with a fair chunk of the money I'd brought from home, but it was *Dummy* that provided the soundtrack for my Vietnam life. In the morning, it reminded me I'd woken up alone. After lunch, it reminded me I'd eaten alone. And at night, under the thin covers of my bed, it told me solitude was all there ever was, ever would be. "And this loneliness," Gibbons sang, "it just won't leave me alone."

I was not, however, entirely friendless. At the Saigon Café, where I'd drunk my first beer on ice, I met Dave Danielson, a squinty-eyed Californian who ran an English as a Foreign Language school called

ELT Lotus. Dave had been a professional skateboarder back in the 1970s, when long-haired dudes carved surf-style across soft SoCal embankments, and I think I trusted him because we shared a four-wheeled past. Also, because I had an EFL certificate, he gave me a job at Lotus, which contracted with companies to teach English to their employees. I would be teaching an introductory course at AkzoNobel, a Dutch paint and chemical concern, earning $15 an hour—about a week's wages for the average Vietnamese worker.

On my first day of work, a Friday, I set off for AkzoNobel by bicycle, and promptly got lost. Maybe not lost exactly, but I couldn't find the damn street the company was supposed to be on. It was hot, and I began to sweat in the dense traffic. Then it began to rain. I was fifteen minutes late, at least, and had no mobile phone to call the company or the school. Suddenly, the traffic parted, and there was squinty Dave on his moped. He pulled up next to me, asked what the hell was going on, and guided me to AkzoNobel, where my sweaty, scruffy appearance (tuck in my shirt? Never!) would turn out, over the coming months, not to be a function of the weather.

That night, Dave took me out to celebrate, getting me drunker—on sour BGI beer—than I'd ever been in my short life. Thankfully, I remember little but the hangover, which lasted the entire weekend, and I'm not sure I ever forgave him.

But meeting Dave proved useful, for he introduced me to another Lotus teacher, Adrian, who was dating the owner of the Bodhi Tree, a not terribly good Pham Ngu Lao café where expatriates congregated. Among them were two I thought I might be able to get along with: Jed, a sharp academic on a Ford Foundation grant, and Ted, like me a wannabe writer, but so argumentative, so New Yorky, so . . . *Jewish* (like me) that I instantly resented his presence in this country. He, I knew, would be my competition.

Among Jed, Ted, Adrian, and their other friends, I was a peripheral figure—literally. Though I knew Adrian slightly from work, I wasn't yet all that friendly with him, so I tended to sit one table over from the gang, hoping I'd overhear a conversation I could participate in. Occasionally, I did; often, I didn't. These people, I sensed, would never be true friends.

But this was Vietnam, and I preferred to make the acquaintance of actual Vietnamese people. I was, however, unsuited to that task as well. Phuoc—Ms. Thanh's student—made an effort for a while, inviting me to lunch once or twice, and then to spend a weekend at his family's house on the outskirts of the city. Phuoc spoke good English and was a stand-up guy, so nice and normal and sweet that his biggest problem in life was convincing his Catholic parents to accept his Buddhist girlfriend. I liked him fine, but couldn't see how our interests matched up in a way that would let us be real friends. On the way to his parents' place, for example, we stopped at a sort of fish-farm café, where we drank iced coffee and sat at the edge of a man-made pond trying to hook catfish. I liked this just fine, but was this Phuoc's primary pastime? Who was this gentle character? Would he be the friend to follow me into the stranger corners of the city?

When we got to his family's house, however, I was thrown into amazed confusion. The house itself was unlike those deeper in the city: it was one tall story, wide and deep, with a *phở* stand out front, a small living room featuring the uncomfortable faux-leather sofas that are de rigueur for Vietnamese decorators, and, a bit farther in, a massive, room-filling industrial loom, fed by four huge spools of thread, beneath a high, corrugated-steel roof. I was transfixed. This . . . this was a typical Vietnamese home? What was it like to live here—to grow up surrounded by light industry?

All through my visit the loom ran, spinning thread into bolts of thin white fabric that Phuoc's family would sell to the burgeoning garment industry. Even after dinner, it kept humming, and when, on occasion, it stopped, due to an unhooked spool or tangled line, someone—Phuoc, a young cousin, a grandparent—would stroll by to fix and restart it. That night, I slept in surprising peace on the uncomfortable couch.

But the next morning, I faced a challenge that proved too much for me: the toilet. It was a squat-style toilet, ceramic and clean, and although I was for the moment free of giardia, I knew that I didn't know how to properly use it, and didn't trust my legs to keep me stable. Worse, there was no way I could really communicate this to Phuoc; we were not yet close enough for toilet talk. And so, though I was supposed to spend another day and night with his family, I bailed on them, making vague excuses, utterly ashamed at my failure and unable to explain any of it to the open-hearted guy who would now never really be my friend. The only good that came of the episode was that I began practicing my squat every day, so I'd never fail again. Pretty soon, I could hold a squat, flat-footed, for thirty seconds to a minute, not long enough to, say, fix a bicycle, but certainly adequate for any emergency bathroom situation.

If only I'd been as successful in learning the Vietnamese language! My second week in Ho Chi Minh City, I'd signed up for an intro course that met five days a week. From the beginning, I struggled. While Vietnamese is written with a modified Roman alphabet, the spoken language is tonal, so the meaning of a word depends on whether your voice stays flat, rises, falls, falls and rises, falls and rises sharply, or falls so far down it gets stuck in your throat. *Anh*, for example, is older brother, while *ảnh* is a photo. I could actually produce these sounds fairly well—or at least better than some of my Australian and Korean classmates—but I could hardly hear them at all, and the confounding preponderance of triple diphthongs and swallowed final consonants didn't help. As the teacher asked questions, I found myself calculating the possibilities of each individual word, trying to guess what made the most sense. *Where is the . . . umbrella? Do I want to buy a motorbike, or sell one? How many friends are in the room?*

Wait, what? Did she really ask that? She did—and to me directly: "*Có bao nhiêu bạn ở phòng?*" I looked around at the class, wondering how many people I could consider my friends after just a couple of weeks. I'd had lunch once with Eun-soon, a Korean supervisor at a clothing factory, but that was about it. Did I dare respond, "One"? How pathetic. Or was I supposed to consider everyone here to be my friend? I opened my mouth. I closed it. I looked around in existential angst.

The teacher called on another student, a young Japanese woman whose language ability outstripped us all. "Nine," she said.

"Good work," said the teacher, then led us in counting all the tables in the room. The tables! Table, I remembered, was *bàn*; I'd heard *bạn*, friend.

Another couple of weeks and I quit the class. I told myself it was because I couldn't wake up early enough to arrive by 8 a.m. every day, but my ongoing failures were the real culprit. If I was going to have local friends, they would have to be English speakers. And as I realized this, I felt the old constraints creeping up—I would not be choosing my friends here. Circumstances would do the choosing for me.

But sometimes circumstances have a way of working out. In the early fall of 1996, the first cybercafé had opened in Ho Chi Minh City. Tâm Tâm, it was called, and it had been started by Tom Rapp, a gruff-voiced, mustachioed New Yorker in his sixties, and his partner, a wiry, hot-tempered young local named Minh. With a half-dozen computers, it was the only public place in the city you could send and receive e-mails, and I spent a lot of time there keeping up with friends and family back home, drinking strong iced coffee with condensed milk, listening to Bryan Adams and annoyingly sweet Vietnamese pop, and chatting about food with Tom, who owned a restaurant on the Upper East Side of Manhattan.

"You should meet Douglas," Tom told me one day. I'd heard this name before, maybe from Tom, maybe from others. Douglas, too, had recently moved to Vietnam, after working in the New York film and TV industry for several years. Right now, though, he was traveling around Cambodia and Laos. To me, that sounded brave. "You'll like him," Tom said. "I'll introduce you when he's back."

Then Tom handed me a CD. He'd bought it in the States, thinking Minh would like it, but it was too dark for Vietnamese tastes. The band's name was Portishead.

Douglas* and I met a couple of weeks later, at Tâm Tâm, as I was coming in and he was leaving, or maybe vice versa. Douglas was laidback and confident, a tall, blondish dude from the Pacific Northwest who'd spent time after high school in a Japanese monastery. About to turn thirty, he'd decided to take a year off from New York and simply see what happened in and around Vietnam.

All of this made him little different from me—or the other Westerners fumbling around Saigon. What linked us, I soon learned over drinks and multiple games of pool at La Camargue, a restaurant in an old French villa, was two things: a shared love of William T. Vollmann, an intense San Francisco writer obsessed with skinheads, prostitutes, homeless people, hobos, crack cocaine, guns, the Afghan mujahideen, the California-Mexico borderlands, and Southeast Asia; and our deep longing to explore.

This was what I'd been missing here—not just a friend but a travel buddy, someone who saw in the gray and empty streets of midnight Ho Chi Minh City an enticement, an opportunity, a dare. I had hung around the backpacker haunts of Pham Ngu Lao long enough. I needed to stretch my legs.

And with Douglas, I began to wander. He rode a Bonus, a big, cheap, traditional motorcycle, and I decided my $40 one-speed bicycle needed upgrading. In its place, I rented a 70cc step-through moped with a little basket on the front. Together, we sped around the city, often with his girlfriend, Dung, a cute youngster with a slightly snaggletoothed smile. In Cholon, Saigon's Chinatown, we marched into a nightclub called Artists, where we stood out in a

---

*Not his real name.

crowd of hip Vietnamese kids. With the Tâm Tâm crew, we cara-vaned on our mopeds to distant, verdant riverside restaurants where we wrapped herbs and grilled meats in rice paper. Frequently, we drove just to see which streets went where, and at the end of an evening we'd return to a Japanese-run downtown hotel, where we'd pay $30 apiece to soak in hot tubs alongside tattooed yakuza. Each night with Douglas was a chance to do something I'd never have done otherwise.

In Vietnam, hierarchy is built into the language. Everyone is either your superior or your inferior, and there's no one word for "you." *Anh*—older brother—is how you address a slightly older male; *chú*—uncle—is a man a generation older than you, but younger than your father; *bắc* is the "uncle" older than your father. Women are addressed as *chị*, *cô*, or *bà*. Anyone younger than you (or just female) is *em*.

In this context, Douglas was *anh*, I was *em*. In Japan, you'd call it a senpai-kohai relationship. In Jedi terms, I was the paduwan. And for a long time, it was nice. I needed someone to teach me, to inspire me, to show me the way by dint of his experience and confidence—even to dress me. The Valentino button-downs Douglas had bought in Bangkok, but no longer liked, clad me for years to come.

But Douglas was not always there, or was always a little distant. When in the midst of a 2 a.m. battle with giardia I called him, he was taken aback. *Were we that close already?* Hanging out together was not a default mode. He had his own life, and Dung, and plans that didn't involve me. Once he got a job as a creative director at a Vietnamese advertising agency, there were work dinners and drinks to go to. I, his little brother, was not at the top of his list anymore, if I ever had been.

I understood this well. Back home, I was the older brother, and while I cared for my younger brother and sister, I didn't necessarily want them around me all the time. For Douglas to feel this way as well was only natural.

And so I continued to retreat to my little room to read weighty novels (Pynchon, Barth, Wallace) and listen to Portishead while contemplating this new variety of loneliness, one that ached ever deeper because it was not complete. I had friends and acquaintances; I spoke with people on a regular basis. But I was still an outsider, with no ties to either the foreign or Vietnamese communities. I might as well have been a tourist, here to drink a few '333' beers, see the Museum of American War Crimes, and bask in the fast-vanishing aura of danger. Vietnam!

On a golden June afternoon in 2007, the Driftless Hills of southwestern Wisconsin bulged with promise. Green woods carpeted the round slopes, fading in places to bald patches of prairie or giving way, abruptly, to the fields of organic farms. The road whipped through and around the hills, and I accelerated my Volvo at each sinuous curve, enjoying the comforting hug of centripetal force and the lush rhythm of late-in-the-day driving. The road, I knew, was dangerous at this time. Deer were coming out to forage. Already, one had dashed across the asphalt in front of me and leapt over a high fence, arcing so slowly it seemed almost to pause, midair, at its apex, backlit and burnished by the setting sun, before vanishing into the tall grass.

"It's not for you to know," Neko Case sang on the car stereo, "but for you to weep and wonder."

Weep and wonder I did. I almost felt I could not go on. The music, the landscape, the unfightable forward motion—they contrived to amplify my isolation. To sweeten it, too. I was a month into a summer-long cross-country Frugal Traveler road trip for the *Times*, zigzagging from New York to Alabama to South Dakota to Texas to Colorado to Wyoming to Seattle, avoiding all interstates, and for most of the twelve-thousand-mile journey, I knew, I would be alone in my car, a creaky silver 1989 station wagon, prone to overheating, that I'd purchased for $1,600 and named Vivian.

Though not exactly alone. Music kept me company. Neko Case sang me across Wisconsin and Iowa, the Flaming Lips through New Mexico and Colorado. Bob Dylan got me past Kansas, Leonard Cohen past Nebraska, Cat Stevens into South Dakota. From my iPod to the tape deck to Vivian's one working speaker, French rapper MC Solaar chanted out his combative prose.

The miles would go by—one hundred, two hundred—and the music kept going. I gunned Vivian around the muddy Mexican borderlands (where her rear bumper fell off) and up Rocky Mountain dirt roads (where her transmission died) and through the persistent rurality of Indiana, and I listened to sad, simple songs all the way, the kind of minor-key music you'd never put on with a real, live friend at your side. But this trip was different, and my solitude needed a soundtrack.

At times, though, the beauty of the landscape and the sound scape would overwhelm me, and I'd be tempted to let go of the wheel and drift off down cliffs and ravines to certain death. The slick Black Hills of South Dakota, those winding pine-lined highways intercut with washboarded logging roads, were a Siren's song. The Texas desert west of Mentone—no gas stations, no population, just empty rock and arid riverbeds—could have been my own personal wastelands. The death wish enveloped me, but not because I wanted this to end. On the contrary, I wanted to go on forever, to preserve this feeling of absolute perfection. As I hurtled across the land in my silver steel station wagon, the world was revealing itself to me, and to me alone, as the musical gods I adored sang to me, of me, for me. I was beholden to no one, in charge of my direction and my destiny, as urgent but unhurried as the loping rhythms of Portishead. And the only way to keep this moment from ending, I kept thinking, was to end it all—to stop any other moment from ever intruding. Sorry, Vivian!

"Do you realize," the Flaming Lips asked me, "that happiness makes you cry? Do you realize that everyone you know someday will die?"

Everyone? Well, yeah. But everyone's death was not what concerned me—I was obsessed with my own fate, and still am. Early on, probably before I was ten years old, I lost whatever faith in a supernatural God I'd once had, and mortality became a pressing concern. At night, I feared sleep, because temporary unconsciousness seemed a mere prelude to an eternity of unbeing. Once in a while, the panic would rise in my chest and spread over my face, drilling into my skull the fact that one day I would be no more—and would not even know it, and would not even for a second be able to feel relief at having come to an end. The universe would, as far as I was concerned, cease to exist. Everyone I know someday will die? Yeah, sure, of course, I cared, but the day *I* died I would no longer be capable of caring.

Over the years, though, I learned to cope, partly through the promise of writing. If I could write, and write well enough to produce something lasting—a book, say—then my words, my ideas, my self would survive my unavoidable end. My work would probably not outlast me by much, a century if I got lucky, but while I'd never know for certain what kind of legacy I'd leave, this was my best chance to avoid being forgotten completely.

I can't say this was a particularly sophisticated approach to life (or death), but it came from deep within me, this visceral fear of death that I could tamp down only through denial and disciplined misdirection. But seen through this lens, it also explains my craving for companionship. By making new friends, I could leave trace memories of myself all over the world. (Had I been more attractive and less ethically bound, I might have left children in many lands.) Luckily, making friends was a virtual job requirement. I needed people for my stories—locals, preferably, to show me around, provide color, and transform my dispatches from the Fabulously Frugal Adventures of Matt into something broader and less personal.

And so I drove into eastern Kentucky with high hopes. This was bourbon country, and a half-dozen distilleries were scattered around among the horse farms and raw limestone hills. Wild Turkey, Jim Beam, Maker's Mark—all had their production facilities and tasting rooms here, and the windowless towers where they aged their liquor in new, charred-oak barrels stood out starkly amid the deep green of the countryside. Bardstown, whose Federal-style brick houses and central square gave it the look of an old town in eastern Pennsylvania, was where I planned to focus my energies, both for its proximity to the distilleries and for the Old Talbott Tavern, a nineteenth-century inn that had supposedly once lodged Abraham Lincoln and, more importantly, was reputed to have the best whiskey selection around.

The dark, wood-paneled bar, however, was nearly deserted when I arrived that Friday afternoon. The handful of patrons were drinking gin-and-tonics and bad bottled beer. The bourbon list was indeed lengthy, with lots of single-barrel selections and rarities from independent producers, and I desperately wanted to discuss it with someone. I loved bourbon, the burn of the alcohol, the illusion of sweetness, the mouth-filling texture. But the bartender didn't seem interested in talking shop. I ordered an old-fashioned and moped.

Perhaps, I thought when I'd finished the drink, I'd have better luck in the tavern's restaurant. I walked through the building, past the gift shop, and into the dining room. But the stone-walled, wood-beamed space was equally desolate. A mother and her daughter were eating cheeseburgers. A trio of older guys sipped sweet tea.

In one corner, however, I spied a single woman. Blonde, mid-thirties, I guessed, and not from around here. When she spoke to the waitress, she didn't have the accent. Maybe, I hoped, she was in Bardstown for the same reason I was—a love of bourbon. But how could I approach her? She was all the way across the room, and I had no pretext for introducing myself. I didn't want to seem like a weirdo, and I didn't want to appear to be hitting on her. (I was married, after all.) I just wanted someone to talk to, to share my discoveries with.

It would be easier, I knew, if I already had a companion—if this woman were already at my side. That's how it had worked in the past. A few years earlier, I'd traveled around northern India with my friend Sandra, a petite, dark-haired graphic designer. We were both involved with other people at the time, but we were friends, and adventurous, and on trains, in restaurants, and on the streets we gave off an aura of approachability. We were not dangerous. We were interesting. You could talk to us—you wouldn't be popping a lovers' bubble. We were together, but we were independent. We could look after each other, but weren't responsible for each other's happiness. We could flirt with whomever we wanted.

This could be confusing in India. On the third-class train from Sawai Madhopur to Agra, a fantastically crowded compartment in which we were the only, and therefore fascinating, foreigners, a conductor pushed his way down the aisle and sat beside me.

After asking my name and where we were from, the conductor looked at Sandra, then at me, and said, "Are you married?"

Yes, I told him.

"Ah," he said. "So this is your wife?"

No, I said without elaborating.

He looked confused, then his eyes brightened. "So," he asked tentatively but eagerly, "she is your girlfriend?"

"No," I said, and smiled.

The conductor frowned. This did not make sense, and he seemed to be wondering whether he'd made a mistake in his English or had misunderstood mine. After a silent minute, he said good-bye and moved on.

Later, I felt guilty for this deception—he hadn't deserved my smart-aleckiness—but at the time I relished our bizarre situation too much to let the opportunity to confound him pass. Sandra and I may not have been an item, but we intrigued, and I loved it.

It wasn't this way when I traveled with Jean. When she and I went to Mexico or Maine or Paris or Taiwan, it wasn't to meet new people but to be with each other. Jean's comfort was my concern; if she wasn't enjoying herself, I couldn't. This is not to say I didn't like traveling with Jean, but it was different. We were a closed circuit.

But with Sandra, it was an open relationship, so to speak, as it was with other friends I'd traveled with: Christine, Sita, Sara, Mary Ellen. If only this mystery woman was at my side already, I wished in the Old Talbott Tavern, I could talk to her, no problem. It was a chicken-and-egg situation, and I was clearly the chicken.

Elsewhere, this would work differently. In Tbilisi, the capital of Georgia, I'd discovered a hip milliner, Nini K., whose boutique sold modern versions of traditional Caucasian fur hats. And when I learned Nini spent half the year in New York, our talk turned to our favorite Lower East Side bars, and then to the party she was planning at her country house that weekend—to which she invited me, without knowing I was a travel writer. I remember walking out into the street, blinded by the summer sun and the hospitality. But apparently, that was just how it works in Georgia: A few nights later, I was walking alone through an area of open-air bars, taking pictures, when a group of teenagers spotted me and called me over, first to ask questions, then to drink beers and accompany them to a disco and hang out all night long.

Here in America (and much of the West), we're afraid. Afraid of being misunderstood or, worse, flat-out rejected. To say hello is to put our souls on the line by confessing our loneliness. Much easier to remain monadic and to suffer than to risk failure. Even for me, after a thousand successes and far fewer failures, I couldn't summon the courage to connect.

And, not for the first or last time, I wished I didn't need to. Why couldn't I just be alone? Why this desperate, flailing craving for human connection? The uncomfortable fact was, I was *good* at being alone. I knew how to eat alone (at the bar), and I could happily go days without a real conversation as long as I had plenty of reading material. Traveling solo was often easier than with a companion— I could wake up when I wanted, go where I wanted, and leave when I got bored. Solitude inspired in me a cheerful indifference, a nothing-left-to-lose sense of independence. I'd survived solitude before; those horrible lonely nights in the Lucy Hotel had transformed into sweet memories of youth. I could survive it again, right?

But then the isolation and longing would overwhelm me, to the point where I would do anything—*anything!*—to make real contact with a stranger like the mystery woman. Anything but go talk to her, of course.

And as some of my readers would later suggest, the mystery woman might have been the wrong target. Maybe the sweet-tea trio or the cheeseburger family were ready for a chat? They looked like locals; they probably knew this town inside and out. But no—I couldn't talk to them. They had other things going on. There were dynamics I couldn't disturb. They had come together, to eat and talk, and I didn't feel like it was my place to interrupt. They did not remind me of myself and Sandra in India, open and inviting.

Instead, I ate my pork chops, alone with my brooding thoughts and creeping dread. But afterward, as I lingered in the tavern's gift shop thumbing through tourist brochures, the mystery woman walked out of the restaurant and up to me.

"Are you from New York?" she asked.

Patricia, I learned over bourbon flights, was from Westchester County and, intriguingly, was a veteran road tripper. Whenever she had a break from her secretarial job, she'd fly off to the Shenandoah Valley or Sioux Falls, rent a car, and roam the region for a week or more, indulging in her passion for American history.

As we talked and drank, I was, in a strictly platonic way, falling in love with Patricia. Here I was, traveling the world as a professional observer and evaluator of the experience, yet this was what she did for fun, and what happened to her on the road did not have to follow a theme and would not be simplified and condensed for public consumption. What happened there mattered to her, and to her alone.

Over the following years, as we communicated by e-mail, I loved simply hearing about her occasionally messy life: the family conflicts, the sexist bosses who denied her promotions and called her on vacation, the crushes on friends (married and single), the realization, after a bluegrass concert attended by senior citizens, that she seemed to "share the same interests as the average seventy year old" and was therefore "a magnet for mandolin players."

In other words, Patricia was a full-fledged human being, neurotic and struggling and occasionally succeeding and, when she had the chance, escaping her life to wander America on a tour of "libraries and cemeteries." I loved how our encounter pulled me out of my morose solipsism and into the world. I loved that Patricia existed, and that I'd had the luck to meet her and fix her in my shaky memory, as I hoped she'd fixed me in hers.

On some level, I wanted to be like her—to have a life full of drama that I'd deal with by traveling. But my life was settled, which was something of a surprise to me. Just a few months before this cross-country road trip, Jean and I had bought an apartment in Brooklyn together. I had a regular column in the *New York Times* and was traveling the world on someone else's dime. I was not addicted to any drugs, did not have any serious health problems, and got along relatively well with my family and my in-laws. Apart from my maudlin fear of death, and the attendant craving for companionship, I had no angst. I may have had amusing stories to tell, but I was, and am, personally boring.

I am also not as good a friend as I'd like to be. In the years after we bumped into each other in Kentucky, Patricia and I exchanged dozens of e-mails—or really, she sent them to me, and while I read with great pleasure of Patricia's peregrinations, her sister's weirdly budding country-music career, her unrequited loves, I never responded speedily or in enough depth to continue the conversation.

In fact, it's only just now I've spotted this line in a message from her in 2011: "It's a little trying, constantly being alone. It seems like there's got to be something better than that . . . but my experience tells me sometimes solitude is the best option."

What I should have told Patricia—what I need to tell her now—what she probably already knows—is that solitude does not last. When its walls seem thickest, that fortress crumbles. You go on Facebook, or Couchsurfing, and make contact. You buy a plane ticket and fly to Kentucky and meet someone in the gift shop. You walk down the street in Tbilisi and wind up in someone's country house. You get lucky—you connect.

And that connection does not have to last. That is, friendship is not diminished by its ephemerality. Patricia and I met, wonderfully, on the road, but what claim do we have on each other? What responsibility can we possibly bear toward everyone we meet? Along with Patricia, I've met and befriended the Signorino family of Columbus, Indiana, and Hannity in his trailer outside Columbus, New Mexico, and Mike the curly-haired Australian snowboarder in Bulgaria, and Henry and Bess, the Australians I met somewhere in Turkey, and those Peace Corps volunteers in Bishkek and the kid on the train from Urumqi to Beijing and my dining companions throughout Malaysia and all the architects and designers of Buenos Aires. There are hundreds more, and while I'd be overjoyed to see them again, in whichever city they like, I harbor no expectation that will happen. The best and most responsible thing I can do is to remember them, to honor the brief joys of our relationships as abstract souvenirs, and to cross my fingers our paths will cross once more.

Because it can happen, and in ways we'd never predict. A few months after Douglas and I became friends—after we'd explored Saigon and taken a trip to Cambodia together and shared many, many Sunday brunches at a grottily cute French restaurant—I began noticing an intriguing crew floating through the Lucy Hotel. There were about eight of them, roughly my age, Americans and Vietnamese-Americans.

Fairly well-dressed, as if they had real, important jobs. I could, I was sure, connect with them—they were my people—but I didn't know how. Or I didn't know how to do so without being obvious.

And so I waited. I had Douglas, I had Ted and Jed and the Bodhi Tree gang, I had Tom and Tâm Tâm Café, and I had Portishead and I had my novels. I was in no rush, but I would make it happen.

As the month of March began, Ho Chi Minh City got hot. The rainy season long since past, the sun roasted the concrete sprawl with ferocity that increased each day. I was at the time deep into my midday routine of pork-chop lunches followed by air-conditioned naps, but that day the heat was too much. I finished my meal, then walked downstairs for an iced coffee with condensed milk in the Lucy Hotel lobby.

As usual, it was cool down there—all those tiles and high ceilings. Across from the front desk was a round wrought-iron table with a glass top and two cushioned chairs. At one sat Lucy Nhung, a gravelly voiced forty-something with big eyes, a bad temper, and a reputation for aggressive business tactics; rumor had it she'd convinced a Korean ex-boyfriend to buy her the hotel, then wound up in full control of the place. She could be loving, but she could also be dangerous.

When Lucy saw me approach, she greeted me and vacated her seat, asking if I wanted a coffee. I said yes, and she dispatched one of her employees into the street to fetch it. I sat down where Lucy had been, directly across from a Lucy Hotel denizen whose name, I would soon learn, was Tuyen Nguyen. Tuyen was thin, almost slight, with wrinkle-free clothes and wire-rimmed eyeglasses. He spoke not only with care but with ironic detachment, and when he wasn't speaking, a small, knowing smile played across his face. He was, I knew, part of the gang I wished to join.

He lifted his own iced coffee to drink, and the tall glass left a puddle of condensation on the table. "Why," he asked me, "don't you tuck your shirt in?"

To be fair, this may not have been the first thing he said to me, but those were the first of Tuyen's words I remember, and typical of his approach—it was a challenge, but a challenge from a friend. He was, I learned, from Bethesda, Maryland, and a fairly recent graduate of Yale who'd spent time living under the tutelage of an older artist in Spain. In Ho Chi Minh City, he was an editor at the *Vietnam Investment Review*, one of several financially minded publications that had launched in the last year or two. To me, this sounded like a very cool job.

From there, the friendships developed smoothly. It might have been that very night, or a few nights later, but Tuyen invited me to join him and his friends in his room for drinks and cards before everyone went out. And that's how I met the gang: Steve and Lien, married architects from San Francisco; Mai and Jason, journalists with bylines in the *Washington Post*; and Hanh and Ayumi, English teachers and friends from Stanford. Other people circulated in and out, but this was the core. We'd begin each evening in Tuyen's spacious room with gin-and-tonics and several rounds of *tiến lên*, the most popular card game in Vietnam, in which players dramatically throw down long straights in an attempt to empty their hands. (There is complex betting involved.) From there, we'd move on to dinner, often at one of the chic Western-style restaurants then opening around the center of the city, but sometimes at street spots, like the riverside auto garage that, come nightfall, transformed into a seafood grill. Then off to the Czech beer garden (run by Vietnamese engineers who'd studied in Prague) for the only authentic Pilsner Urquell in the city, and maybe a little karaoke in its private rooms, where Hanh would belt out Madonna songs with utter conviction and I would find nasal solace in Dylan. After which more drinks and viciously competitive games of pool and, when we all at last gave in, breezy motorbike rides back to the Lucy.

It was a routine, and a community, and I was part of it all, as accepted as anyone else. We spoke the same language—the language of very young people with forthright ambitions and undisclosed fears, overeducated twenty-somethings who'd temporarily turned their backs on the United States in favor of this unknown new land. Among these friends, I was an equal, and while I wasn't sure what my role was supposed to be, I also wasn't sure it mattered, so long as I was there to participate in the drinking, the gambling, the eating, the chatter.

This was utterly different from hanging out with Douglas. Here I was not the little brother, even though Tuyen might call me "Matty." Nor did this circle have the tensions and competitions I found among the Bodhi Tree gang. I didn't need to prove myself. No one would take advantage of me. These people were the friends I'd wanted for months, and half of them had been living right in my building.

I developed crushes on all the women. Lien had a rough, sexy voice and laughed at everything with total confidence, and once, after lunch, we napped together, clothes on, in my bed; but she was married to Steve. Mai was short, with thick glasses, and was incredibly tough—she'd grown up a refugee in Oakland, California—and one night she rode pinion on my moped back to the Lucy, hugging me from behind; but she was with Jason. Hanh was cute, her face composed of perfect circles, her emotions raw and naked; but she had a boyfriend back home, and I didn't know how to approach her anyway. With none of them did anything happen, and I was glad. I was terrified of upsetting the delicate balance of this perfect ecosystem.

But for a long time, that balance was maintained by the Lucy Hotel itself, the antics of whose tenants and staff we observed with equal parts fascination and horror. Mr. Bob, the middle-aged American on the first floor, had lived there the longest, having moved over from the Philippines after the closure of the U.S. naval base at Subic Bay; red-faced, paunchy, and only too happy to show off his full set of the *Encyclopedia Brittanica*, he seemed to move through a different Vietnam from the rest of us, speaking Vietnamese with a terrible accent (he didn't care) and enmeshed in the operations of his store, the Yankee Peddler, which sold weird, off-brand perfumes and T-shirts. Mr. Bob was also responsible for having discovered Lucy's front desk clerk, skinny Ms. Luc, who'd had a hard life; the French-speaking daughter of a South Vietnamese policeman, she'd spent the postwar decades going mad, winding up homeless, carrying her young daughter on her back as she sold lottery tickets on the street—which is where Mr. Bob had found her and given her work at his shop. At the Lucy Hotel, she was the mild-mannered rock, kind, approachable, and patient.

Which is to say, quite unlike her boss, Lucy, who could transform in an instant from girlish and helpful to pure raging evil. We guests were mostly safe, but each of us, at one point or another, had stumbled upon her in mid-rant, screaming at one of the desk clerks or security guards about some infraction or another—before she'd turn to us, flash a smile, and ask if we needed anything, bottled water, fresh fruit, new sheets. She'd pay off the police so American guys could have their Vietnamese girlfriends spend the night, and she knew where to find good deals on motorbike rentals. But she also spared no one her wrath—not even Thuy and Duyen, the sweet-faced cleaning girls, whom she fired when they asked to be paid the past two months' wages.

The next month, however, Lucy hired them back, and it seemed part and parcel of the comedy that was life at the Lucy Hotel—a dramatic but consequence-free interlude in all our lives. Or maybe just in my own naïve, innocent life.

One night, though, things blew up for serious. A Filipino engineer who lived alone at the hotel had been enjoying a visit from his wife, who'd come over from Manila for a week. But the wife's presence was a problem, because the engineer, as we all knew, had been having an affair with Lucy. For a few days, Lucy and the engineer kept up the landlady-tenant charade, but then, somehow, their cover was blown, and an epic fight began, one we could hear from up in

Mai's room on the fourth floor, where we'd begun another round of cards. And that battle ended (as we pieced it together that night and the next morning) with the engineer's wife slashing her own wrists with a kitchen knife, after which the engineer drove her to the hospital—in Lucy's car.

Even though my friends and I had observed this all from the outside, and even though it had nothing to do with us, it was a sign that seemingly stable dynamics might suddenly shift—or collapse. The next crack appeared when Lien left to return to San Francisco. Her last night in Saigon, we celebrated with a vodka-fueled party at the Siberian Hunting Lodge, and I heard whispered rumors she was on the outs with Steve. Then I took off, on a ten-day trip to Taiwan to visit Tammy, my ex, and when I got back, Lien had returned. Had they patched things up? Or was there something else going on? I heard more rumors of other hookups among our crew, and while no one showed anything on the surface, the sudden tensions frustrated me. We'd all been so good together; why did it have to end? Why did there have to be secrets among us?

The thing is, it didn't end—none of it did. It got a little harder to raise a quorum for cards and drinks in Tuyen's room, but we still went out together, still rode home to find the Lucy Hotel's security gate being groggily opened by a shirtless night watchman. New people appeared in our circle—Susie, Wynn, Hien, Khue—and old ones changed jobs. As far as I knew, there were no fights, no cut ties, no subtle breakups. Even Lucy, the engineer, and his wife worked things out somehow; the wife went back to the Philippines, and Lucy and the engineer resumed their affair. But life at the hotel was feeling different, less special.

Even as I was spending time with the Lucy crew, I was also, to my surprise, growing tighter with the Bodhi Tree gang. Jed, the academic, introduced me to the Ubiquity record label and its compilations of dancehall jazz; his girlfriend, a Japanese woman with whom he communicated solely in Vietnamese, lent me a CD by UA, the quirky Tori

Amos of J-pop. Ted, the annoying New Yorker, helped me form a bi-weekly writers' workshop with Douglas and a couple of other wannabe writers, and although I bristled at his personality and heartily criticized his short stories (and he mine), we seemed to have come to an understanding. We didn't necessarily like each other, but we related—we were in this together. And we all spent nights drinking and smoking pot on someone's balcony, playing silly memory games ("One duck, couple of sheep, three brown bear, four running hare . . . ") and flirting with friends of friends who'd come over from London for a few weeks, or were moving to Phnom Penh next month.

Once or twice, I tried to integrate the groups—the Bodhi Tree gang and the Lucy crew. Steve, Mai, and Tuyen were aspiring fiction writers, so I invited them to my workshop, but they just didn't fit in with Douglas and Ted—different goals, different sensibilities. The conversation was stilted, unfree. From then on, I kept my circles of friends separate.

But "from then on" did not last long. June rolled around, bringing with it clouds, humidity, the prospect of an end to the intense heat, and the looming certainty that soon I too would be leaving Vietnam behind. In the early spring, before I'd found my rhythm and my place in Saigon, I'd applied to graduate school—and gotten in. I'd looked into the future and seen none for me in Vietnam, and so now, at the end of July, I'd return to America. And without regrets, I figured. A month earlier, you couldn't have dragged me away from these new friends—the first people who'd accepted me, so calmly, as an equal. Now, after the ups and downs, our parting seemed natural and inevitable, and therefore not something to be mourned. There must have been a going-away party—probably at a goat hot pot restaurant with loads of rice wine—but I don't remember a thing.

Fifteen years later, here's how things stand: Mai and Jason moved to Africa, married, then split up almost immediately, and Mai moved to New York and eventually married a guy who used to date

Tuyen's sister; their kid and mine play together happily, though less frequently than we'd like. Steve and Lien lived apart, got back together, had kids, got divorced. Hanh married her college sweetheart and lives in Massachusetts. After stints in Philadelphia, Washington, D.C., Manila, Hanoi, and, once again, Saigon, Tuyen lives in Mongolia, and remains single. Douglas and I were roommates for awhile in New York, then drifted apart; now we get together for drinks or lunch a couple of times a year. Ted moved to New York and now is one of my closest friends. I guess he mellowed out. Maybe I did, too.

Vivian I sold in Seattle for $1,800. I never heard from her again.

After what felt like thirty minutes but was probably no more than five, I sensed movement on the other side of the police car. The lights were still in my face, and I squinted to catch a glimpse of what I thought would be Cassady's bruised, handcuffed form being dragged into the road.

Instead, Cassady and the policeman had their arms around each other's shoulders, and were laughing enthusiastically, like old friends. I didn't get it. They'd been hurtling toward a confrontation, but it had become something else entirely. The cop clapped Cassady on the back, told us to be careful on the road, and left us in the dark. I was too dumbfounded to ask Cassady what had happened.

"This is my island," Cassady said as we walked on the shoulder. "I built that road, ha!"

The party was just up the road, in the front yard of a ramshackle house. Twenty men and women on the verge of being rednecks sat around drinking beer and smoking weed, which they eagerly offered me when they heard I was from New York. "Gotta try some of this B.C. bud!" was the refrain.

But the initial welcome soon turned sour. Cassady decided to bring up my *New York Times* affiliation again and again, and his words had a nasty edge to them, like some kind of taunt. Others joined in the sneering, too, though with less vigor than Cassady. He was drunk, sure, but I was pissed. Hadn't I stood by him when the police threatened? Did that count for nothing? Instead of showing my anger and resentment, I took another hit off the joint, finished my beer, and said good night. I was pretty sure I would never see Cassady or the others again, and that was fine by me. I'd done my duty, and they'd done theirs: We'd been ourselves, for better and for worse.

～

## Chapter 4

# *Poor Me*

How I Learned to Travel Frugally and
Got the Best Job in the World—
and Why I Gave It Up

*From: Stuart*
*Subject: Re: Back in NYC . . .*
*Date: March 31, 2006*

*Matt:*

*How about coming by on Tuesday? I have a meeting
from 11–12 and then from 3–3:30, but otherwise I'm
free. Meanwhile, something to think about: How would
you feel about a three-month, round-the-world trip later
this spring, blogging from the road and gathering material
for a couple of features along the way, if we were able to
make it financially feasible for you?*

*From: Matt*
*Subject: Re: Back in NYC . . .*
*Date: April 1, 2006*

*Let's try for 3:30 on Tuesday. That'll be best for me.*
*A three-month, round-the-world trip? Sure, why not?*
*See you Tuesday . . .*

Bologna sucked. I only went because I'd already fucked up Venice. And I only went to Venice because the €50 nonstop flight was the cheapest out of Barcelona, an early stop on the round-the-world summer adventure that launched me as the *New York Times'* Frugal Traveler, the gig that everybody called "the best job in the world"— and an opportunity ripe for fucking up.

I didn't realize how bad things were until I got to Venice. Actually, I thought I was pretty smart. For example, I'd heard that lodgings were cheaper on Venice's Lido Island, so I'd booked a room there (via LastMinute.com) at the Hotel Windsor, on Viale Venezia. But when, after a bus ride from the airport and a vaporetto journey across Venice, I showed up on the Lido and asked around for the Windsor, no one had heard of it. Nor did they know where Viale Venezia was. Finally, the manager of the cell phone store where I was buying an Italian SIM card asked to see the confirmation e-mail from LastMinute.com. I showed him.

Oh, this was easy, he said as if it happened every day: I had the wrong Lido. This right here was the Lido di Venezia, but I wanted the Lido di Jesolo, an hour or so northeast by ferry and by bus— and an eternity from the romance and mystery of Venice. What could I do? I'd already paid for the room, a condition of LastMinute.com, and since my Frugal Traveler budget limited me to $100 a day, or about €80, I couldn't change course. I took the ferry and the bus, and spent a night in a hotel I've since forgotten. The next morning, ashamed of my mistake and unwilling to commute, I fled south to Bologna.

There things improved, but only temporarily. For a couple of midmorning hours, I walked around the city's historic center, loving the bricks and the cobblestones, the arched windows and arcaded passageways, the feeling of being in a true, old Italian city. At a café near Piazza Maggiore, I heard the echo of choirs singing somewhere and watched thin sunbeams fighting their way through a glittering light rain.

Over successive espressos, I hatched a brilliant plan for staying here on the cheap. It was late May, and the semester at the University of Bologna (founded in 1088!) was coming to an end. Many of the school's one hundred thousand students were leaving town, and those who were staying were losing their roommates; on notice boards near university buildings, I'd seen flyers advertising vacant rooms. Surely, at least one student would be happy to put up a thirty-two-year-old New Yorker for five or six nights in exchange for several dozen euros. When the rain slackened, I got up and rolled my suitcase down the street toward the university.

At first, I got lucky: roommate wanted; starting May 24; €17 a day. I called the ad's number on my cell and explained myself in halting Italian.

Okay, come on over, the student said, explaining that I'd have to take a bus or two from Piazza Maggiore to reach his place. Might take thirty minutes. Maybe forty-five.

See you soon, I said. Then I walked back to Piazza Maggiore to wait for my bus.

That's when it began to rain, harder this time. In about thirty seconds (maybe forty-five), I went from elation to absolute dejection. It all seemed so hopeless. I was tired, wet and getting wetter, and I didn't really understand where the apartment was or how to take public transportation there, not to mention that the now-heavy rain was (I was being told by fellow straphangers) delaying the bus line by two hours. A taxi was an exorbitant impossibility. And I wasn't sure I'd want to stay there anyway, since it seemed far from anything I might actually want to see in Bologna. And then what? I'd have to look at another apartment, and another and another, dragging my crap behind me. As I stewed in the rain, a procession of priests and the faithful made its way across the piazza, carrying an image of the Madonna to the Basilica of Saint Petronius.

My phone rang. It was Sarah, a graduate student at the Johns Hopkins University's Bologna Center. A few days earlier, I'd e-mailed her entire class, telling them I was an alumnus passing through on a round-the-world trip "and since I don't actually know anyone there, I was wondering if any of you would be up for having a drink or meal with me." (I did not mention the *New York Times*.) Now Sarah was asking if I wanted coffee. Sure, I said.

A couple of hours later, I'd landed myself a complimentary spare bed in one of Sarah's colleagues' half-vacated dorm room. (I didn't ask, they offered.) Fine, so I wouldn't have an Italian student guiding me through Bologna, but I did have a posse of Americans willing to show me the city's best bars for aperitivi, where drinks are served alongside free, often grandiose spreads: cured meats and salty cheeses and dark olives and slightly overcooked pasta—a dream come true for impoverished scholars and travelers alike.

But after the first night of wine, camaraderie, and complimentary snacks, my Bologna fractured. With exams to take and papers to finish, the students were busy during the day, leaving me to wander the city alone. And that was what I did, clueless and aimless. I slept late, I glanced at the remains of the old Roman stock exchange, and I hiked up through 666 arches to the Sanctuario di Madonna di San Luca, one of many Western European religious structures that failed to impress me. And in a region known for having the best food in Italy, I was eating terribly—cheap pizza by the slice, mostly, with aperitivi-based dinners. All around me, I imagined, Italians were drowning in ragù bolognese, while I subsisted on oily, free focaccia.

Each day I wished I could figure a way to wrap my head around this town, to find something new and exciting, to fit into its strange rhythms, and each day I failed. The problem was, I didn't understand what I wanted to do here, and when you don't know that, it's impossible to even begin looking for a solution. I kept hoping I would stumble upon it by chance, but instead I simply kept stumbling. And although I was living within my $100 budget, I was barely living.

Still, I had a job to do, and Monday morning, after four days in Bologna, I punched out my Frugal Traveler column: 1,200 words that covered almost everything you've just read, minus the maundering. I e-mailed the story and photos to my editors in New York, dealt with their queries and changes on Tuesday, and prepared to return to Venice for another shot at conquering La Serenissima.

Wednesday morning my Bologna column ran—"In Bologna (Thanks to a Cheap Flight) on My Trip Around the World" was the not-written-by-me headline—and I awoke to a long e-mail from Stuart, the editor of the Travel section. Its subject line was Your Column, and its point was this: get your shit together.

With my stomach churning in fear and embarrassment, I read Stuart's criticisms. The column, he said, was turning into a picaresque account of Matt Gross's adventures, not at all the colorful-but-useful series of narrative travel tips he'd hoped the Frugal Traveler would be. By accepting free accommodations from my alma mater, I'd done something no reader could do—a grave violation of the column's precepts. The writing was flat. I'd even failed to provide the names and addresses of the aperitivo bars I'd liked so much. And this wasn't the first time. My two previous columns, from Lisbon and Galicia, were just as disappointing.

What, he asked, was the problem? Was I taking on assignments for other publications, and thus ignoring my primary responsibilities? Or did I just not get it?

"If things don't improve," he wrote, "both in the quality and depth of your reporting—if I am not convinced by the next couple of columns that you are taking this assignment as seriously as we are—then I am going consider pulling the plug on it. We'll get you home—as promised—but I am not going to continue to subsidize a column that doesn't meet our needs or give the readers (or my bosses, to be frank) what they expected when they responded so enthusiastically to its launch. To do so would undermine the progress we are making on the Travel Web site with Web-only material, and also risk tarnishing the name 'Frugal Traveler.'"

I packed my bags for Venice, trembling. This was serious. Stuart was right: My columns had been terrible—lacking in both relatable, replicable adventures and money-saving advice for would-be frugal travelers. I thought of excuses. The too-brief word count of each column meant I had to squeeze too many things together: The Lisbon story was, for half its length, about the basic premise of the trip—circle the globe, living as well as I could on $100 a day—and my attempts to price out airfare, followed by an account of my first days in Portugal. My material circumstances, meanwhile, were frustrating: I was writing not on a laptop but on a Palm Pilot, with a flimsy, erratic wireless keyboard, and I had neither a reliable Internet connection nor a calm place to work. I was constantly on the move, constantly reporting, constantly collecting experiences. How could I write decently at the same time?

Those excuses, however, were just excuses. I couldn't go back to Stuart with such lousy complaints. But what could I do? What did he and the *Times* expect from me? It's not like I'd ever trained to do this work. I'd become a travel writer almost entirely by accident. I'd become a writer because I didn't know how to do anything else. And I'd learned how to travel frugally because I had no other choice.

The lecture hall was a cement cavern that stretched at least fifty feet, and my voice would have echoed throughout the space had it not had to compete with the roar of trucks, the honking of motorbikes, and the barking of wild, sad dogs that bled through the paneless windows and open doors. My students—young, fresh-faced, barely able to understand a single word I said—filed in and took their seats among rows of wooden desks. There were fifty of them. Maybe sixty. It was the first day of my Introduction to Literature class at the Ho Chi Minh City Open University.

I wrote "Matt Gross" on the blackboard, but the humidity and my light touch—I have a visceral hatred of chalk—rendered it nearly illegible. I began speaking, then almost shouting to be heard over the noise from outside, trying to keep my syntax simple. We had a textbook, a tragically photocopied thing bound in transparent plastic, and its first short story—the first work of English-language literature I would be teaching these kids—was about a girl and her dog on a presumably Australian sheep farm. To my eyes, it appeared to have been written for middle-schoolers; although I can't remember the plot specifics, it was earnest and uncomplicated, with minimal sub-text. The students, Ms. Thanh had told me, were supposed to have read it already, but like freshmen everywhere, they hadn't.

To get them accustomed to speaking in class, I had each read aloud a paragraph. This was, as I'd expected, a slow and painful process. No one spoke English particularly well, and fewer still were comfortable performing for their peers. But little by little, we got through the text.

When I started asking the class questions about the story, it immediately became clear we were all in trouble. Silence—utter silence. Even the barking dogs and honking mopeds seemed muted. As I asked more questions about the story's theme and meaning and characterization, I could tell these concepts were too sophisticated for students struggling not only with a foreign language but with a teacher who, probably unlike every instructor they'd ever had, wanted them to participate in the discussion of the work. I had to change tack.

In my EFL training course the previous summer, I'd been taught that students—or "learners," as we were supposed to call them— often felt shy speaking imperfectly before a native speaker, and that the way to get them more comfortable was to have them speak to one another. So, I had an idea. I broke them into ten small groups and assigned each group an investigation based on one of the five W questions: Who was in the story? Where was it taking place?

When was it taking place? What was happening? And why did the author choose to tell the story?

Incredibly, they understood, and got to work breaking this flimsy tale into its constituent elements. For ten minutes, they brainstormed, and I even heard English phrases and sentences floating among the Vietnamese. When I asked each group to present their work, they actually got things right, dissecting the characters not only of the girl but of her dog, too, even if they were slightly confused about where (France?) and when (present day?) the story took place.

But the question of *Why?* was more complicated. Both of the groups assigned to contemplate the deeper meaning of the story saw it solely as moral instruction—this was a tale designed, as all tales were, to show us how, or how not, to behave. The girl's actions were representative, symbolic, with no weight or impact outside of their commentary on society and an individual's proper place within it.

This was, of course, pure Marxist-Leninist literary thought, as taught to generations of students throughout the communist world. Literature exists to improve us and our country; it is unambiguous; it is written with purpose.

There were only a few minutes left in class, so I spoke, again raising my voice to be heard over the outside noise. Maybe, I suggested, the author of this story had written it for other reasons—to try to understand the thinking of the young girl, to make sense of something perhaps she herself had gone through as a child, to capture a particular historical moment in Australia, or even, possibly, for the pleasure of conveying a minor drama in elegant language. These were not deep interpretations, but I needed to get the students to consider other possibilities—anything but the "moral lessons" of literature.

Class ended. I'd survived it, and invented a reading framework that I could apply throughout the semester. The students had spoken aloud, and one, a cute girl named Marie who spoke English surprisingly well, thanked me personally afterward. My anti-Marxist-Leninist approach to literature might one day bite me in the ass when

I applied for Communist Party membership, but for now I was relieved. In the past sixty minutes, I'd earned a whopping thirty thousand Vietnamese dong—just under $3.

This, I knew as I rode my Chinese-made bicycle back to the Lucy Hotel, was going to be a problem. Ms. Thanh had come through with this teaching gig, but a weekly hour-long lecture wouldn't come close to paying my bills, even if I covered other teacher's classes now and again. The $15-an-hour courses I taught for ELT Lotus helped, but those were still only two or three days a week. And Suzanne, an Indonesian woman who lived at the Lucy Hotel, had hooked me up with a friend of hers who needed a tutor for Ferdinand, her chubby eight-year-old son.

Altogether, I was bringing in a few hundred dollars a month, barely enough to pay my fairly meager expenses. Foremost among these was my rent at the Lucy: $300, which was reduced to $210 when I asked not to receive three liters of bottled water per day. Still, I investigated even cheaper options in the backpacker zone. Following a tip, I walked down one of the alleys that thread through Vietnam's urban blocks, climbed several interior staircases, ascended a ladder, and popped my head through a hatch into a dark attic where a young Japanese guy sat in his underwear. Sharing the room, explained the landlord who'd led me there, would be $4 a day.

"I'll think about it," I lied.

Beyond that, the Vietnamese food I was trying to learn to enjoy cost very little; if I spent more than $5 or $7 on a meal, I was splurging. Beers and gin-and-tonics ran a dollar or two, depending on whether I bought them at a dive like the Saigon Café or at Q Bar, a cavernous, multichambered lounge installed under the city's Beaux-Arts opera house.

And that was really it. I had a small cushion—$2,000 my parents had given me—but that was slowly disappearing as I dealt with issues both serious (flying to Bangkok to arrange a proper long-term visa) and trivial (buying a nice Aiwa CD player). I even had an American

Express card, although opportunities to use it in undeveloped, unconnected Vietnam were few indeed.

Soon, I knew, something would have to give: I was making almost nothing, and I was unwilling to ask my parents for a cash infusion (although I would let them pay the occasional small Amex bill). All my life, they'd given me everything, and apart from the money I'd earned in college—as a delivery guy for Domino's and a video clerk in Baltimore—I'd had to rely on them. For years, I'd looked forward to finishing college and striking out on my own, and now, in my first stab at independence, halfway around the globe, I was flailing.

More frustrating still, I was surrounded by glamorous expatriates with flashy jobs. At Q Bar, I met bright young architects and graphic designers and video game producers and filmmakers and entrepreneurs and admen (and women) staffing the newly opened offices of Saatchi & Saatchi. They bought vintage Vespa scooters and lived in castle-like villas in the suburbs and ordered Scotch and sushi and foie gras like those were everyday snacks for twenty-five-year-olds. They bought tailored suits in Hong Kong and went scuba diving in the Philippines. I didn't resent them—I wanted to *be* them, for they all seemed to have come to Vietnam knowing what they were there to do: make money and live awesomely. Meanwhile, I couldn't even tuck my shirt in and had to turn down bottled water to make the rent.

There was, of course, another option: I could become a backpacker. When I moved to Vietnam, I hadn't even known such a lifestyle existed, but I became aware of it quite quickly. They were everywhere throughout the Pham Ngu Lao area, bearded guys in tank tops and tie-dyed pants, willowy girls in long skirts, all tanned, all musty, all with enormous high-tech, high-capacity backpacks towering over their skinny bodies. They drank the cheapest beers, slept in un-air-conditioned misery, and subsisted not on street food but on banana pancakes and french fries in the restaurants that catered to them. They would hang around seemingly forever, then vanish to the next low-budget destination, or maybe back to finance jobs in London or New York, leaving behind thumb-smudged bootleg copies of last year's Lonely Planet.

The Vietnamese called them *tây ba lô*—literally, "Westerner with a bag"—and looked down on them for their shabby attire. As did I and the other semipermanent expatriates. Though we inhabited the same quarter of town, and often the same bars and restaurants, I rarely spoke to any backpackers, and so most of my impressions of their lifestyle were just assumptions. Were they really as cheap—and as trust-fundedly rich—as everyone said? I didn't know. All I knew was that I wanted to keep away from them, for fear of being perceived as a filthy transient myself. And I knew, too, that unless I could improve my circumstances, the distance between us would shrink to nothing.

One morning in mid-November, I biked to the offices of ELT Lotus, housed in a middle school whose female students all wore white ao dai, the long, nearly transparent traditional gown of Vietnam. At the long table in Lotus's common room were strewn local English-language publications—*Vietnam Economic Times, Vietnam Investment Review*, the *Saigon Times*, and *Viet Nam News*, the state-run daily newspaper. After murmuring hellos to Dave and Adrian, I took a seat and flipped through the *Viet Nam News*, my eyes settling on an intriguing story. Next month, it seemed, the Hanoi International Film Festival would be taking place. Over an eighteen-day period, it would feature movies from Germany and India, China and Italy—even the United States was involved: Warner Bros. was premiering *The Bridges of Madison County*, the first major American postwar production to be subtitled in Vietnamese for official distribution.

This was intriguing. In college, I'd been a serious movie geek: film society, student shorts—the whole mid-nineties cinéaste schtick. But I knew movies, and in a way I figured few others in Vietnam did, and I hatched a plan to exploit that knowledge.

A week later, I'd quit all my jobs—to no one's real surprise, it seemed—and was on a Vietnam Airlines plane to Hanoi. At my side was Ms. Thanh, who had an academic conference to attend in the capital. Her visit gave me the perfect opportunity to combine job hunting and sightseeing; if the former didn't work out, well, I was going to do the latter anyway. For the next few days, she and I rode cyclos down tree-shrouded lanes (Ms. Thanh didn't trust motor-bikes), strolled past the cafés around Hoan Kiem Lake, ate remarkably good vegetarian "duck," and toured the Ho Chi Minh Museum, whose exhibits included a replica of Uncle Ho's one-room cottage and a selection of industrial products manufactured in the Socialist Republic of Vietnam. The electric fan behind one display window was, I noticed, identical to the fan blowing humid air in front of it.

One day after lunch, I took a break and visited the offices of the *Viet Nam News*, in one of the gray concrete buildings, stained with damp, which contrasted so sadly with the capital's surviving French colonial structures. I climbed a few flights of stairs to the newsroom, a wide-open space where young Vietnamese and a few older foreign-ers were bustling around computer terminals. It looked, it felt like a real paper—the first I'd ever visited.

I introduced myself and asked to speak to Nguyen Cong Khuyen, the editor in chief, and was led over to a thin, distinguished man with smart glasses and a sharp black mustache. In careful but perfect English, he asked what I was doing here. And I told him—about my background, about my love of film, about the festival, about my desire to write. I handed him a résumé. I explained that I hadn't come empty-handed: I'd brought some fodder for Dragon Tales, the weekly humor column written by one of the paper's expatriate staff; it was a copy of a hilariously mistranslated menu from one of Ho Chi Minh City's most expensive French restaurants. Dishes in-cluded such delights as "Brains to the citrus fruit" and "Pave of wolf in his sauce Dutch."

"Okay," Mr. Khuyen said calmly and quietly. "Our features editor has just quit. You can have her page."

Features page? Sure, why not? And so, like that, I became a newspaper columnist. A night or two later, after Ms. Thanh had flown back south, I attended my first film festival screening: *Aguirre: Wrath of God,* the Werner Herzog masterpiece in which Klaus Kinski plays an increasingly unhinged conquistador in search of El Dorado. On grainy video. Without subtitles. In a mostly empty theater whose air-conditioning was set somewhere between "walk-in freezer" and "Arctic whaling station." The result, as I hurriedly wrote a couple of hours later in an attempt to fill up my page (*my page!*), was absurdity—a frozen theater playing an insane and unintelligible (but awesome) movie to a bare handful of shivering weirdos.

For two and a half weeks, this was my approach—to write not only about the movies themselves (which were playing only once or twice) but about the weird delight of watching them in this foreign context. One afternoon, I found myself in a theater full of hyperactive Vietnamese eleven-year-olds who, when they discovered me, rushed up to practice a single sentence in English: "Give me money!" Another day, another theater, I sat down next to a small, round eighty-something-year-old Vietnamese man bundled up in vest, jacket, and beret. He and I were seated next to each other, and when we began a conversation in French, I had to tell him repeatedly I was American—whether because he couldn't hear well or simply couldn't believe it, I don't know. Then the old man reached into his jacket pocket, removed a small notebook, and handed it to me. I opened it to find page after page of French poetry, written in a neat hand. I picked a poem at random and as I read through it realized: this was serious stuff, precise in its rhythm and diction. Then I flipped the page, reached the end, and saw how he'd signed it: "—Charles Baudelaire." The whole notebook, it turned out, was transcribed, with contributions from every major French poet. For a moment I was disappointed—but only for a moment. Okay, so he hadn't written his own poems, but his dedication to poetry, his obvious love of the language, and his attachment to this foreign culture were in some ways more impressive, more touching, more beautifully sad.

Every evening I'd rush back to the newsroom to pound out my reviews and lay out my page. Occasionally, I'd supplement the reviews with reported sidebars—about how ticketless foreigners were often let in but paying Vietnamese customers turned away, or an interview with an Italian director, conducted in a three-way mishmash of English, French, and Italian. I loved the adrenaline rush of working late at night, fighting the approaching deadline.

Frankly, I don't know if the writing was any good, but it served a purpose. Most of the time, the *Viet Nam News* was heavy on the Viet Nam part, light on the News. Official visits by minor foreign functionaries, dubious agricultural statistics, abstract health initiatives—these were the paper's meat and potatoes, not the kind of hard reporting (I thought) the country needed. "Ca Mau Province Gets New Tractor" was the joke headline I'd use to convey the tedium of the paper's subject matter, and it's not far off from a real one I read today: "Children and Mothers Given Vitamin A and Iron on Micro-Nutrient Day."

In this context, the mildly humorous writings of a young, movie-mad American—and, moreover, a native speaker of English!—were a balm, something that the paper's expatriate audience could actually read, beginning to end, and understand. So what if it was rushed, juvenile, or at times inaccurate? It was at least a break from socialist propaganda and a glimpse of the strange fun lurking under official surfaces.

Occasionally, those official surfaces thickened and hardened. One movie I loved was *Back to Back, Face to Face*, an obscure Chinese comedy in which the acting director of a local cultural center fails, due to corruption, cronyism, and bureaucracy, to officially take over the organization. When Mr. Khuyen read my review, however, he asked me to tone it down—the governmental system stymieing the movie's protagonist was awfully similar, he said, to that of Vietnam. But if I praised the movie in less universalist terms—this particular fictional theater troupe, not the Chinese communist bureaucracy—all would be okay. So I did. His paper, his country, his call. Also, I liked Mr. Khuyen's quiet, fair attitude, and would have hated for him to get in trouble with the paper's censors, who allegedly gathered each morning to go over every word of every story—an after-the-fact strategy to encourage self-censorship.

And, naturally, I would hate to lose this gig that was putting money in my pocket. The *Viet Nam News* paid ten cents a word for articles—barely a tenth of American standards, but since I was writing roughly a thousand words a day, every day for more than two weeks, the cash was building up faster than I could spend it. The hotel I was staying in, on one of Hanoi's ancient 36 Streets, cost $8 a day, and the Halida beers and fat burgers at the Roxy, a dark, funky theater-turned-nightclub, didn't add much more. By the end of the festival, I was being handed thick white envelopes full of cash—enough so that, when I went back to America for a brief visit after Christmas, I had more than $800 to spend on whatever I wanted.

Finally! I had money. Finally! I didn't have to depend on my family for support. Finally! I was doing work that I loved, that I had some measure of talent for, and that gave me a certain status in the eyes of my peers. I wasn't just a college grad bumming around Vietnam—I was a writer, a working journalist, living off the words I put together.

When I returned to Ho Chi Minh City after the winter break, Vietnam suddenly became much more manageable. Now I was working at the local bureau of the *Viet Nam News*, copyediting stories alongside my frenemy Ted Ross, the annoying New Yorker from the Bodhi Tree gang. The job was amazing: I'd show up every day at 2 p.m. and attempt to turn news stories—written in Vietnamese, then translated into pseudo-English by the paper's Vietnamese staff—into readable prose. I'd cut, edit, and rejigger the stories, line by line, trying hard to figure out not only which facts were, in fact, facts but which were relevant to the story. Once, I reduced a four-paragraph story, about the failure of an experimental oyster farm, to a single sentence, retaining only the original headline: "Oysters Die a Lot." (Oddly, it did not run the next day.) In articles like that, it was as if the original writer had just crammed in as many points of data as possible, maybe to stretch out the piece, maybe because a publicist had paid him or her to do so.

This happened all the time, my Vietnamese colleagues explained to me. A press conference would be held to discuss rice exports or a new hotel project, and the publicists would duly pay off the reporters—100,000 dong here, 200,000 there. This was essential. It was how you got coverage from journalists whose government-set salaries were unlivably low: $40 a month, $60 if they were lucky.

And many of the journalists at *Viet Nam News* were people with long, serious careers. Mr. Minh had been the foreign desk editor at *Tuoi Tre*, one of the country's top papers, until a traffic accident landed him in the hospital; while he was recuperating, *Tuoi Tre* fired him. Mr. Hoanh, a good-humored fellow who every evening changed into a leather motorcycle outfit to ride his Harley home, had lived and studied overseas; he'd returned to Saigon to visit his family just weeks before the South Vietnamese government collapsed in April 1975. It seemed like a tragedy, but he'd laugh as he'd tell the story.

Naturally, not every employee was so illustrious. One young, pretty woman seemed to do nothing but gossip with friends all day— because, rumor had it, the head of the Vietnam News Agency, the national wire service, was her uncle.

But good for her! Ted and I, too, appreciated the leisurely aspects of the job. Between edits we'd all retrieve little pots of fresh yogurt from the fridge in the break room, and sometimes, as we struggled to reshape awkward copy, one of our colleagues would set a can of beer next to our keyboards. Beer! By 5 p.m., we'd be finished anyway, and it was time to have a glass of snake wine—strong rice liquor from a glass vat filled with dried cobras—with our bureau chief, Nguyen Tien Le, a kind man with a thick black mustache and a voice so soft we could barely hear it above the air-conditioning.

For my efforts at the paper, I was paid a salary of $700 a month—crisp hundred-dollar bills in a white envelope—with the standard ten cents per word for any additional restaurant or movie reviews I wrote. I wasn't rich, certainly not compared with the admen at Q Bar, but I could, at last, upgrade my room at the Lucy to the air-conditioned one with the patio. Beyond that, though, my lifestyle changed little. I could splurge on meals if I wanted, but I ate Vietnamese food whenever possible. Buying a motorbike and a mobile phone would have been nice, but they weren't strictly necessary, so I rented the former and did without the latter. If I left town, I took buses and slept in the cheaper (but never the cheapest) hotels. I didn't have health insurance, but I was twenty-two—why would I need it? Above all, I was simply satisfied with what I had, as if my now-comfortable circumstances were a magical gift, a secular blessing.

And now that I was, officially, a journalist, more work came my way. A colleague passed word that *Billboard* was looking for a stringer, and I landed myself a couple of stories, about the impending U.S.-Vietnam copyright treaty and a new CD production facility. Another business magazine launched in Ho Chi Minh City, and I sold it a story about *cơm bình dân*, the "people's food" restaurants. I e-mailed an editor at *Might*, a U.S. magazine started by Dave Eggers, to pitch an article on Vietnamese ear-cleaning; he said it sounded great but the publication was going out of business. With Ted, Douglas, and a couple of other creative expats, I started the Saigon Writers Workshop, which met each week to discuss (or destroy) the short stories and novels we considered our true calling.

My life was nearly ideal. I woke up late, read the *International Herald Tribune* (and did the crossword) over black coffee and fresh croissants, met people for lunch, napped, worked a few hours, and spent my nights eating, drinking, and exploring the city with an increasingly close circle of friends. I had renewed my study of Vietnamese at what I dubbed Đai Học Đường Phố—the University of the Streets. I danced until morning on a barge floating down the Saigon River, and I was planning to shoot a sixteen-millimeter short film, about love and mopeds, called "Honda Dreams."

This is when I decided to pack it all in and return to America.

My thinking made—and still makes—a certain kind of sense. Although copyediting at the *Viet Nam News* was the best job I'd ever had, I could tell that it was not a job with a future. I could do it, I knew, for years without ascending the masthead or fundamentally changing the paper's culture. Mr. Lê, the bureau chief, was proof enough of that: Though he certainly had the professional and political chops to take over the whole publication, he was—everyone knew— a southerner, and therefore limited. The *Viet Nam News* would always have as its editor in chief someone from the more historically communist north, and that was the way it was. If Mr. Lê could only go so far, what could I, a foreigner, possibly accomplish?

And although I had my new freelancing opportunities, I didn't know how to develop them. What was a story? How did one pitch it to an editor? The answers eluded me (the questions, too), and there were few people I could ask. We were, I imagined, all competing to cover the same small, strange country, with clueless me at a great disadvantage. And what else could I, with my pitiful language skills and nonexistent network of local contacts, do here? Work for Saatchi? Open an import-export business? So I left—left Vietnam, my new friends, my hard-won independence.

My new apartment in Manhattan was on the edge of Chinatown and the Lower East Side, a converted two-bedroom tenement with windows between the kitchen and the living room. My roommate was Wayne, a gay Maori who worked in the TV and film industry and knew Douglas. My share of the rent was just over $500 a month. My New York life was about to begin.

Within six weeks, I had a job: copy editor at *Shoot*, a weekly trade magazine covering the TV commercial industry. ("Why did you hire me?" I later asked the managing editor. "Because," she said, "you had copyediting experience—at the *Viet Nam News*.") I had regular hangouts: Happy Joy, an excellent Chinese-Malaysian restaurant around the corner; Good World, a Chinese barbershop turned Swedish bar; Limbo, an East Village café whose customers would sometime O.D. on drugs in the bathroom. I even had a girlfriend, Jean Liu, a fellow Johns Hopkins alum whom I'd met when a visiting college friend invited me to a group dinner in Koreatown. Now a fashion student at Parsons School of Design, Jean had impressed me with her gorgeous smile, easy laugh, and enthusiasm for food (*raw crab kimchi? no problem!*), and we'd started dating soon afterward.

It was a good time to be in New York. The first Internet bubble was still inflating. Kozmo.com was delivering pints of Ben & Jerry's all over Manhattan essentially for free (since new members were given $5 coupons, you'd create a new membership for each order), and Pseudo.com was hosting random, raucous parties in its building at the corner of Houston and Broadway. Not every corner of downtown had been gentrified, and relatively little of Brooklyn; a no-cover club like Fun could open under the Manhattan Bridge and fly under-the-radar for months. An Asian-style night market spontaneously appeared that summer in Sara D. Roosevelt Park, with permitless squatter-vendors selling everything from socks to pot stickers, until the city shut it down. Maybe this is every young person's first feeling about New York, but it all felt truly new—newly invented, newly discovered.

The excitement of New York also served to distract me from what was to become a series of only partially fulfilling jobs. At *Shoot*, I was learning the copyediting business in a far more professional way than I ever had before, but I had no inkling that copyediting—correcting prose for grammar and style—was going to be my métier. After six months there, I received an invitation, out of nowhere, to apply for a similar job at a Web site I'd never heard of before: FoxNews.com. In early 1999, no one had ever heard of it, not even the Fox News Channel, the conservative cable network it was supposedly run by. For the next two years or so, I would help manage the site's front page, placing wire copy, writing headlines, and helping cover breaking news events like the Columbine massacre, the Serbia-Kosovo conflict, and the crash of the Concorde. Then, shortly after George W. Bush's inauguration, the dot-com collapse hit FoxNews.com, and I, along with a few hundred other people, was laid off. Within a few months, however, I landed a new gig, as a copy editor at *New York* magazine, one of whose editors had also gone to Hopkins. Once again, I was inserting and deleting commas, perfecting verb tenses, and setting the titles of novels and feature films in italics.

Copyediting may not have been sexy, but it was at least stable. I earned a decent salary—never more than $50,000, if you're wondering—but that was enough to cover my rent, eat out (in Chinatown more than at Le Bernardin) with Jean, and, most important of all, travel without going into debt. The first year in New York, for instance, I visited Jean in Paris, where she'd gone to study abroad, then a month later visited my family in Denmark for Thanksgiving. The following April I flew back to Vietnam for ten days, and I spent New Year's Eve 1999 in Cambodia. Once Jean had returned to New York, she and I visited Mexico twice, enduring a thousand-mile road trip on which I was stricken, as usual, with giardiasis. One winter I even went snowboarding in Switzerland.

Was this extravagant? The thought never occurred to me. I bought my plane tickets online or through Chinatown travel agents, usually for less than $1,000, and I stayed with friends whenever possible. I ate street food and in small restaurants, and I rarely went on shopping sprees. All the things I liked were already inexpensive, so I didn't have to stretch my budget.

More than making travel affordable, my incidentally frugal approach made it *normal*. That is, I never saw these trips as strange, as special, as my sole chance to see Angkor Wat or Oaxaca. I worked some job, I saved some money, I went somewhere. And yet even that cycle was not so consciously crafted. To fly halfway around the world was not a release valve for an otherwise staid lifestyle. Rather, these adventures flowed naturally into everything else I did, not least because I had a foreign-born girlfriend who wanted to see her family in Taipei every year or two. I traveled because . . . there was no because.

As the years went on, though, the return to life at home became ever more disappointing. At *New York*, I was not only copyediting but also editing the film critic, the theater critic, and the crossword page, plus writing short articles on smoked salmon, dictionary illustrations, and the mutant bicycle Olympics in Brooklyn. I freelanced a little, too, even writing a short piece for *Travel + Leisure* about the opening of Libya to foreign tourism. But rarely did I have the chance to write anything substantive, or even anything longer than a few hundred words. My old dream of being a writer—a real writer, whose words might outlive him—was fading.

The solution to that was obvious. As I had in Ho Chi Minh City, I put together a small writer's group and embarked on a new novel, *The Jungle Always Wins,* a noirish detective story set in 1950s Cambodia, the hazy era of optimism and violence after the country won its independence from France. Every week or two, my friends and I met to share and discuss our work, and chapter by chapter *The Jungle* grew. By the time it reached 150 pages, in the summer of 2004, I knew what had to be done. I began saving money, writing as many extra articles as I could for *New York,* and by November I had $5,000 stashed away. I gave notice and bought a ticket to Southeast Asia.

(There were at least three other factors in my decision to leave: 1. Jean was living in Columbus, Ohio, for work, so I felt less tied to New York. 2. I'd hurt my knee while training for the New York City

Marathon and was depressed. 3. George W. Bush had just been re-elected president.)

The plan, as I saw it, was this: spend at least three months in Cambodia, studying the language, researching at the National Archives, and finishing and rewriting the book. I had friends of friends living there; I'd stay with them. Five grand would go a long way, and Jean would support me if I absolutely needed it. Eventually, I was confident, *The Jungle Always Wins* would find a publisher, and the book would come out. Then it would fail—as many, many books do. But, I hoped, my novel would also catch the eye of an editor at some travel magazine, who would then send me back to Cambodia to write a feature. Thus would begin my difficult, poorly paid career as a travel writer.

Before I left, though, my friend Andrew Yang, a design and architecture writer, suggested I e-mail Mary Billard, an editor at the *New York Times*. Mary was part of a team that had just taken over the Travel section, and they were making many changes, including commissioning several pieces from Andrew himself.

So I e-mailed her, dropping Andrew's name, informing her I'd be in Cambodia (and Vietnam) for the next few months, and asking if there was anything I could look into. This was not a request for an assignment, I made clear, just a note to say that if she'd heard of something worth checking out, I could do it, I was in the neighborhood, it would be easy to see if there was a story.

Mary's response came two days later—lightning-fast in the New York media world: No thanks. The *Times* already had someone in the region, Mary said, so don't worry about it. But have fun!

Fine. I wasn't pinning all my hopes on a *New York Times* assignment—I had a novel to write. And so, on December 1, 2004, I boarded the long, economy-class flight to Southeast Asia. If Mary wanted me to have fun, I would have fun.

The life I established for myself in Phnom Penh was bizarrely idyllic. After bouncing around the country for a couple of weeks, from the ghost town atop Bokor Mountain to the temples of Angkor (with a side trip to Ho Chi Minh City to visit old friends), I moved in with Gordon, an American writer and Web designer, his British girlfriend, Aarti, who worked for an anti-human-trafficking organization, and Peter, a Swedish writer researching a book on his country's involvement in the Khmer Rouge era. They all lived together in a concrete house that, while not luxurious (no air-conditioning), was at least spacious and had both functional Wifi and an Xbox.

For several weeks, I was quite disciplined. In the mornings, I would ride my rented motorbike to the National Archives, a small building adjacent to the National Library, and pore over crumbling French newspapers and colonial government documents with the help of an archivist named Dara. The novel took place largely in Pailin, a small town on the Thai border that was later a base for the Khmer Rouge, and I was eager to find any reference I could. At noon, I'd break for lunch—chicken with rice at a Singaporean joint, American-style fast food at the shame-inducingly addictive Lucky Burger, or maybe a salad at the Foreign Correspondents Club. In the mid-afternoon, I went to my Khmer class, where the awful teaching did not diminish my love of the language, the way complicated aspirations and clipped triple diphthongs masked what was at heart an easy and playful tongue.

By five o'clock, I'd be running laps at the 1960s-era Olympic Stadium, inhaling the evening-ritual scent of garbage burning all over the city. I'd eat dinner with my roommates—we took turns cooking—or out with other new friends, but sometimes I stayed alone at home, playing Halo on the Xbox until I noticed the mosquitoes sucking me dry. I'd go to sleep under a thin sheet, an electric fan keeping the skeeters at bay, and in the moments before drifting off marvel at the distance—psychological more than physical—I'd traveled in just a couple of months. Here, tangled in routines and research unimaginable to my New York peers, I felt at home.

A surprise e-mail in early January changed all that: "just checking in . . . looking for destination stories. . . .1000 or so words . . . any thoughts?" It was Mary Billard, and by now I definitely had some thoughts. Within two days, I'd sent her three story ideas: a general guide to Ho Chi Minh City, a report on the up-and-coming Vietnamese kite-surfing town of Mui Ne, and a piece on the developing area around Kampot, Kep, and Bokor Mountain, in southern Cambodia. Sounds good, she said over the next few e-mails: Write 'em!

And so I did. I put my novel aside and returned to Ho Chi Minh City to eat, drink, and shop, and I interviewed Mui Ne's kite surfers and I ate Kep crabs and I drank Mekong whiskey with friends around a mountaintop campfire. I turned those experiences into words and sent them to New York. Mary liked them; so did her boss, Stuart. Even before they were published, she asked for more. Could I go to Chiang Mai, Thailand? I could, and I did.

On May 1, a week after my first two stories appeared in the *Times*, I flew back to New York. I'd spent five months in Asia—Vietnam, Cambodia, Thailand, Hong Kong, and Singapore—and had accomplished a lot of research on the novel. But now I found it hard to focus on fiction. The *Times* was calling. I went in to meet Mary and Stuart in person for the first time: She was fair-skinned with an angular smile; he was a preppy Floridian with arched eyebrows; both were in their early fifties, and both seemed very excited about me. By the time I left the building, I had new trips assigned—snowboarding in Argentina, exploring the untouristed east coast of Jamaica—and was going to write an installment of a series called "The Frugal Traveler."

As Stuart explained it to me, "The Frugal Traveler" was being reinvented. The previous columnist, Daisann McLane, had written the series since the mid-1990s, following from its originator, Susan Spano. Now that Daisann was gone, the column was up for grabs—anyone could pitch a Frugal—and Stuart wanted it to change focus. Henceforth, the column would be about famously expensive destinations done cheaply. The joke would be in the headline: Frugal Aspen. Frugal Monaco. Frugal Tokyo.

The budget was $500 for a weekend (not including airfare or, often, rental car), which seemed reasonable—after all, I was not supposed to be a backpacker. These were, by definition, unaffordable places, so finding affordable hotels would be the primary challenge. But to make it more challenging yet, I decided to bring Jean along to my first Frugal destination: Newport, Rhode Island. Could two people not only survive a weekend in Edith Wharton's Gilded Age haven but enjoy themselves as if money were no object?

This was not to be an easy weekend. Jean and I stayed in a $175-a-night motel (the best deal we could find) and in a homey hostel. We spent too much on parking, and on Mexican food, and on disappointing chowder. We felt too old at the beach, and too young touring the mansions. We missed out on free amusements—a polo match, a brewery tour—and we hiked until our feet hurt, then discovered our destination was closed. I fretted constantly about the budget; if I went over, would I incur my editors' wrath? "I hate Newport," I told Jean at one point.

And yet we had a wonderful time. We ogled Doris Duke's wardrobe and ate at the hostel's barbecue and drank California sparkling wine on a sunset cruise. We learned a video arcade had once been the city's biggest brothel, and we found a delicious, inexpensive cup of chowder. We were together, in a new place, doing whatever we wanted because the *New York Times* had asked us to. This—this insane, expenses-paid undertaking!—was my job.

When I returned home, I began writing almost immediately. "For a beachy vacation spot," I wrote, "Newport has an unusual theme: anxiety."

In Edith Wharton's day, one worried about impressing the social set. For one longtime resident, Doris Duke, shyness mutated into Paxil-worthy pathology. In *Reversal of Fortune*, the Hollywood adaptation of the Claus von Bülow trial, the objects of anxiety are dire: murder, justice, truth. Even those old Newport cigarette ads straddle the line between pleasure and terror, as the media critic Mark Crispin Miller once pointed out: Are those tan, rich folk laughing or screaming?

My anxiety, however, was purely of my own making. I was planning a last-minute weekend in Newport—land of Vanderbilt mansions and America's Cup yachts—with a spending cap of $500. This sum was supposed to cover not only myself but also my travel companion, Jean, a fashion designer who, although laid-back and undemanding, deserved to experience a bit of the glamour for which Newport is famous. And glamour, as fashionable people know, rarely comes cheap.

This approach worked. The editors liked it, and readers seemed to as well. And it made sense to me. A travel story, I felt, shouldn't just convey information about how to travel—service, as it's called. Even if its raison d'être was to tell people how to save money while traveling, a good story should be a real narrative: with a beginning, middle, and end; with some goal that needs to be accomplished and isn't certain until the end; and with a theme, some unifying element that deepens it beyond the basic tale of a journey from A to B.

From that point on, this was my model, for both Frugal Traveler stories (next up, Palm Beach and Jackson Hole) and the other articles I was writing. After Argentina and Jamaica, the *Times* sent me back to Southeast Asia for a month, and I produced my first 2,500-word cover stories, "To Be Young and Hip in Bangkok" and "Why Is Everybody Going to Cambodia?" By early 2006, my editors were hinting they wanted me to take over the Frugal Traveler column permanently, and when that "three-month, round-the-world trip" e-mail came in from Stuart, I was on a foodie road trip up the west coast of Malaysia. A year ago, I'd been hoping a novel might turn me into a travel writer. Now a dream I'd never even let myself dream was coming true.

Which made the failures of this Frugal Traveler's first official weeks so maddening. What had I forgotten? Maybe I'd never known how to do this at all, and had just gotten lucky. Now I was being exposed for what I was—a copy editor out of his depth, with little talent for either traveling or writing.

On my way back to Venice, Stuart's deputy, a young editor named Denny, called my cell phone, and we had a long conversation that boiled down to two things I needed to do. These were things I'd known I should do, but had never quite thought of them that way. As soon as he said them, I felt like an idiot. What Denny said was this:

My blog posts needed to (1) convey a sense of place, and (2) give a few frugal tips.

A sense of place? And some frugal tips? It was one of those head-slapping moments. How could I not have seen that that was all I needed to do? I mean, here I was riding into Venice—if I couldn't convey a sense of that place, maybe I didn't deserve the column. And frugal tips? Ditto.

But you know, I told myself, I can do this. Sense of place, frugal tips, sense of place, frugal tips—that was the mantra that ran through my mind as I roamed Venice, struggling through the throngs of tourists in Saint Mark's Square, getting takeout calamari in a paper cone (€5 versus €10 to eat in), and sipping spritz cocktails in the mob-free bars of the Dorsoduro neighborhood. I focused: I took notes, I took photos, I took a cross-canal gondola ride for €0.50. Purple flowers sticking out a back-alley window. Passersby practicing arias at sunset. Toddlers blowing soap bubbles and schoolkids playing soccer. A fishmonger I'd spotted earlier, now dolled up in exquisite leather.

Nothing profound happened in my few days there, but nothing needed to. All I wanted was to get back to basics, and give myself enough time and space to produce a decent story. I'd figured out I'd have to change my schedule, too. No more trying to travel and write at the same time. From now on, I'd be active only from Wednesday morning through Sunday night, and devote Mondays and Tuesdays to nothing but my writing. I knew I could do this—I just needed to breathe, calm down, see things clearly.

The story that came out the next Wednesday was not great. But it was good enough. It did what Denny and Stuart had asked—sense of place, frugal tips—and they were happy. So was I. I was safe, and could concentrate on the next week's destination (Croatia), and the next (Montenegro), and the next (Albania).

With each week, my confidence grew, despite the regular sniping of my readers in the comments section, who complained that I was either spending far too much money ("How dare you call yourself the Frugal Traveler?"*) or living like a backpacker. Denny and I argued occasionally about wording or structure, but these were minor matters, the normal things that always get hashed out between editors and writers. (Even if I sometimes sputtered with frustration at his inability to see the importance of my near-death experience in the mountains of Georgia! Although, really, as the adrenaline rush faded, I didn't mind so much changing the lede.) I had a handle on things. Sense of place, frugal tips.

———

*"How dare you call yourself the Frugal Traveler?" wrote a commenter named "Steve," who said that in 1983 he and a friend had spent $6,400 (about $12,800 in 2006 dollars) on a six-month round-the-world trip. "Even with inflation your budget just for food and lodging is higher than that of the majority of American families vacations. We've been on several similar trips as recently as five years ago, without ever even approaching your bloated level of expenses. Shame on you, change your name to the Privileged Yuppie Traveler."—Steve

Accepting these basic constraints slowly freed me up to once again tackle more complicated themes and experiences. In rural Turkey, where I spent a handful of days at an apple orchard, the frugal tips were minimal, consisting primarily of this: There is an international program called WWOOFing, or World Wide Opportunities on Organic Farms, whose network of thousands of farms offer volunteers free food and lodging in exchange for their labor.

It sounded easy enough, but there were other challenges. The farmer, a fifty-five-year-old named Kemal Görgün, spoke about four words of English—*yes, no, okay,* and *wow!*—which was almost exactly how many words of Turkish I knew. As no other volunteers were around to translate (Kemal's cat, Simi, was little help), we had to make the best of things, and so each morning we'd walk across his seven acres, set in the softly rolling green hills of Anatolia, and tie down the young branches of his apple trees, giving them an arcing silhouette. Kemal tried repeatedly to explain which branches to tie down, and how, and why, but I could never follow his logic, and always had to present my choices for the silent approval of his kind brown eyes.

At midmorning, we'd break for glasses of *ayran*, a salty yogurt drink, and when the muezzin sang out from the rocket-ship minaret of the village mosque, Kemal would chuckle and comment: "Pavarotti." At noon, we'd lunch on hearty vegetable stews served with yogurt and crusty bread, then explore the countryside, skipping stones in a pond or drinking sweet tea with Kemal's friends in the village. (Preparing me for the social encounter, Kemal would mime shaking hands and say, "Ahmet, Mehmet . . . Ahmet, Mehmet . . . ") In the evening, after a couple more hours working in the orchard, we'd make a new vegetable stew and play backgammon while listening to Keith Jarrett or Maria Callas on the stereo. Then Kemal would start a wood fire to heat water for our evening showers.

It was easy to sink into the placid rhythms of life on the farm, but with each day my curiosity grew. Kemal, I could see, was not like Ahmet, Mehmet, and the other farmers in the village. His clothes were sharper, his teeth in better shape; he didn't have the weather-worn look of a man who'd spent a lifetime in the fields. Instead, he invited me to do yoga in the morning before breakfast. ("Matt," he said, "after after after, yoga, please, okay?" In the future, I responded, I would try to keep it up.) And he had a "master trainer" certificate in neuro-linguistic programming.

After three nights, I wrote in my column that week (the first from that summer I'm comfortable quoting), my curiosity got the better of my reticence, and I broke out my Lonely Planet phrasebook and Kemal's Turkish-English dictionary:

> Through a mixture of basic vocabulary, hand gestures, exaggerated facial expressions, and frantic diagrams and doodles, Kemal told me of his life. He'd grown up near Konya, the hometown of the poet and founder of the Sufi sect, Rumi, and had spent his adult-hood working as an engineer for various Istanbul companies. Fi-nally, he'd gotten sick of the grind and was casting about for something new and more fulfilling to do when he had his Isaac Newton moment: apples!
>
> In 2002, he bought the land at Beypinar, built his house and planted 2,500 apple trees. His plan was to get the orchards certified organic according to both Turkish and European standards, with the ultimate goal of selling his crops to Milupa, the big baby food company. So far, he's accomplished the former, but not the latter.
>
> That will come in time, I thought; after all, the farm is less than five years old. My more immediate concern was Kemal him-self. The night before, he'd grown dizzy during backgammon and had to lie down and check his blood pressure; he was out here in the countryside alone, his two grown daughters unwilling to follow

their father's dream. Their mother . . . I couldn't figure out how to ask about her.

"Are you sure you're okay living by yourself?" I asked him in primitive, ungrammatical Turkish. "Don't you get lonely?"

Kemal tapped his heart, smiled and said, "Apples." Translation: Don't worry—I'm finally doing what makes me happy.

The next day, Kemal and I drove to the coastal town of Priapos, named for the way its peninsula juts into the sea, and wandered among the Greco-Roman ruins before eating a long, lazy, late lunch of grilled fish, meze, and lots of raki, the cloudy, anise-flavored liquor that is Turkey's national drink. As dusk approached, we drove home, past fields of wheat and sunflowers catching the last golden rays, and although we were mostly silent, Kemal eventually spoke a few words.

"Matt Gross, Kemal Görgün," he said. "*Arkadaşlar, kardeşler.*"

*Arkadaşlar*, I recognized: friends. But I had to flip through my phrasebook to translate *kardeşler*. Finally, I found it—brothers.

Wow.

I wrote the story on a bus back to Istanbul, tapping it out letter by letter on the screen of my PDA (the wireless keyboard had finally died). And when I sent it to New York, I knew it was right—not only in need of little editing but philosophically perfect. I had conveyed a sense of place and offered a frugal tip or two, and had gotten down to the business of exploring the world and making new friends, which was all I'd ever wanted to do. Frugality, I believed and tried to explain, was not an end unto itself but one of many traveler's tools, a means of getting closer to exotic lands and foreign peoples.

For the rest of the summer, I relaxed. I knew what I was doing. And my bosses knew it too. In August, I wrote about taking a forty-eight-hour train trip across China, from Urumqi to Beijing, and woke one morning to a new e-mail from Stuart, sent to his entire staff. "When you get a chance today," he wrote, "be sure to read Matt's latest installment, now on the Web, about his train trip through China. It's one of his best. As he winds down—there are just two more to go—he's gaining steam, not losing it."

For the next roughly four years, I was the Frugal Traveler—or, as the *Times* preferred I phrase it, I wrote the Frugal Traveler column. My stories appeared irregularly. Maybe every six weeks or so, I'd have a piece about a $500 weekend in some expensive destination: Punta del Este, Dubai, Hong Kong, Barcelona. Some features were frugal-themed without being labeled as Frugal Traveler stories: drifting around the Caribbean on EasyCruise, the hard-partying budget cruise line, and an insane seven-day jaunt from Geneva to Prague to Copenhagen to London to Fez to Paris to Budapest and back to Geneva, taking a different low-cost airline (RyanAir, FlyBaboo, and so on) every day. And as the following summer approached, I planned a new saga: a cross-country road trip during which I'd not only write a weekly column but would also shoot a weekly video segment. The summer after that, I'd circle Europe for the Frugal Grand Tour.

I was working, and constantly. In total, I was spending three to six months a year on the road, away from Jean (whom I'd married a few weeks after returning from the round-the-world trip) and my friends in New York, but writing about fascinating places. And the more I wrote, the more I developed a formula for my Frugal stories. It began with the anecdote that opened the article. In a normal story, I would want something that simply evoked that sense of place, or set up the drama to unfold, but in a Frugal Traveler piece I had to add an economic angle.

When I wrote about Istanbul, for instance, I started off with getting the bill at a cybercafé: "One million lira!" piped the cashier. She meant, I quickly realized, 1 million *old* Turkish lira, which would be 1 *new* Turkish lira, or about 65 cents. Whew. The Frugal Traveler dodges a bullet—and also gets an opportunity to talk about how in Istanbul, it's not simply the hoary travel-writer trope of old and new clashing but is actually something weirder, more complex, and more interesting: old and new so jumbled up that no one really knows (or perhaps cares) which is which.

Likewise, when I first wrote about Rome, I described drinking a civilized Negroni at a tony piazza, a brief splurge that was interrupted when a seagull violently attacked a pigeon amid the well-dressed Romans, while the bells of a nearby church rang out. This show was worth the €10 price of admission, a cost that included not just my drink but a host of free snacks. Frugal Traveler paradise—plus a way to hint at the Felliniesque (or should that be Pasoliniesque?) turmoil lurking just under the surface of the Eternal City.

Now, "formulaic" is not necessarily the most laudatory way to describe a piece of writing, but for a very long time I was happy to be working within a formula. There's something comforting about knowing intimately your constraints (sense of place, frugal tips) and not struggling against them. Most professional writing—that is, feature stories written for newspapers and magazines—follows a formula, and the formulas exist because they work well for conveying information. The opening anecdote sucks you in, the nut graf explains why you've just been told the anecdote, and the rest follows through on the narrative premise, with the final few paragraphs wrapping everything up in a way that's neat, but not so neat as to seem pre-programmed. Fulfilling the formula so that it doesn't feel like a formula is just about the apex of professional writing.

Writing for the *Times*, however, involved additional constraints that tweaked my experience in unusual ways. The first, and most famous, of these was the Travel section's absolute ban on writers taking press trips, those junkets sponsored by airlines, hotel chains, tourism boards, and P.R. firms. No writer, says the paper's Policy on Ethics in Journalism, "may accept free or discounted services or preferential treatment from any element of the travel industry." It didn't matter whether you were working on a piece for the *Times* or someone else. The ethics questionnaire that freelancers were required to complete asked whether they'd taken a press trip within the last two years; if you had, the section simply would not—could not—hire you.

This caused some consternation among many travel writers, who relied on press trips to get around the world and report the stories they'd then pitch, to the *Times* or wherever. How could they afford to do research otherwise? To the *Times*, it didn't matter, and justifiably so: The paper was constantly under attack—usually politically, but sometimes from the standpoint of how it practiced journalism—and it didn't need any further conflicts of interest, real or perceived. Few writers, however, fell victim to this policy, as the Travel section's editors seemed to operate according to "don't ask, don't tell," trusting prospective freelancers to come clean from the beginning and only acting when a contributor's "ethical lapse" inadvertently came to light.

For me, this was not a problem. Though I was a freelancer*, the paper had me traveling and writing enough that I didn't need to seek out alternatives, and the paper paid my relatively frugal expenses. (Expenses for cover stories rarely topped $2,000—that's airfare, food, lodging, supplies, and so on, for maybe two weeks of travel.) Once in a while, I'd receive an e-mail offering a trip somewhere—a twenty-two-day round-the-world-by-private-jet tour of Four Seasons resorts, for example—and I'd politely decline, citing *Times* policy. Although I occasionally wished for a bit more comfort on the road, I liked living by this rule, and not having to deal with the favor-trading world of publicists and comps. And besides, when it came to writing, I appreciated the built-in drama of traveling on my own, on a budget. What could I possibly say about a trip where everything was provided for me?

---

*No one at the paper ever discussed hiring me full-time. Once, early in my Frugal Traveler stint, I asked a copy editor if I should push for a job offer. "Why," he asked me, "would you want to work in this vale of tears?"

Another *Times* rule was more troublesome. "Writers of travel articles," the ethics policy says, "must conceal their identity as journalists during the reporting, so that they will experience the same conditions as an ordinary consumer."

In theory, this made sense, especially for my Frugal Traveler stories. If I was to help *New York Times* readers travel smarter and cheaper, I couldn't rely on my vaunted status to get better treatment. I had to be—and to write as—an Everyman. But in practice, that was not so simple. While I could easily hide my identity from hotels and restaurants—the professional travel world—many of my stories revolved around civilians: friends of friends, random strangers, normal people whose livelihoods did not depend upon a favorable mention in the *New York Times*.

How should I treat them? Should I simply lie when they asked what I did for a living, or would that violate other clauses of the ethics policy? And if I told them the truth, wouldn't that, too, alter how they treated me? No longer was I just that interesting (or dull) traveler but the one and only Frugal Traveler, in need of aid and advice! Or was this just a fantasy? Would anyone care who I was?

Early on, I got a sense of how this all worked. In September 2005, I flew to Jamaica to explore the area around Port Antonio, a region that was the first to develop tourist facilities but, because it was always hit hardest by hurricanes, had failed to keep pace with Negril and Ocho Rios. It was a rough, wet, wild, and beautifully green place, at once rundown and vibrant. Hotels could be damp and crummy— or pristine and far beyond my budget. I sat on the sidewalk talking with old barefoot Rastas, and I drank Hennessy from fresh-cut coconuts in rented villas, and I heard famous names: India Arie, Francesca von Habsburg, Ian Fleming.

My guide through the area was Jon Baker, a British music producer and a friend of a friend. With him, I saw no reason to hide my identity, nor with his weird circle of friends and acquaintances, ranging from Kingston high-society types to strippers. And for one week of hiking, dancing, and eating jerk chicken, the fact that I was a *New York Times* writer did not matter to anyone.

But on my last night in Jamaica, I checked in to Strawberry Hill, a luxurious resort in the mountains right above Kingston, fairly far from Port Antonio. Owned by Chris Blackwell, the founder of Island Records and discoverer of Bob Marley, Strawberry Hill was a collection of studios and villas straight out of some nineteenth-century colonial fantasy, and in line with that fantasy, the first thing I did after putting my bags in my room was head to the bar for a gin-and-tonic.

After placing the drink in front of me, the bartender asked for my room number. I told him, and his response was, "Oh! Hello, Mr. Gross."

This was strange, I thought—or maybe it wasn't. Maybe at these small high-end resorts, it was standard practice for employees to know the names of guests.

"So, Mr. Gross," the bartender went on, "what brings you to Strawberry Hill?"

"Well," I told him, "I've been in Jamaica a week, and I'm leaving tomorrow, and I just wanted to spend one night somewhere beautiful and quiet where I could relax."

The bartender wiped down some glasses, then said, "Are you by any chance a writer?"

"Yes," I said, slowly and with great suspicion. "How did you know that?"

"Oh, no reason," he said. "It's just that when people come here for quiet, solitude, and relaxation, they tend to be writers. That's all." *Uh-huh*, I thought. "Excuse me," he said, and went to take an order down the bar.

This was beyond strange—this was nerve-wracking. Had I really been made? What would this mean for my story? Could I even spend the night here, or would I have to check out?

"Look," the bartender said a few minutes later, "I knew who you were when you walked in. They told me, 'If Matt Gross comes in here, he's a writer—take good care of him.'"

My mind raced. Someone I'd met had told someone else who I was, and the news had spread through secret channels around the island. But where was the link? How could I trace the trail? "Who," I asked, "is 'they'?"

He didn't want to answer, but in the end he said, "the chef." I told him I'd need to talk with this chef—but first I had to eat dinner: a marvelous jerk lamb with guava sauce. Was it always this delicious, or was I getting a special cut of meat?

Afterward, the chef—Darren Lee, a third-generation Chinese-Jamaican—came out of the kitchen to chat. And although he was incredibly friendly and open, he did not disclose his source—"blame the bush network," he joked—adding that he was the only one at Strawberry Hill who knew, not the front desk or management. Then he handed me a bottle of his homemade chili sauce, a fiery green slurry of Scotch bonnets and vinegar that was the best I'd ever tasted.

Fine, I thought, I guess I can spend the night here. And luckily, when time came to write the story, I found I didn't have space to mention Strawberry Hill at all. Ethical dilemma averted!

In the future, though, I swore to be more circumspect. From then on, when people asked me what I did back in New York, I'd deflect. I'd answer, "Not much!" Then we'd all laugh and move on to the next topic. (Once, a fellow New Yorker sitting next to me in a cruise-ship hot tub said, "No, seriously, you live in New York. What do you do for work?") Sometimes I varied my response: "I have a small regular income that allows me to travel regularly, but not luxuriously." After my daughter was born, I'd explain that I was a stay-at-home dad (mostly true), that my wife's job supported us (very true; at best, I was making no more than I had at *New York*), and that for every thousand diapers I changed, I earned myself a week's vacation (less true). Usually, these quips were amusing enough that no one delved deeper.

Still, I hated deceiving civilians, especially those I quickly grew to consider friends, and often, after I'd sussed them out, I'd reveal my true identity, like Spider-Man lifting his mask to Mary Jane—if slightly less exciting. Usually, people demonstrated little surprise. It never seemed much of a stretch, I suppose, for me to be, at one moment, a funny sort of traveler, and at the next a funny sort of professional traveler. For a second, the news might impress them, and they might remark on how awesome my job was, or even mention they'd read me, but soon they'd realize: Matt Gross was just Matt Gross, *New York Times* or not, for better or worse.

This is not, however, how Hannity reacted. I met Hannity (not his real name) outside Columbus, a small town on the American side of the New Mexico–Mexico border, during my cross-country Frugal Traveler road trip. Columbus was famous for two things: In 1916, it was raided by Pancho Villa's forces, prompting a retaliation that included the first military deployment of airplanes. And partly because of this history, Columbus had become a mecca for hobbyist pilots, who lived together in compounds, their houses equipped with hangars that opened onto central runways.

After a few days in Columbus, wandering its history museum and crossing the border for street-taco dinners, I was anxious to find a pilot who could take me up in a plane. The owner of my $40-a-night bed-and-breakfast suggested Hannity, who lived not in a compound but in a trailer on a big, empty, dusty lot outside town. When I found him and broached the idea of going up in his ultralight, Hannity was amenable, although he noted it had been raining, and his runway was a little soft. If it didn't rain overnight, though, we could go up the next morning.

Great, I said. Do you mind if I shoot some video while we're airborne?

"Sure thing," he said, then: "Wait. You're not from the media, are you?"

Faced with such a direct question, I couldn't lie. In less than a week, this video would soon be on the *New York Times* Web site, seen by hundreds of thousands of people, maybe millions, and Hannity had a right to know what he was getting into. So I told him who I worked for.

"The *New York Times*?" he said. "Why, I'd just as soon shoot you as talk to you."

Evidently, Hannity had a problem with the paper. Whether it was the *Times'* political coverage or something else (the *Times* tends to attract cranks), I didn't know, but I tried to explain things to him: what I was doing, which section I was writing for, my mission this summer—to stay off the interstates, see how people lived in different parts of the country, and save money. I offered to show him the Frugal Traveler site, and we moved into his trailer and turned on his satellite-Internet-linked computer. All the while, Hannity kept nodding and listening and not shooting me in the face, and I got the sense that, out here alone with the dust, his plane, and his dog, he craved company, even if it was that of a liberal *New York Times* writer.

After I'd explained myself for half an hour, Hannity relaxed. "If it doesn't rain tonight," he said, "be here at seven o'clock and we'll go up."

That night, it did not rain. At seven the next morning, I returned to Hannity's plot, and he wheeled out his plane, a home-built ultralight consisting of hollow piping, PVC wings, and open cockpits. It weighed, Hannity said, about 250 pounds. It did not look all that sturdy, but I had to trust Hannity, even if Hannity did not trust the FAA, which he complained wanted too much oversight of rickety contraptions like the one he was just now firing up.

And then we were aloft! Cruising over the wide flat expanse of Columbus, tracing the line of the barrier fence between Mexico and the United States, arcing toward the low Florida Mountains in the shrinking distance. Up there, supported by so little, my face buffeted by winds, I had a sense of how big the planet was, and how open. I'd asked to go up, and my wish had been granted. Did other travelers know this was possible? Did other travelers know how simple this was? And could I communicate it to them in a way that would make sense?

These were the eternal questions of life as the Frugal Traveler, and as the years went on and the stories piled up they became ever more vexing, mostly because they were not the primary questions my column existed to answer. Instead, I had my frugal tips to discover, develop, and sometimes invent, but after dozens of articles I didn't know quite how to come up with anything new. As I saw it, the way to travel frugally had been laid out sufficiently:

**Air:** Search Kayak.com, ITASoftware.com, and (for international flights) Vayama.com for low prices. Use AirfareWatchdog.com to set up alerts on routes you'd like to fly, and if those routes are to well-known destinations like Beijing or Rio de Janeiro, look into a U.S.-based consolidator, such as uschinatrip.com. Buy the ticket directly at the airline's Web site whenever possible, and always join the loyalty program (and set up points-gaining credit cards; see cardratings.com for details). In Europe and Southeast Asia, fly low-cost carriers. Check in online. Be prepared to spend more than you want, and don't complain too much.

**Lodging:** The cheapest option is to stay with friends, or friends of friends. The next cheapest is CouchSurfing.org, the international network of two million people willing (in principle) to give you their couches, floors, spare bedrooms, or guest cottages in exchange for no money whatsoever. (Yes, it's safe.) Almost as cheap is WWOOF, but you must be willing to plan your vacation around farmwork. Next up are services like AirBnB.com, Roomarama.com, and Wimdu.com, which let you rent rooms, apartments, and whole houses around the world, like a user-friendly version of Craigslist. (Yes, they're safe.) If you don't trust these services, then you've got (in generally ascending order of expensiveness) hostels, motels, bed-and-breakfasts, inns, and real hotels. Again, join loyalty programs. Don't take TripAdvisor too seriously. Never wire anyone any money (ever).

**Food:** Search Chowhound.com for recommendations, and Google your destination plus "food blog." Buy ingredients at farmers' markets, small grocery stores, and supermarkets—and taste every free sample. Really nice restaurants often have cheaper menus at lunch or at the bar. Eat a bigger lunch and a smaller dinner. Skip breakfast, unless it's included with your room. Seek out church dinners. If you're Jewish, seek out Chabad House for Sabbath dinners. If you're hungry, seek out Sikh festivals. Eat street food. Eat fast food. Eat bad food.

**Other:** Use Skype. Go in the off season. Unlock your cell phone and buy local SIM cards. Find friends of friends (of friends) through Facebook. Buy citywide multimuseum passes, or skip museums and go to art galleries. Make sure your credit and ATM cards don't charge foreign transaction fees. Take public transportation. Hitchhike, if it feels safe. Ride a bike. Walk.

So: There, in less than four hundred words, is everything you need to know about traveling cheaply—the sum total of my Frugal Tips, the material I spent four years, and hundreds of thousands of words, writing about in depth. To me, it all seemed so obvious, and repeating the same advice, week after week, in slightly different scenarios (today Paris, tomorrow Chiapas!) was maddening. Often, the advice boiled down to: *You want to save money? Then just spend less, and care less.* In a way, I felt like the copy editor I'd been at *New York*, only instead of offering the same grammatical and stylistic advice to the same writers every week, now I was giving readers the same money-saving travel tips they would have learned from me long ago, if only they'd been paying attention.

To be fair, every once in a while some new system or business would appear, and I'd jump on it. AirBnB.com, for instance, was only founded in 2008, and I wrote about it as soon as I could. But for the most part, I was recycling the same tips and techniques. Worse, I was getting jaded about the whole experience—about what was supposed to be the best job in the world—and I resented my audience even more bitterly for making me jaded. I wanted to be friendly and peppy, enthused about each new discovery, but instead I'd turned dark and sour. Why couldn't I just enjoy myself?

Maybe because I felt I was failing to convey the subtleties of frugal travel. That is, none of my tips would mean anything to a traveler unless that traveler could prioritize. Would you sacrifice a four-star hotel room so you could afford three-star restaurants? Or would you subsist on Ritz crackers so you could stay at the Ritz Carlton? The answers, naturally, would vary from reader to reader, and depend on their level of travel experience. You don't know what you truly care about as a traveler until you've traveled widely—by which time you've doubtless wasted lots of money on things you now realize you didn't need or want. And those were things that I, as the everyman frugal traveler, couldn't warn you about.

Moreover, as frugal tips came to dominate my thought process, I realized I didn't give a damn about traveling frugally. Not that I wanted to go the luxury route, it was just that saving money was a secondary concern. Making friends, exploring unseen corners of the world, eating well, understanding how different people lived—those were the reasons I traveled, and the frugal aspect of it was just a means to that end.

But for too many of my readers, saving money was *the* goal of travel. Or it seemed that way. Maybe I was too sensitive, maybe I cared too much, but in comment after comment posted on the Frugal

Traveler site, readers complained I was spending too much money, that I was doing things wrong, that they could do it better. I wanted to respond to them, "But it just doesn't matter! It doesn't matter whether you save money or spend money. It's how and why you travel that matters." But that's not the kind of thing the Frugal Traveler is expected to go around saying.

I tried to ignore the commenters, to dismiss them. Clearly, the naysayers were blindered idiots, convinced of their own skinflint greatness and oblivious to the broad range of travelers and interests I was attempting to appeal to. For them, frugal travel was about hostels, camping, supermarket meals—and nothing else. Their self-righteousness infuriated me, for I knew frugality carried no moral weight.

But the fans, too, bothered me. They'd praise a story, it seemed, solely because I'd visited the same place they'd been twenty years earlier; never mind that our experiences and insights utterly diverged, all they cared about was that I'd triggered their nostalgia of that Turkish honeymoon or that postgraduation Mexican backpacking trip.

I told myself and my friends I didn't care what people said or wrote. "Embrace the hate," Ted from Saigon, by then my friend and colleague, told me again and again. But the truth is I cared. I wanted my audience to get what I was doing, and why, and to sign on to my nascent philosophy—to accept frugality as a mere premise, to open their eyes to the world it would unveil, and, ultimately, to cease thinking about money at all. And while some surely did, it was never enough. The high of publication was always followed by the low disappointment of feeling misunderstood.

Making this even worse was the guilt. I had, everyone agreed, the best job in the world, and yet all I could do was to look at the bleak side, to worry and moan over my failures, to discount the possibility that I might truly be helping people through my advice. What kind of ungrateful monster was I? Why did *I* deserve to travel constantly—and get paid for it, no less—while others scrimped and saved and waited for their once-in-a-lifetime shot at Paris?

Or maybe . . . Maybe I didn't deserve it? I might not be fucking up as my editors once worried, but maybe someone else could do the job better, with more energy and dedication than I could muster after four years and two hundred stories. I wouldn't, I knew, quit traveling or writing about travel completely, but I needed to get back to doing it how I wanted, focusing on what I felt was important: the unparalleled joy of bewilderment.

And so, as I had before and no doubt would do once again, I quit—while, I hoped, I was still ahead.

≈

## Chapter 5

## *The Best Policy*

In Which I Try to Come Up with an
Ethical Response to Developing-World Tragedies
and My Own Role in Perpetuating Them

Lina's skin was dark, even for a Cambodian, and her kinky hair was pulled into two short ponytails. She couldn't have been more than five feet tall. She was sitting next to me at the Walkabout, an Australian bar in Phnom Penh, wearing a black sundress that seemed to be covered in thin, white, diagonal stripes—they were actually the words "sex girl" printed over and over again in very small type—and she had just offered to give me $40 to spend the night with her.

"I like you," she said in English, faking a pout. "Let's go home."

This was awkward. I gulped my Angkor beer and tried to figure out how to tell her no. This was going to be difficult, not least because I wanted to say yes—to take her to the apartment I'd rented by the river and strip her of that obscene outfit. But I had a girlfriend back home in New York, and I didn't want to have to lie to her. And so I told Lina the truth.

"I can't," I said. "I have a girlfriend. I can't."

She pouted for real now. My honesty didn't matter. Every expat in Cambodia had a girlfriend or a wife, and that never stopped them from taking home prostitutes like her. "But I want to," she said. On the stool next to Lina, her Vietnamese friend Quyen looked skeptically down her nose at me.

On my other side, Mark, a photographer friend who was just a few years older but whose red face was deeply lined from sun exposure, shook his head, then exchanged a few sentences with Lina in Khmer.

Our artist friend Buckminster, he explained to me, had taken Lina to his place the previous night and—who knows why?—paid her far too well: He'd given her $50. Now Lina was feeling flush and generous.

"She's a nice girl," Mark said. "You really don't have a choice. Say yes."

Mark was entirely right. Lina was a nice girl—energetic, sassy, silly, chatty—and to refuse her was to insult her, to remind her that she was nothing but a hooker, no match for the nice, official girlfriend in America. And if I accepted—well, so what? I could come home from this monthlong vacation, my premillennial jaunt in 1999, and tell the easy lie, knowing that, like most people, my girlfriend would believe me unquestioningly. Plus, I'd make $40.

So why did I say no? I had many reasons: For one, I don't like lying. I don't mean this altruistically, in the sense that it is simply, universally better to tell the truth. Rather, it's because I find lying easy—so easy that when people believe my lies, I'm disappointed in their gullibility. With strangers, this matters less, but with friends and family, I have high expectations. I don't want to think poorly of them, I want to believe they're as bullshitproof as I am, and so I try to tell the truth, even when it hurts.

But I had a more immediate reason for saying no. Because—and neither Lina nor Mark knew this, nor do most people—I had a history with hookers. A lousy history.

Spend twenty-four hours in Southeast Asia, of course, and you've got a history with hookers. They are tragically, stereotypically, everywhere: at the bars in the tourist districts, smiling at you from the motorbike cruising next to your taxi, hovering in the lobby of your mini-hotel, slurping noodles with their johns at the all-night Chinese restaurant you've drunkenly wandered into for after-hours dumplings. They can be aggressive, bashful, bipolar, stoned, confused, haughty, alluring. Their faces can be caked to lighten their complexion, or they can look untouched, peasant girls trucked in from the countryside. They can be crude, broken, looking only for the next $10 fuck, or they can act so sweet you're tempted to call them your girlfriend. Indeed, there's often a fine line between the girl you pay for sex and the girlfriend for whom you buy clothes and drinks, whose little brother's education you fund, whose mother's medicine you pick up from the pharmacist. And this is only the beginning— there's a whole rainbow of prostitutes, an infinite spectrum of the savvy and the innocent, the willing and the enslaved, the vigorous and the ailing and the desperate.

How to deal with them—and with all the other tragedies of life in the developing world, from beggars and thieves to street children and adults still suffering from birth defects or wounds suffered in the war—is a real dilemma for travelers, men and women, backpackers and jet-setters. Are you supposed to be offended by the intrusion of their presence into your vacation? Or amused, as if they're scenery in the louche, Third World atmosphere? Are you supposed to be crushed by the unfairness of it all, that some should go hungry and legless and abused while others should fly halfway around the world in search of adventure? Or should you be moved to do something about it, whether by dropping coins into the gnarled, outstretched hand of the man at the noodle shop, or by seriously taking up a cause and working with aid groups to alleviate poverty and injustice? Is there a single right answer?

These were issues I dealt with almost from the day I moved to Ho Chi Minh City—and indeed, almost everywhere I've traveled since. Back in 1996, I would walk out the door of the Lucy Hotel and in the damp heat of the rainy season instantly encounter evidence that, well, Vietnam had a ways to go. The sidewalks were cracked, uneven, unnavigable, crowded with parked motorcycles and food carts, smelling of trash and sewage. Half the street was composed of makeshift shanties. Little kids squatted at the curb edge and shat into drains that did not lead to treatment plants. Beggars, some able-bodied, others on crutches—one, I remember, with twisted, useless legs, crabbing around upon a makeshift plywood skateboard—would put out their hands and ask for a dollar.

At night in the bars, I'd see street kids. A sweet eight-year-old girl had been taught to say, in near-perfect English, "Would you like to buy a fan?" Others sold sticks of gum. One kid in particular captured my attention: He was short, with an overlarge head and eyes that never focused properly. He spoke with a bit of a slur, and he called everyone *di già*—old whore. We called him Peanut Boy, or Peanut Head, and rumors about him swirled: He was thirteen but looked five. He was a heroin addict. He was an Agent Orange victim. Whatever the truth, he was simultaneously sweet and sour. He could be cute, a damaged baby you wanted to cradle, until suddenly, out of nowhere, he'd grab your nipple through your shirt and twist it hard, and laugh. When he tried to play pool, it was heartbreaking—he could barely peek over the edge, and you got the sense he would never grow tall enough to see the felt.

This scene wasn't just taking place in rough-and-tumble Pham Ngu Lao. After dark, in the center of town, amid the graceful old French colonial buildings, homeless families slept on cots, or sheets of cardboard. Every time I'd leave Pho Hoa Pasteur, the most famous noodle shop in the former Saigon, a man whose legs were missing below the thigh would smile at me and hold out a baseball cap. Elsewhere, thin women with thin babies would mime putting food into their mouths.

In the face of such depressing moments, it was hard to figure out how—or even whether—to respond. My first instinct was always to hand over some small amount of money, one thousand or two thousand Vietnamese dong, about ten or twenty cents. But as I quickly learned, that merely drew other beggars over: If I had a thousand dong for one, surely I had the same for all? And if I did give out money, how could I be sure that the cash would go to its recipient? In Bangkok, where I and others would go to renew our visas, we heard rumors that panhandlers were organized by the mafia, with some of them intentionally crippled in order to bring in donations.* Who's to say it was any different in Saigon?

The same seemed potentially true of the street kids. Where were they getting these fans and packets of chewing gum to sell? Who would the money truly go to? With them, in a way, it was easier. Peanut Boy and Fan Girl didn't really expect anything of you, and if you bought them a Coke or a bowl of noodles, they were happy and, a little to my surprise, politely grateful. They took what they could get. There was no pressure—only an aura of desperation that lingered after they'd left.

With the beggars and the kids, there was always a simple alternative: Walk away. Ignore them. Make your face a blank, impassive mask that sees nothing but what it wants to. And if you must acknowledge the poor filthy creature before you, it is solely by a slow, subtle shake of the head, your eyes half-closed, as if you'd just remembered something shameful that someone else, somewhere else, had once done long ago.

It sounds callous, but when you feel beset by demands for your money and your attention, when you just want to sit on a plastic chair in a leafy alley and enjoy a twenty-cent iced coffee with condensed milk, when the trauma of witnessing the hell that, for hundreds of thousands of people, is everyday life in Saigon—or Bangkok

---

*The rumors were not entirely well-founded, it turns out. While many Thais believe Cambodian mafias run the child-beggar racket, a UNICEF study in 2007 showed that most beggars were independent operators who'd come to Bangkok with their mothers.

or Mumbai or New York City—grows to be too much, you sometimes have no choice but to shut it out entirely.

This is what I would do from time to time: make myself blind. What cripples, what orphans, what buckling pavement and excremental stink? I had my coffee and croissants at the French café, my air-conditioning (from time to time) and studio apartment, a credit card, and a passport that would get me the hell out of there if and when I needed to get the hell out.

But that attitude took its psychic toll too. Willed blindness is only temporary, and in startling moments that dim veil reverts to Honda exhaust and the smoke from burning garbage, which clear to reveal a shattered but spirited populace clamoring for your charity. How sweet that sound!

For months, I yo-yoed between affection and impassivity, bestowing or withholding generosity with all the capriciousness of a Greek god. And it worked—these twin attitudes made my life in Saigon bearable. If I seemed to be turning gullible, I'd shut down, and when I seemed like a jerk, I could pay off my conscience with a spontaneous gift to someone in need. And when I felt like a sucker, the wallet would seal up again. It doesn't sound like an attitude to aspire to, and it was hardly a unified philosophy, but the human brain does not demand consistency to get through the day. All it needs is relative peace. And with my mind at rest, I began to feel that maybe I had a place here in this strange country.

Except when it came to the prostitutes. Frankly, I was scared of them. There were bars—darkly illuminated by neon and Christmas lights—where the only women inside were working girls, and these girls would stand in the doorways, in long, cheap evening dresses, their faces overly made-up, and try to lure you in, sometimes by actually running out and grabbing your arm and yanking you inside. They fawned and spoke little English, and I couldn't see how anyone would find them attractive. They smelled desperate. But so did I, probably.

I was also afraid because they reminded me that although I felt like I was slowly getting a grasp on the country, I really had no idea what I was doing there. First was the language barrier: Their English was minimal, my Vietnamese was worse. But this difficulty with the language served as good protection against prostitutes. If I couldn't talk to them, I couldn't even come close to sleeping with them, right? Or could I? All around me, it seemed, were guys for whom mutual incomprehensibility was no obstacle to sex. They wanted a girl, they bought her, easy as that. And when they'd got her back to the mini-hotel or the shiny, shoddily built suburban villa, they knew just what to do with her—or so I imagined, because at the time I had no idea what to do with a woman. Oh, I'd had girlfriends, including a long-term relationship through college, but sex had been awkward at best, and more often disappointing. I had neither stamina nor dexterity nor confidence; forget performance anxiety—I was in *terror* of what I might have to do.

Not that I had much chance to do anything anyway. In my first few months in Vietnam, I'd had two not-very-close calls. One was with Marie, the cute, bright student from my literature class at Ho Chi Minh Open University, whose energy and enthusiasm brightened up the lecture hall every week. The day I announced to the class I was quitting, she and I spoke for a while afterward, then rode our bicycles home together, a wonderful ride marred only by its end: We turned off Pham Ngu Lao onto the Lucy Hotel's side street, but then I forgot that she didn't actually know where I lived, and when I swerved over into the stretch of sidewalk that served as the Lucy's parking lot, I rammed my bike into hers, knocking us both to the ground in front of Lucy, Ms. Luc, and assorted other hotel denizens. Marie and I exchanged phone numbers, and Band-Aids, but we never spoke again.

The other near-hookup was with Loc, a well-spoken Vietnamese guy I'd met in my first days at the Saigon Café, that fluorescent-lit corner bar. Loc didn't announce his sexuality right away, instead just chatting me up, and since I didn't know anyone in Ho Chi Minh City at that point, we made plans to go riding around town on his motorbike. The tour was brief and random, and after we'd sped past the French-built Catholic church, he asked me, seemingly out of nowhere, "Do you want to see the Jew?"

"The Jew?" What could that mean? Was there a synagogue in Saigon?

"Yes, the Jew. The place with lots of animals?"

"Oh, the zoo."

Instead, we went to his family's place and, sitting in his tiny bedroom, which opened onto a billiards parlor the family owned, Loc played his acoustic guitar and told me about his last girlfriend, an Australian businesswoman who'd brought him along on a trip up the Vietnamese coast, and his current boyfriend, another expat who was away in Singapore or Hanoi. "Sometimes I go with boys, sometimes I go with girls," he said. Then: "Have you ever done anything with boys?"

"No, sorry," I said, shrugging. "I guess I just like girls." From my backpack, I pulled out my notebook and showed Loc a drawing I'd made of Tammy, copied from the photo I took of her after our car crash on the Eastern Shore. The drawing was terrible, and I felt bad for us both—for disappointed Loc and for my own tragically incompatible tastes.

"That's okay," Loc said. Then he strummed his guitar and sang me a Bryan Adams song: "(Everything I Do) I Do It for You."

In March 1997, the *Viet Nam News* sent me to Phnom Penh to cover the First Biennial Southeast Asian Film Festival, a grand series of new releases from all over the region, mixed with several old French movies starring Alain Delon, who was rumored to be making an appearance. The Cambodian capital was then at the height of its post–Khmer Rouge Wild West phase. Large bags of marijuana were sold at the central market. Armed men, some of them soldiers, others unaffiliated, drove around in glistening Toyota 4x4s. The morning after I arrived, a peaceful protest against corruption in the judicial system was attacked by men with grenades; at least sixteen people were killed, and many more injured.

At night, after the screenings had ended and I'd written my reviews and faxed them back to Ho Chi Minh City, I'd hit the bars with Douglas, who'd come over from Vietnam to show me around this seedy town. Douglas would lead me to Heart of Darkness, Sharky's, and Martini's, a notorious hooker bar with a flesh-packed dance floor and a slightly less claustrophobic garden with concrete tables and benches. That was where I found Ali—or rather, where she found me. She'd spied me and Douglas right away and sauntered over in her peach blazer—a dark-skinned, short-haired tough girl jutting out her chin and telling me in a low, defiant voice she wanted me to fuck her. Flattered, terrified, I refused. But I danced with her anyway, until she left to pursue surer clients.

Douglas, who was far more at home in this underworld, was, I sensed, disappointed in me, and after lunch the next day we embarked on a trip to Svay Pak, a brothel village eleven kilometers from the city. Why did we go? I can't speak for Douglas, but for me it was simple fascination that there existed in this country, on planet Earth, a village of brothels. To this twenty-two-year-old, it sounded fantastical, unreal, something out of Bukowski or Vollmann. Or maybe it was because I wanted to test myself, to see how far I'd descend into Cambodia's dark heart. Or maybe we had no reason— it was just something to do, *something that one did*, on a hot afternoon in Phnom Penh.

We found two motorbike taxis, told them "Kilometer 11"— Svay Pak's distance marker on the highway—and soon we were wandering around a sleepy compound of shacks and long, low, warehouse-like buildings with corrugated tin roofs. It was in one of these that we found ourselves sharing a beer with two Vietnamese girls. I can't remember their names, only that they both had long hair, loose white dresses like Edwardian heroines, and too much makeup. Douglas chatted comfortably with his girl in Vietnamese, while I struggled to ask basic questions like "How old are you?"

After his beer, Douglas announced, "I'm going to get a massage." I'd like to say that Douglas winked at me, but he probably didn't. Then he left me alone on the long, sticky black nylon couch with my girl.

This was awkward. I asked her where she was from, how long she'd been in Cambodia, did she want to go back. I sipped my beer, and pulled out my camera. She tried to look alluring—pouting, draping herself across the couch, giving sidelong glances, even kissing me on the cheek—as I took a few shots. But clearly, this was not going where everyone—she, Douglas, Douglas's girl, the middle-aged mama-san who'd met us at the door, the taxi drivers who smirked and dropped us off—assumed it should go.

I asked about her mother. She said she missed her.

My Vietnamese conversational skills exhausted, we lapsed into silence.

Douglas and his girl returned. He looked refreshed. He may very well have had a massage.

"Ready to go?" he said.

It was not many more days before Douglas and I were back at Martini's, along with Ravudh, the young desk clerk from our hotel, and his friends, most of whom were the well-heeled children of government officials. I was half-drunk. Or mostly drunk, I can't remember. Ali cornered me, rubbed up against me, restated her desire, and I led her back to our table in the garden, where we ordered snacks. I got Chinese dumplings. Ali got a mango and sucked lasciviously on the sweet, fuzzy pit. Ravudh and his friends departed. Without my ever saying anything, everyone understood that Ali was coming home with me.

There was one problem left to deal with: Douglas and I were sharing a hotel room, and he was not going back there alone. Ali got up, walked over to the dance floor, and returned with a baby-faced girl for Douglas.

"How old is she?" Douglas asked.

Ali spoke to the girl in Khmer, then turned to us: "She says she's eighteen."

Thirty minutes later, Douglas and I and our dates, Ali and Baby Face, walked into the lobby of the Morakat Hotel, where the night clerk and the shirtless, gun-wielding security guard were watching a porno starring a black guy and a white girl.

Upstairs, we got down to business right away, no drinks, no TV, no lights. Ali was not much for kissing or foreplay, and while I wasn't sure where to begin, I also had no clue how to ask Ali to help me out. Luckily, we were interrupted by Douglas and his girl in the next bed.

"I can't do this," Douglas whispered to me, turning on the bedside lamp. "She's too young. There's no way she's eighteen. Ali, how old is she?"

"She says she's eighteen." Ali's voice was suggestively neutral.

"Tell her she can go home. I can't do this. She's just lying there doing nothing."

Ali relayed the message, Douglas handed over $10, and Baby Face left.

"It's too bad. She's going to think it's easy to make money now," Douglas said. He turned out the light. "You two can carry on."

We carried on. Ali put a condom on me, I got inside her, and soon I was done.

"Did you come?" she asked me quietly.

As I curled up with Ali that night, I couldn't help noticing how relaxed she'd become, how soft her skin felt against mine as we spooned. Was this the brazen mango-sucker?

The next morning, Ali put her blazer back on, accepted my $20, and left, her face once again hard and proud.

This is where I'm supposed to talk about the rightness or wrongness of what I did that night, and yet I find that a really difficult thing to do. Obviously, prostitution is bad. Except in supposedly enlightened places like Amsterdam or San Francisco, no one ever really aspires to the world's oldest profession. Most prostitutes have no choice—they're trafficked by mafias far from their homes to places where they have little recourse to legal help or nongovernmental support. African women wind up in Italy, Vietnamese girls in Cambodia, Moldovan women just about everywhere. Many of them are taken against their will, some are sold by their families, and a sickening number are children. When men take advantage of the sex industry, especially in the developing world, they perpetuate a system that ruins lives and keeps countries hobbled and poor. It is bad.

At the same time, I find it hard to condemn the younger me for his behavior. Knowing what I know now about the evil depths of the business, knowing that the experience would be less than good, I think I might still have done the exact same thing. For all his naïve ambitions and literary pretensions, the younger Matt Gross was trying to figure out, on a very basic level, how to relate to other people, people whose lives and experiences were light-years from his own. But to do so, he first had to find his own limits, to see what kind of person he actually was, or could become. An insensitive brute? A sucker? A timid aesthete? Or—and maybe this is what he learned from the whole episode—a confused young man whose capacity and desire for empathy could be dangerous.

Two and a half years later, I was back in Cambodia, biding my time in Phnom Penh before heading to Angkor Wat for the millennium. The capital felt different already: Since I'd left, a power struggle between the first prime minister, a royalist prince, and the second prime minister, a one-eyed ex-communist, had erupted in violence that left the latter prime minister, Hun Sen, the clear victor.

Few Cambodians, and fewer foreigners, thought Hun Sen would be anything over than a kleptocratic dictator, but many were relieved nonetheless: For the first time in decades, one person (and one party) had firm control over the entire country. I saw fewer armed guards in the streets. Peace was in the air.

It was therefore only appropriate that I spent my first few evenings at the Café Santepheap—the Peace Café. Unlike almost every other Phnom Penh bar, it wasn't fast or wild, hookers didn't congregate there, the wayward teenage children of Cambodia's ruling class didn't start fights and leave without paying. People went for an Angkor beer and a basket of fries and a chat with the British owner, Dave, whose Cambodian wife had recently given birth to their son.

At the Santepheap I met Cambodians from the emerging middle class, like Pepsi, whose income level and English ability allowed him to drink and talk about sports, politics, and the weather as, essentially, an equal to the foreigners like me who surrounded him. So when Lina walked in one night, climbed onto the barstool next to mine, ordered a Bailey's on the rocks, and complained about her long, tiring day, I figured her for a regular, albeit a young-looking one. We made small talk. I left, impressed at the clientele the bar had managed to attract. This was the new Cambodia!

A few days later, however, I ran into Lina at Martini's, and all became clear. At Martini's, guys could be there for sex, or just for a drink (and an ogle), but women, especially Cambodian women, were there for one thing only: work. On the dance floor, the bass excruciating, I told Lina I'd met her at the Café Santepheap. She didn't seem to remember, but at the same time, I think, she could tell she'd made an impression on me.

I began to see her everywhere: at Heart of Darkness, where I played pool, or back at Martini's. Always we talked a little, and I learned a little about her. Her father lived in Bangkok, and she missed him terribly. She sent him money. I listened to one of their phone calls: She spoke Thai fluently, and insisted to me she wasn't Khmer at all. ("What are you talking about?" Mark said later. "She's completely Cambodian.") She was sweet and energetic—she may have been a prostitute, but she didn't let that demean her. Like Pepsi, she considered herself my equal. She may have needed a cell phone, but she didn't ask me for one, and I didn't buy one for her. She wasn't my responsibility, and I liked it that we could speak without her demanding I fuck her for money, and while I wasn't naïve or romantic enough to think she had a heart of gold, I started to think maybe she wasn't like all the other working girls—that she remained capable of having relationships that weren't predicated on sex and cash.

Until that night she offered to buy me out. Until I stammered in shame. Until I wrecked the evening even further by failing to play along with a linguistic game started by Lina's friend Quyen, whose difficult accent had me constantly asking, "What?" To which Quyen would reply, "Wat Phnom." At which point Lina would chime in with "Phnom Da."

As Mark explained to me, Wat Phnom was the temple on the hill near the river, and Phnom Da was a big hill near Takeo, to the south. "They're trying to help you save face," he said, "so it doesn't look like you don't understand them."

But I didn't understand them, and I understood even less why I was clinging to my virtue. I was halfway around the world with people I'd most likely never see again, and I could lie. I'm good at that. People want to believe me. They really do.

Afterward, I didn't bump into Lina for a while. She had vanished into the limbo prostitutes vanish into whenever you don't want to find them. But I did want to see her again, if only to take her picture. This was the compromise I made with myself, and I considered myself very clever for having made it: I would see Lina before I left, and I would invite her to my sublet apartment, where I'd ask her to undress for my camera. I'd pay her whatever she asked. I wouldn't touch her—that would be cheating on my girlfriend. Still, it was dirty, so I felt obligated to pay her something. After all, that was her job, to accede to the filthy wishes of the rich-by-comparison. Denying her altogether would be like refusing a Michelin-starred chef's offer to cook you dinner, provided you pay for the groceries.

Of course, I did nothing at all to make my tepid fantasy a reality. I left Phnom Penh for Angkor Wat, where I caught the flu and missed out on all the fun, then returned to the capital for a twelve-hour stopover before catching my flight home to New York. Twelve hours—my last chance to find and photograph Lina. But instead of tracking her down at Martini's, I spent the afternoon hanging around the Foreign Correspondents Club of Cambodia—probably the least sordid bar in the country. It was full of brown leather club chairs and burnished wood, and diplomats and businessmen met here to relax and gaze out across the Tonle Sap River, their pints of Angkor beer covered with their coasters to keep out flying green bugs.

Three tourists of the high-class variety sat down in the chairs near me. They were in their forties and dressed fairly well: khaki pants, not shorts; shirts buttoned up and tucked in; no visible cameras or backpacks. They had just come from Ho Chi Minh City, and we traded intel: I asked about places I used to frequent there, they asked about the tourist attractions and political situation in Cambodia. I'd only been there a month, but I knew about the shaky government, the corruption, the crazy stories about cheated-on spouses of high officials who threw acid in the faces of their younger rivals. As I told these stories, I gave off—possibly intentionally—the image of being a bright young man, an adventurer in the dangerous zones of the world, eager to put things in literate perspective for my fellow Americans. I could see these tourists were hanging on my words, impressed.

And then Lina walked in, looking more like a prostitute than she ever had before. It wasn't anything she was wearing, not a miniskirt or too much eyeliner or cheap, Chinese-made high heels. She was simply young and local and brazen, with alert eyes always seeking something, or someone. Girls like her didn't come in here, ever.

Within seconds, Lina and I had greeted each other and brusquely left the tourists behind. For a few minutes, we stood at the balcony, watching the wide, muddy river below, the awkward encounter of a week earlier forgotten, or at least unmentioned. This was my chance.

"I'm leaving tonight," I told her. "Come back to my place—I want to take your picture." As we walked out, I could feel the tourists watching me, no doubt horrified.

The apartment, around the corner and down an alley, belonged to a reporter for a Spanish news service, and Lina regarded everything inside with a detached air. Why should she care? She'd surely seen its equal, and she'd probably see this place again, especially since Buckminster, her benefactor that one night, had lately been crashing here as well.

"Take off your clothes," I said, but not out loud. "Take them off right now."

Instead, she spoke first. "Tell me about your girlfriend," she said.

I gave Lina the bare facts—I was dating a pretty fashion student from Taiwan who had a lovely smile and a great appetite—while telling myself that what I really wanted bared was Lina's body. But telling myself and telling Lina were two vastly different things, as distant from one another as America and Cambodia, honesty and betrayal, wealth and poverty. If only she would ask . . . but she didn't, not even when I led her up to the airy, lofted sleeping area and showed her my mosquito-netted bed. It was as if by refusing her that other night, I had exempted myself from the world of sex, and that by so strenuously insisting—against all common sense—that she and I relate as human beings, as equals, I had actually succeeded. I had gotten what I wanted, even if what I wanted was changing.

Finally, meekly, I told Lina I wanted to take her picture, and she followed me out to the deck. Beyond us was the river at dusk, and beyond that a Muslim neighborhood whose landless inhabitants worked the local slaughterhouses, and beyond that fields of rice and land mines, and I took a few long-exposure shots of her face. She looked defiant in them, but then again, with her fierce eyes and up-turned nose, she always looked defiant. Then I walked her downstairs to the street.

Before we parted, Lina said: "Don't show the pictures to your girlfriend."

"I won't," I told her. "I promise." I wasn't lying.

Five years later, I was back in Phnom Penh to research my novel. Much of the city's anarchic quality had been tamped down, restrained by Cambodia's expanding economy, not to mention the dictator in charge of the country. Martini's, Sharky's, the Heart of Darkness, and all the other hooker bars still existed, but I avoided them. They didn't fascinate me any more. They were real, I knew, and their reality was too much for me to handle. My life would be, for a few weeks, regular and calm.

But I did make it back to the Café Santepheap. Since I'd last been there, Dave's wife had been killed in a grenade attack (the accidental result of a dispute at a neighboring karaoke bar), and he'd moved the bar across town, down to where all the NGOs he loved to bitch about had their offices. He'd remarried, his son was now five, and he remained as intense and gregarious as before, railing on about Cambodian corruption in light of the Stalin biography he was reading.

"The hooker with a heart of gold?" he said when, inevitably, I asked after Lina. "She's in Kompong Som"—a backpacker-filled beach town better known as Sihanoukville. "She hooked up with the Starfish Project, you know them?"

I nodded. The group took street kids in and taught them useful skills: baking, handicrafts, restaurant work. Starfish were good people;

at least, they didn't receive the whiskey-and-Coke-fueled abuse that Dave heaped on World Vision, UNICEF, the Assemblies of God, the Mormons . . .

"Well," Dave continued, "she went down there and adopted a few of the Starfish kids. Lovely girl. Works in a couple of the bars down there as a waitress. Lovely girl. Of course, she was always a problem at the bar. Would drink too much and puke. You puke on my bar, I give you a bucket and you clean it up yourself. That was her. She had a boyfriend for a while named Mark. She'd get drunk and nostalgic about him and then puke all over my bar . . . She's older now, and maybe not as cute. She doesn't want to be a hooker anymore. 'Course, who wants to be a hooker?"

This was good news. Amazing news, really. A prostitute of unusual verve and spirit had, on her own initiative, gotten out of the business and was now keeping kids from following the path she'd followed. My own path was now clear—I had to find her, hear the story from its source and offer any help she might require.

Sihanoukville was not an impressive place. Like many Cambodian towns, it felt haphazard and unorganized, encompassing a series of beach areas of varying quality: the backpacker-friendly Victory Beach; the private, guarded area at the five-star Sokha Beach Resort; the long, long stretch of sand at Ochheuteal Beach, where everyone from tourists and expats to street vendors and middle-class Cambodians would hang out. To the north was Cambodia's main shipping port. Inland was an uninspiring downtown and a bunch of cheap guesthouses on a hill above Victory Beach. I'd been through here before, and while I didn't mind soaking in the warm waters of the Gulf of Thailand, I found Sihanoukville dull—a beach town that existed solely because Cambodia felt it should have a beach town. But I'd come this time only partly to sunbathe, and as soon as I had a chance I made my way to the Starfish Project's café in downtown Sihanoukville to ask after Lina.

She wasn't around, the Cambodian employees said. They seemed wary as well, reluctant to talk, and suggested only that she might be down at Ochheuteal Beach. A Scandinavian woman working for Starfish asked me if I was sure Lina was Cambodian. "It doesn't sound like a Khmer name," she said.

At Occheuteal, I asked anyone I could find if they'd heard of Lina. A woman selling snacks seemed to recognize the name, but said she hadn't seen Lina in a few weeks. Maybe she'd gone back to Phnom Penh?

I wasn't sure what to make of this. If she'd adopted children, wouldn't she be here with them? Or was the Cambodian sense of "adoption" something different? Or had Dave been wrong?

No, people here at Ochheuteal knew Lina—or at least knew a Lina. At the Sea Dragon restaurant, a foreign bartender reacted strongly and happily to the name. "Oh, sure, Lina," he said. "Tall girl? Light-skinned? Works with Starfish?"

Now I was in a quandary. Were there two Linas in Sihanoukville, both of whom had turned their lives around to help street kids? Dave had definitely known who I meant, but this bartender seemed fairly certain himself. Well, I thought, whichever Lina I find, I'll be happy.

But no Lina turned up that day or that evening. The next day I tried asking at Victory Beach, whose vendors and bartenders sent me up to Weather Station Hill, where the town's crummier backpacker hotels and bars were located, to see the owner of a guesthouse, who might know. The owner pointed us to a room in the compound where, he said, a friend of Lina's was staying. Lina herself might be there, too—he didn't know.

I approached the flimsy door and knocked. A young woman who looked Vietnamese answered. "Lina not here," she said. Behind her

I could see a man with his shirt off. Quickly, so as not to interrupt further, I apologized and backed away.

Again, I asked at the front desk for help, and finally the owner lit up. He led me out of the hotel and down the street, to a small, low concrete house with a portable sandwich cart out front. The guesthouse owner pointed at the old woman running the cart and said, with evident pride, "Lina mama!"

Could this be Lina's mother? She certainly resembled Lina with her dark skin, kinky hair and slightly upturned nose. In my beginner's Khmer, I began to explain: "I'm an old friend of Lina. I knew her five years ago. I am trying to find her. Please, do you know where she is?"

"She's gone back to Phnom Penh," the old woman said, hardly looking up from her cart to answer.

"Do you know, was she working with Starfish? Was she helping kids? What is she doing in Phnom Penh now?" I could feel my questions getting more desperate, and the woman growing more indifferent. She'd told me Lina—some Lina—was in Phnom Penh, and that was all.

Suddenly, I realized what was going on. To her, I was just another foreign john looking to sleep with her daughter, the daughter who, for one reason or another, had left again to work as a hooker. With every question I asked, with each insistence that she was a smart girl and just a friend, I was reminding her she'd raised a prostitute—just as, so many years ago, I'd unintentionally reminded Lina of the same thing. I wanted to help, but I couldn't help hurting.

A week or two later, I was back in Phnom Penh, and I did what had to be done: I went to Martini's. The place was bigger now, with a sprawling outdoor space that led to a small stage. Electronic music thundered in the night, and the crowd looked the same as ever: foreign guys drinking, local girls dancing. I ordered a Tiger beer and sipped it as I walked around, shaking my head sadly as girl after girl approached me with a slightly scared smile. I climbed the steps up onto the stage and looked out at the sea of prostitutes and their potential clients, but I saw no Lina—no Linas, either, no one who showed the slightest bit of individuality or energy or wit.

Or rather, they were all Linas, all wearing "sex girl" dresses, all equally trapped in a system that rewarded fuck-machine tactics and laughed at any expression of hope or determination. It was stupid of me to expect otherwise. I left my half-finished beer on a concrete ledge and went home to sleep.

The French millionaire was barefoot. It was a cool day in May 2008, and, like me, he'd just gotten off the ferry from Dover to Calais. From the ankles up, he looked the picture of the cosmopolitan Gaul: pressed pants, cashmere V-neck, clear blue eyes, close-cropped silver hair. An air of confidence and self-satisfaction emanated from him. He was returning to his home turf, happy.

But he wore no shoes. His feet were clean, but tough-looking, and I didn't even catch a glimpse of his presumably leathery soles. On the taxi we shared from the port into town, he explained that he'd first gone barefoot sometime in the 1960s, and from that point on, he'd never reverted. Unless a social occasion or sport activity absolutely called for it, he was shoeless. In winter and summer, in first class and in restaurants. Sure, he sometimes got looks from people, but what did he care? He had money, he knew who he was, and he didn't want to wear shoes. A few weird glances were worth the freedom.

The taxi dropped me off in the center of town, not far from Rodin's famous *Burghers of Calais* statue, memorializing six prominent citizens who'd surrendered themselves to British forces to ward off a siege during the Hundred Years' War. To my eyes, Calais looked as proper as the French millionaire. Its stately buildings, artsy atmosphere, and clean, slightly chilly air were what I thought a northern French town should be, and the local appetite for beer and *pommes frites* gave it a human aspect, too. As I checked into Le Cercle de Malines, a meticulously designed but still whimsical bed-and-breakfast—there was a taxidermic crocodile in the Indochine room, a huge claw-foot tub in the Rome room—I had the sense that Calais might be a place where I'd feel at home, on that fine line between highbrow and low.

I knew, however, that Calais had another side. In the past several years, it had become a magnet for refugees, who'd come from all over the world and hoped that here, where the English Channel was narrow and cargo trucks plied the tunnel beneath it, they'd manage, at last, to reach Great Britain. Until 2002, many of the refugees had stayed in a nearby camp called Sangatte, but Nicholas Sarkozy, then the interior minister, had closed it, and officials had declared the problem solved.

But that hadn't stopped refugees from arriving. Hundreds of them, I'd heard, lived in hiding around Calais, and as the Frugal Traveler I felt it was my duty to learn what I could about these travelers who were frugal not by choice but out of necessity.

One day I walked over to an empty lot near one of Calais's canals, where Anne-Sophie, the proprietress of Le Cercle de Malines, had told me the refugees gathered each day to receive free meals. Two hundred or so were milling around, waiting for La Belle Étoile, one of three aid organizations that feed the refugees, to open up its trailer. The majority—I learned through interviews—were Eritreans, Iraqis, Afghans, and Palestinians, many of whom had paid tens of thousands of dollars to escape their homes and would give what little they had left for illegal passage across the channel. Some had spent eighteen months getting to this point—others longer—and their voyages were never easy.

"You cannot imagine," a young Eritrean man told me before turning away to join the lunch line.

Life was tough for them, sometimes in nonobvious ways. France would not give them asylum, nor would it deport them, nor would it allow them to stay and work temporarily. Worse, refugees and aid workers told me, the police would generally arrest them for walking in public during the day—simply for being in the country illegally. They'd be held twenty-four hours, then released, perhaps to be re-arrested mere hours later.

For some, this was a minor inconvenience. Many were being trafficked in a semi-organized way, and would wait only a few days in Calais before getting word of a truck that would take them to the port, then—if they were lucky—to England.

In this respect, Roshan and Ahmed, a Sri Lankan and a Somali I was introduced to by aid workers, were atypical. Both had fled their war-torn homelands, but not with asylum in England as their goal—they'd simply fled for their lives. Roshan, a round-faced, kindly bus driver in his twenties, had run away after his conductor was murdered; he'd received word he himself was next. His seven-month boat journey brought him via India first to Italy, then to Paris as well. As for Ahmed—known to aid workers as Eddie Murphy for his good humor and *Delirious*ly red jacket—when both his parents were killed in a single day (his father in the morning, his mother in the evening), he took a boat to Djibouti with four friends, who then locked themselves in a container on a cargo ship, and several days later found themselves in France.

Neither Ahmed nor Roshan had the aid of organized trafficking mafias, and neither had any money. They were trapped in Calais, and life in Calais was hell. They shared a donated tent in a wooded area known as "the jungle," and survived on donated meals (two a day, if they were lucky) and donated clothes. Another aid organization handed out tickets for showers—but with hundreds of refugees needing to bathe, this was at best a once-a-week luxury.

"Dogs don't live like this! Cats don't live like this!" Ahmed told me. Then he laughed bitterly as he told me about his attempt to win asylum: He'd been rejected because, without access to an embassy, he was unable to prove his story—and yet France also refused to deport him, saying Somalia was too dangerous to go back to.

Despite their miserable circumstances, they had not lost their basic humanity. If anything, it appeared their deprivations had made them more human. When Roshan had arrived in Calais, he had no idea what to do, or even where to go to find food, but Ahmed took him under his wing and showed him how to survive. They were both the sole representatives of their countries, both calm and intelligent (each said he spoke at least six languages), and they'd bonded deeply.

Once, Ahmed said, he'd been invited to join several other refugees on a midnight truck to England, but when he'd asked if Roshan could come, too, the others said no. They were Muslim, as was Ahmed, but Roshan was not. And so, faced with the prospect of freedom in the U.K.—or at least slightly better living conditions and a community of Somali expatriates and refugees—Ahmed turned them down. He stuck by his friend, stuck in Calais. Could I have done that? I wondered. Would anyone have done that for me?

The second day I met with them, I brought sandwiches—chicken, tuna, cheese—and cans of Orangina. But when I arrived at the empty lot, I found Roshan and Ahmed already in line for their free meals and didn't have a chance to remove what I'd brought from my bag. Nor did I want the other refugees to see me giving them anything, for fear it would upset the equilibrium of the larger group. So the three of us sat near the canal, under a warm, early-summer sun.

Ahmed and Roshan opened their lunches: platters of canned tuna, mini-baguettes, cheese, fruit, yogurt. And as they were getting ready to eat, they noticed that I had nothing. Immediately, they started dividing up what they had, handing me a can of tuna and half a baguette. I tried to refuse, insisting I wasn't hungry and preparing for the waves of horrific guilt to wash over me. How could I take what they had when they had nothing? But they, too, insisted. If they were eating, I should as well.

So I accepted. I broke off pieces of bread and dug them into the shallow can of tuna salad, and I ate slabs of cheese that reminded me of what had been served on the flight over from New York. We shared our bottled water, and we ate, and we talked.

And the guilt that I'd imagined never quite materialized. I think I understood what was going on—that their instinct to share was so strong, so ingrained, that they would let nothing block it, not even the fact that they had next to nothing. Sharing food—with friends, with strangers, with the needy—was what they had done at home, was what had sustained them during the months of hard travel that had brought them to the jungle of Calais, and it was what they would continue doing in order to preserve what dignity remained. It was a way of asserting their equality—they didn't have much, but they had enough to give away—and of reminding me that I was not so far removed from them. I, too, was hungry. I, too, felt gratitude in the depths of my soul for this act of kindness. For half an hour, we could simply be three people from different parts of the world, lunching as friends together in this place we'd never expected to wind up.

I don't know where Ahmed and Roshan are now. In 2011, a representative of La Belle Étoile confirmed for me they were in England—"but we don't have anything more precise," she wrote—and my further attempts to locate them failed. Instead, I have to make the assumptions one makes about refugees in the abstract: that they survived the journey; that they found asylum, or government aid, or community support; that they continue to live and try to maintain some semblance of dignity, despite the hardships. Or: La Belle Étoile was wrong; they died en route; they were discovered and deported—to another limbo, to a newly pacified home, to certain death.

But the truth is I hate to have to think this way, to lump them in as mere members of the group of refugees, with typical histories and typical destinies. As with Lina, I want to imagine them as individuals, as unique human beings with personalities and families and quirks— with stories that separate them from the mass of stereotypes and statistics, that prove they were alive and that for a few minutes or hours we shared a can of a beer or a can of tuna, the same slab of concrete or mosquito-buzzed balcony. And while I wish we could have shared more (and, yes, that I could have honored Lina's humanity by accepting her offer), I also know that I don't know where we'll all be tomorrow. Our paths might cross, our situations reverse. I've wandered enough, and worried at the future, and sketched out in my head what I'd do if it all went to shit, and I hope that when it comes time to split my last soggy baguette with a stranger, I'll act as they did—without hesitation, as an equal, as if I had all the bread in the world.

⌒

## Chapter 6

# *The Orient*

### On Learning, and Unlearning,
### How to Navigate a Messy World

The first Émile Zola book I read was *The Beast Within,* a novel of lust and murder on the railroad line between Paris and Le Havre. I'd found the book during my research stint in Phnom Penh—it was lying around the house I was staying in, and, having nothing else to read, I picked it up and was immediately absorbed into its twisted, violent world. The story concerns a railroad station manager, Roubaud, who discovers that his wife, Severine, had as a child been sexually abused by the president of the railroad, whose house she'd grown up in. In a fury, Roubaud forces Severine to help him kill the president, and then, believing their crime has been witnessed by Jacques, a railway engineer, cajoles his wife into romancing Jacques so he won't turn them in. Only Jacques, too, has a secret: Any time he's sexually attracted to a woman, he gets an uncontrollable urge to kill her, savagely, and drag her naked corpse through the streets. Now that's what you call dramatic irony!

I loved the darkness of the novel, as well as its suspenseful plotting, but perhaps more than anything I loved its setting, which turned out to be the setting of all Zola's dozens of books: France in the late nineteenth century, a time of not just social mobility but literal mobility as well. Railroads had tied the country together as never before, and now people from Provence were moving north to rebuild Baron

Haussmann's Paris, while folks in Le Havre could take day trips to the capital and come home in time for dinner. Travel was remaking people's lives, challenging the traditions of the past, and inviting the ambitious to start anew wherever they could imagine.

Over the course of my own travels, I read many more of Zola's novels: *Nana,* about a hustling concubine in nouveau riche Paris; *L'Assommoir,* about Nana's mother, an aspiring laundress tempted by booze; *The Belly of Paris,* about the intersection of politics and gourmet cuisine at the city's famous food market, Les Halles. I read these books at home, sometimes, but mostly I read them while traveling. They attuned me, I felt, to the way travel changes the world, and the hyper-precise language allowed me to fantasize that I, too, might one day be able to describe my own adventures in such crystalline detail. The stories took me out of myself, into a strange and fascinating and startlingly complete universe—a place so distant from my own life that I wished I could stay there forever.

Which is why it should have been no surprise that one evening in the spring of 2007, as I was reading Zola in bed, I looked up from my book and realized I didn't know where I was. Not the city, not the country—I was nowhere at all. Terror hit me like a locomotive. My heart slammed in my panicky chest, and I was seized by the fantastical fear that at any moment a government official would storm into the room and demand I reveal our location. What would I say?

And why hadn't this happened more often? At the time, I was on the road months out of every year, visiting a dozen or more countries, and yet never in one longer than two weeks. *Veni, vidi, fugi.* Just a couple of months before, I'd spent seven days flying from Geneva to Prague to Copenhagen to London (via Berlin) to Fez to Paris to Budapest to Geneva, and moving so speedily that in London I didn't bother to get a hotel room—I just walked the rainy streets all night. My personal velocity was accelerating every day, and I half-expected to get confused, to mistake Budapest for Prague or forget what had come after Copenhagen.

But that didn't happen. I'd always known where I was, where I'd been, where I was going. Not that I'd ever felt *stable*, as if I truly inhabited any of the places I happened to be passing through. I'd speed-walked through Kafka's Prague, tipsy on nettle beer, and I'd spun unthinkingly through the alleyways of the Fez, and I'd never come close to losing my way. Movement was my natural state. My orientation was forward. I was in the zone. I could go on like this forever.

So why had I come unsprung only now, while reading in bed? And why was I so terrified at the prospect? And most important of all, where the hell was I?

I tried to think. I scanned the room, hoping I'd find in its décor the hint I needed. Wooden four-poster bed. Antique desk sticky with air-conditioning. Sponge-washed peach walls. Framed prints of blue gods with many arms. I knew this, I knew this!

India! I was in India, and, and . . . in the former French colony of Pondicherry! I'd arrived a few hours ago, and I'd leave in five days. Next up: Darjeeling, then Mumbai, then Brooklyn.

Relief welled up inside me. I read my book and fell asleep. And when I woke up the next morning, I was still in Pondicherry.

In the weeks and years that followed, however, I began to regret my quick thinking in that Pondicherry four-poster. Why couldn't I have held on to that feeling of lostness that had invaded my body? Why couldn't I have savored it, rolled it around my mind, tried to enjoy for a few more minutes the sensation of utter disconnection? It was there, I'd had it in my psychic grasp. For the first time since I was seven years old, I'd been lost! And yet it had slipped away so quickly I was left with nothing, only puzzlement and a lingering aftertaste of fear.

Fine, then, I'd have to rely on what had happened in Denmark, twenty-five years before.

After the adult bookstore, after the bad hamburger, after the restorative french fries, there was at last Tivoli Gardens, the amusement park. Rides and shows, lights and the legs of towering Danes. My father had learned a fireworks display was imminent, and we hustled through the crowd. I remember a metal fence as high as my own not quite four-foot head, and I remember being unable to see as well as I wanted to. I scooted this way and that, darted around bodies, squeezed through gaps, and caught only glimpses of sparking pinwheels and cannons of flame—earthbound pyrotechnics, not the Fourth of July skyrockets my family would watch, unblocked, on the UMass campus.

When the fires were finally doused and the audience dispersed, I found myself alone. Dad was gone, and I couldn't recognize my surroundings. Where was the hamburger stand? Where had we come in? Where was I? I was nearly eight years old, with dirty blond hair and blue eyes, and I must have looked like any other Danish child. Maybe I cried. Maybe people came to help me, speaking a language I couldn't understand. How long did this go on for? How long until some mother brought me to a security guard, who brought me to an office, where my father was waiting to take me home—or did I arrive first?

I can't remember. I can't remember, either, what it actually felt like to be lost. Did I panic? Did I try to reason my way back to my father? Did I notice landmarks, or follow that metal fence back to where I'd been before? By that age, I must have seen the classic *Sesame Street* cartoon in which a young boy gets lost in a psychedelic landscape where women have butterfly heads, a plastic house pulsates like a Wurlitzer jukebox, and a green-clad pimplike figure steps out of a yo-yo string to inform the poor confused kid, "Well, you should figure it out for yourself, little guy. But I'll give you a hint: Try to remember everything you passed, but when you go back, make the first thing the last. Ha ha! Yeah!" At which the kid simply retraces his steps—past the animal fountain, past the hippo eating chocolate—

to his home, into whose entryway (framed in Corinthian columns) he runs, yelling, "Hi, Mom! Boy, was I lost!"

But I can't say that, because I don't remember that feeling. What I do know is that in the thirty years since that evening in Copenhagen, I haven't come close to being lost—not once. It's difficult to say for certain how I developed my sense of direction. (Although wouldn't it be great if I could point to the trauma of getting lost at Tivoli Gardens as its catalyst? Alas.) In fifth or sixth grade, I know, we were taught to read maps: how to examine the legend, understand scaling, measure distances between two points. Or maybe it was even earlier—all those maps in the J.R.R. Tolkien books fascinated me more than the garbled plots ever did.

And that Tolkien obsession grew and mutated. One of the first things I bought in Vietnam in 1996 was a map of Ho Chi Minh City, its main roads well-marked, its districts clearly numbered and set in different colors. The map's informational quality far exceeded that of its paper, and I had to replace it two or three times; and each replacement evolved, with new landmarks added and old streets removed—it made me feel I was truly witnessing the city's growth. A year later, in Baltimore, I bought a 1967 *Times* of London atlas, whose rich detail and antiquated political lines were (and remain) fodder for an afternoon's daydreams. Yahoo's, MapQuest's, and Google's products began to consume my hours. In Brooklyn, I hung a 13 x 9-foot map of the world in our second bedroom, and a three-foot laminated map (unfortunately lacking today's newest country, South Sudan) now faces me when I look up from my laptop in my office. On a bookshelf at home rests a French globe from, I believe, the immediate postwar period: vast blotches of colonialism, a not-yet-divided Germany.

You look at these maps long enough and you start to fall into them, to connect the infinite dots of the world. That huge wall map shows shipping routes—Montevideo to Miami, Cape Town to Port Saïd—and another Mediterranean map, purchased in preparation for that first round-the-world Frugal Traveler trip, picks out oases in the North African deserts. In the center of Brazil, I see the Mato Grosso Plateau and wonder when I'll meet my "big jungle" namesake. Norwegian islands in the South Atlantic, Attu Island in westernmost Alaska, and cities I'd never noticed before—Jask, Mbuji-Mayi, Caniapiscau, Piolesti—and now long to visit. And when I do, I'll know where I am.

But then I can read maps. Many people cannot—some not effectively, others not at all. Often, this depends on which country you're from; in some, maps make no sense.

"I ran across this a lot in Phnom Penh in the mid-late nineties," my friend Rich Garella, who worked at the *Cambodia Daily*, wrote me on Facebook. "Most notably, one time at the newspaper office we were putting up a huge topographical map of Cambodia. It came in about a hundred sheets, so I asked a member of the admin staff to help piece it together. She had no idea what it was or what I was asking her to do. I had to get her to imagine she was flying high like a bird and looking down, and then showed her home village to her. She was absolutely awestruck."

I got a taste of this, too, when I was reporting one of those first stories for the *New York Times*, about the sleepy Cambodian river town of Kampot. In the center of Kampot, I'd noticed a new-looking hotel, the Borey Bokor, and went in to find out more information. At the front desk was a young woman, friendly and enthusiastic, wearing gold jewelry and stylish makeup. I asked her about the hotel, the rooms, the rates, then, finally, its address. She didn't know.

"Okay," I said, "what's the name of this road?" Outside was a medium-sized street leading to Kampot's central traffic circle.

"I don't know," she said in English, then her eyes opened wide as she had a brainstorm. "I don't know," she repeated with excitement, "because I don't care!"

What she meant, more specifically, was that the street names just didn't matter to her, or to anyone in Kampot. The Borey Bokor was near the traffic circle, and that was as much direction as was necessary.

It would be easy to dismiss this attitude as the natural state of much of the developing world, but surely there are complicating factors—like Cambodia's depressing twentieth-century history of colonialism, war, autogenocide, and invasion. With a semiliterate population inhabiting a land where names change with each new ruler, why fixate?

But I've found similar phenomena all over the world, sometimes with interesting variations. In Japan, for instance, mailing addresses are hyperprecise, but don't function in the same linearly progressive way as in the West; rather, they identify buildings not on specific streets but on specific city blocks, making them useful primarily for the post office, the police, and the government. So while streets do have names, those names won't necessarily tell you where a particular business or home happens to be.

Which is not to say no one knows where anything is. In many of the places where maps have no common use—including the United States, which is likely as map-illiterate as anywhere else—people navigate by methods linked to their personal point of view and landmarks. This is how many of us function by default ("cue-response strategy" is the technical term) and why turn-by-turn GPS mapping is so successful. Rather than by giving you an overview of a route, and requiring you to understand, as a whole, the relationships and connections between multiple points, the devices adopt our outlook, telling us at each moment what to do and where to go.

This human's-eye view approach has deep roots not just in our psyches but in mapmaking as well. In the archives of the Austrian National Library is a remarkable document, the Tabula Peutingeriana. A thirteenth-century copy of a fourth- or early-fifth-century map, the Tabula lays out the incredible network of roads that criss-crossed the Roman Empire. Yet instead of taking the now-default bird's-eye view, the Tabula unfolds as a scroll—about one foot by twenty-two feet—with Rome at its center, and the roads leading outward, roughly east and west, from the Iberian peninsula to Antioch, Mesopotamia, and even the Ganges. The roads, inked in red, with interstitial hooks to denote a day's journey, progress landmark by landmark: buildings of varying size, rivers, mountains, lakes, and well-identified cities and towns. It's exactly what a traveling courier, soldier, or diplomat would have encountered along the way—an imperial Roman version of Google Street View.

The Tabula is transfixing—so much that I spent thirty minutes writing that last paragraph because I kept getting absorbed in scouring the digital version of the map for recognizable place names, like Palestina and Bactrianos. And as amazed as I am to behold it, my wonder must be nothing compared to that of an actual fifth-century Roman, who could have gazed the length of the scroll and imagined it not only contained the entire world but rendered it navigable, accessible—human scale.

Before the Tabula, maps of the world—at least those we know of—were different. Some were symbolic, such as a Babylonian carving of seven islands surrounded by a "bitter river." Others from antiquity, which we mostly know through later reconstructions, took a more recognizably geographic approach to rendering the continents and bodies of water—Italy's boot, for example, is obvious in many of these—although the limits of human knowledge are evident, too.

What unites these earlier maps—and what makes the Tabula so revolutionary—is that they are attempts to depict the world *as it is*. Cities and landmarks may appear upon them, but the world's natural, objective shape is of paramount importance. Not so with the Tabula, which maps instead the manmade world. Roads are now the organizing principle, the cities of humanity supplanting god-wrought geography as the fundamental unit of existence. The Tabula is a monument to mankind's dominion over the earth, and a map of the possibilities of existence. "What is the world?" was the old question.

With the Tabula, we now ask, "Where am *I* in the world? And where else can I be?"

These are questions that, with a map before me, I can ponder for hours. But take away the map, and I have answers instantaneously. I know where I am, and I know how I got there. I might even be able to give you relatively accurate lat-longs.

What I don't know is how it feels to be lost—how *you*, one of the millions or maybe billions of human beings with neither a sense of direction nor map-reading skills, feel when you look around and realize that nothing gels, no landmark strikes your memory, no path leads back to the familiar. This matters to me because it is so widespread, and as a traveler who wants to understand why and how we travel, I don't want to assume you are filled with panic or fear. Perhaps you're like my friend Don George, a perpetually sunny writer and editor who's been roaming the world for decades, yet had to ask me for directions when he gave me a ride through San Francisco—even though he lives right across the bay. For Don, getting lost is something he has to live with, but he thinks of it (he told me in an interview in 2010) as "the gift of being directionally challenged."

"My instinct is pretty much always to go the way that is opposite of the way I should be going," he said. "And this has served me extremely well professionally. When you get lost—when you, essentially, always go the opposite direction from the way you should—all kinds of marvelous and illuminating adventures ensue."

In Cairo, he went on, he'd started out one day heading (he thought) for a neighborhood full of "touristy attractions," but instead wound up going deeper and deeper into a maze of ever-narrower alleys. "I saw all kinds of everyday, working-class shops and houses I probably wouldn't have seen on my planned excursion," he said. "Eventually I ended up walking down an alley lined with down-and-out people looking covetously at my watch. The alley got so narrow that I was literally stepping over their legs in some places. Clearly I was lost and I thought that I was headed for big trouble. But then, just when I was beginning to get desperate, a young boy materialized and wordlessly took my hand. He turned me around and walked me out of the maze and into ever broader and broader streets, until he deposited me in a main square. I looked around and realized that I recognized where I was. Then I turned back to thank him. In that instant, he had melted away into the crowd."

What struck me about Don's Cairo story was not its climax and resolution but its beginning. I, too, have had more than my share of magical help-from-nowhere moments—in Slovakia, in Georgia, in British Columbia—but to get into such predicaments, I've had to act deliberately. I've had to understand maps or the layout of cities, and consciously turn away from the touristy areas, moving step by knowing step into the neighborhoods I hope will contain those untarnished working-class shops and houses (or whatever). This is maybe not the greatest thing to complain about, but when I hear the stories of people like Don, I feel crude and calculating: I *know* I can get myself to the place where the kid will lead me to safety, where the old man will pour me a drink and tell me tales in the Italian he learned as a boy, where the *babushka* on the shared minibus in rural Kyrgyzstan will hand me one of the loaves of bread she baked for her niece. I'm not sure I believed Don's way was better or purer than my approach, but I understood, too, that knowing how to manipulate these situations told me nothing about myself. My mastery of maps and directions preserved my illusion of control, and kept me from reaching that point of utter helplessness, that terrifying point when I would—well, what would I do?

The first thing you do when you arrive in a strange city and want to get lost is put your bags away. Getting lost involves—requires—intense wandering, and a suitcase or heavy backpack is only going to slow you down and make you long for a hotel, a shower, and a change of clothes. If you're lucky, you're already at the bus or train station, and the left-luggage office is perfectly equipped to care for your things as long as you like. And then, swearing never to glance at the map on your phone, you just set out.

Ideally, you'll have taken some getting-lost precautions. You won't have read a guidebook, or looked at a map, or been there before, so you won't know how the city is organized at all. (Except, of course, that you can smell the salt air blowing up from the Straits of Gibraltar and through the Tangier medina, and from anywhere in the nighttime desert you can spot the glowing palaces of the Vegas Strip.) All you know of the place is its rough history and its reputation, gleaned from half-remembered high school classes, movies that favor stereotypes over subtlety, news reports from questionable sources, and friends' post-vacation praise and complaints.

Maybe you know even more than that. Maybe you're there because you understand that this place is thematically apt for getting lost. Like Tangier, a gray zone that lies at the northern tip of Morocco, a jumping-off point for both Arab invasions and European colonialism, and thus not really one or the other, instead a jumble of French and Spanish and Arab (and American) people and languages and ways of living. Or like Paris, whose nineteenth-century flâneurs redefined the aimless wander as a sophisticated modern pursuit. Or like Chongqing, the city of thirty-three million whose steroidal skyscrapers spread, uncontrolled, across a swathe of mountainous, river-cut southwestern China twice as big as Switzerland.

Venice? Not a bad idea, but maybe you've been there already, and realized how terribly small it is. In Venice, you can lose your way for five minutes, ten minutes, but then you'll intersect a horde of tourists, or stumble upon a vaporetto stop, and you'll instantly reorient. Ditto hundreds of other locales, both familiar and foreign, whose chaotic layouts seem to promise you'll lose yourself, but whose limits—size, variety, complexity—are all too obvious.

You consider the wilderness. The forests of Montana, the sands of the Sahara, the mangrove swamps of the Sundarbans. Yes, getting lost might be easy. But you want, eventually, to get un-lost, too, and emerge at the end of a week or two alive and intact. To want to get lost is not a death wish. Rather, it's the desire to block out the noise of expectation and structure, to experience surprise and the challenge of disorientation, to travel as if you'd never traveled before.

To pretend I'd never traveled before was impossible, of course, but it's what I attempted to do starting in the summer of 2010, after my stint as the Frugal Traveler came to an end. A new editor, Danielle, had recently taken over the Travel section, and over steak-frites and red wine in a diner near the *Times* building, she asked me to pitch her a new series of travel stories, one that was ambitious in scope but had no service element. These adventures did not need to be useful to or replicable by readers, she said; they only had to be great stories and well written.

So I began to talk to Danielle about what had happened at Tivoli Gardens and how, in the years since, it had never happened again. What I wanted to do, I told her, was to get lost, and to do so I needed to go to extremes: I would travel without a guidebook or a map, without contacts or a plan, without even booking a hotel to crash at upon arrival.

To her credit, Danielle saw this idea as more than one weird traveler's crazy mission. Getting lost—or, as the series would be called, "Getting Lost"—was a way of casting off the shackles of checklist tourism, GPS-based driving directions, and Internet advice forums, all in the hope of finding something more engaging, more true, more real. Which is, I think, what I was hoping for, too, even if I couldn't yet articulate it. All I wanted to do was go somewhere, blindly, and with these artificial constraints governing my behavior, I would see what happened.

What happened was this: Every day for a week in July, I stormed through the Tangier medina, a maze of ochre alleyways, thick wooden doors, and shadows that provided fleeting protection from the Mediterranean sun. Trying urgently not to consider my route, I turned left and right and left again, marching up stairways and under archways and ignoring children who bobbled soccer balls and warned me certain pathways were *fermés*—closed. (They were always right, those routes always dead-ended, and I always had to backtrack.) I watched women carrying bundles of pungent mint to market and old men shuffling in loose, hooded djellabas, like retired Jedi.

And as I maintained my forward momentum, I realized: this was not working. As labyrinthine as the medina was, it lay on a hill that sloped down toward the sea—which meant I was, almost unconsciously, orienting myself. Every step uphill took me inland, every step down led to the shore. And as my paths crossed each other and repeated, I could tell that, even if my brain had not yet processed the exact route from one end of the medina to the other, my legs were figuring it out. Traitors!

Not exactly helping things were all the guides (licensed and ad hoc, old men and young boys), who cooed at me in English, French, and Spanish, "What are you looking for? Where are you going? You want the Casbah? Hashish?" I didn't want to ignore them—that seemed rude—but no answer, especially the truth, could satisfy them. Indeed, any answer only invited them closer. One, a tall, thin guy named Abdul whom I met outside the riad, or traditional house, where I'd decided to spend my first night, announced to me that he was not a guide, just a neighbor, that he'd grown up in the Casbah, the old walled citadel atop the medina, and that he wanted to accompany me as I walked around. He would, he promised, not ask me for money.

As clearly and eloquently as possible, I explained to him that I had come to Tangier for no other reason than to get lost, that getting lost was something one could only do alone, and that while his offer was very generous, I had no choice but to refuse.

In that case, he countered, he would let me go, but would follow well behind me—several meters at least—available to explain whatever might need explaining. A fair compromise, I thought, and so off I walked—with him right at my side, explaining absolutely everything: Behind this wooden door was Mick Jagger's house; that minaret was the only octagonal one in Tangier; Kofi Annan once went to that café. I tried to argue, asked for space, turned on my heel, ducked around corners to hide when I thought he wasn't looking, but to no avail. Fine. If I couldn't lose him, I'd put my losing-myself plans on hold for the evening and take advantage of Abdul's expertise. I asked if he knew a leather worker who could fix the ancient canvas shoulder bag I was carrying; indeed, he did, and we spent a very long hour in front of a tiny storefront in a skinny passageway, watching a one-handed man with horrific scars across half his face mend and rebuild the bag. It was a frustrating interlude, and when it was over I wanted desperately to get away from Abdul and be on my own.

As we parted, he asked me for money. I gave him the coins in my pocket. And as I did so, I knew I was not about to get lost—not in Tangier.

But over the next week, I discovered other forms of lostness. Tangier's mix of languages—French, Spanish, English, and Arabic—was joyfully disorienting. I could begin a sentence in one, throw in a word or phrase from a second, and end in a third. Thirsty in the afternoon, I'd seek out a café, but since I couldn't remember the French word for watermelon, I'd order *un jus de sandia. Shukran!* And I'd be understood, as if this were an everyday request! Indeed, it was.

In Tangier, hearing, not seeing, was the key. At a nightclub, I drank too much with a group of German, French, American, and Korean expats and closed my eyes to focus on the babble of languages, and the live band's surprising segue from Miles Davis to salsa. Another day, my wanderings led me to a secluded hilltop spot where the frenzied drumming of a wedding procession whirled up from the unseen lanes of a neighborhood below. As hard as I tried to pinpoint the party, I never caught sight of them, and the intensity of their rhythms wavered only with the strength and direction of the breeze.

These alternative losts may have made sense when I wrote about them in the *Times* (and now here), but on the ground in Tangier I still felt like a failure. There—and on subsequent "Getting Lost" treks to Ireland, Chongqing, Jerusalem, and Paris—it was impossible to step back, understand what was going on, and enjoy the myriad nongeographical ways I was losing myself. Instead, I was caught up with the concrete, step-by-step, practical process of getting lost. Do I turn right or left here? Have I seen this store, this intersection before? How can I shield my eyes from those maps on display at every bus stop?

Paris in particular presented a challenge, as I'd been there at least five times before, and had walked—and walked and walked—across it on each visit, from the hills of Montmartre to the Marais to the corner of the 15th Arrondissement where Jean had lived during her year abroad. I'd shopped at flea markets on the far edges of the city, and picnicked on pizza by the Canal St. Martin. I knew Paris, not perfectly but well, and I thought getting lost there would require an extra effort. So, before I arrived, I immersed myself in research: I read about the flâneur, the aimless urban wanderer who became an icon of nineteenth-century poets like Baudelaire, and about *le dérive*, literally "the drift," a theory of "psychogeography" developed by the situationist Guy Debord in the 1950s that described how we move through urban spaces without hesitation. Or something. Frankly, I couldn't see much difference between *flânerie* and *le dérive*, but I did appreciate how very French it was to impose a highbrow intellectual framework upon something normal people already do all the time.

In fact, I probably got too "French" or Debordian in my own thinking, because immediately upon landing in Paris one rainy

September day I was consumed with imposing a theoretical framework on every single footstep. Any time I saw a landmark I recognized—the Carnavalet Museum, say, or the bar Prune—I'd turn around and walk the other way. Except that meant retracing my steps along the path I'd just come from, which also felt verboten. So . . . should I turn right or left? Push on through past the familiar into the unknown? And to what purpose? What was the point of this, except as an intellectual exercise? What would Baudelaire do?

The walking was wearing me out, too. The first night, exhausted, I'd crashed in a small, nondescript hotel near Place de la République (though I was no longer officially Frugal, the *Times* hadn't bumped up my budgets), and as I set off the next morning, a heavy pack on my shoulders, I knew I wouldn't be able to go another day like this. Up in Montmartre, I happened upon a short-term apartment rental agency, and arranged to stay in a renovated seventh-floor garret for the rest of the week. The apartment—the Eagle's Nest, they called it—was tiny, clean, and spectacular, with a jaw-dropping view of the city from Montreuil to the Bois de Boulogne. Every evening I'd sit at that window, drinking Sancerre and eating warm, prize-winning baguettes and imagining what might be going on beneath that sea of mansard rooftops.

And that was the problem: my imagination. I had set off for Paris with a too-fixed idea of what I might find if I got lost—eccentric museums hidden in fourth-story apartments, lively cafés in little-touristed quartiers, Parisians who would, unlike every other Parisian in Paris, greet the arrival of a moderately Francophone American with surprise and glee. (Or whatever passes for glee among Parisians.) But I didn't really know if such things existed, and I'd denied myself Internet access to find out. Instead, I relied on advertisements in the Métro, and I fixated on strategy: How could I get to the areas I hadn't yet seen? This was a vexing question—I was staying in Montmartre, from which walking to far-flung parts of Paris would not only take hours but also drag me through those familiar areas again and again.

There was the Métro, of course, but if I rode it blindly, I still might resurface somewhere I knew. Unless . . .

Unless I looked at the subway map.

So I looked at the subway map.

In full contravention of my own "Getting Lost" rules, I picked out corners of Paris, plotted my Métro connections, and emerged in Passy, at Tolbiac, at Bel-Air, at Pré-Saint-Gervais, fully prepared to discover what no other travel writer had yet discovered. Which was that my longed-for eccentric museums did not really exist. Instead, I walked past beautiful buildings and saw on their brass nameplates that all those mysterious third-floor suites and garden studios were the offices of gynecologists and physiotherapists. I sat in those side-street cafés and ate duck confit and braised lamb shanks that were, as far as I could tell, awfully similar to the duck and lamb I'd eaten at cafés in other neighborhoods. Innumerable little roads leading up to Père Lachaise, through forgotten swathes of the Marais, or toward the Bourse were lined not with underground boutiques but with wholesalers of crappy Chinese-made clothing.

It wasn't that every neighborhood in Paris was the same. Not at all. Passy was crammed with teenagers and bourgeois families browsing international chain stores, while couples in their twenties lounged in the sunny, quiet public parks of the 15th. The primly designed region around the Bibliothèque François Mitterrand had pockets of color—an artists' collective housed in an old cold-storage warehouse, a shop devoted to Japanese manga, anime, and video games—and La Butte aux Cailles, in the 13th, was precisely what I'd been looking for: the kind of tight-knit, old-school village no one believes still exists in Paris. (It's not like it's unknown, but somehow I'd never heard of it.) And yet, when I reported back this discovery to my Parisian friends, they dismissed it. La Butte aux Cailles, they said, was too far from anything to bother visiting—never mind that it's about five hundred feet from three different Métro stops.

What I began to understand was that the parts of Paris I already knew—the Marais, the Bastille, the cheap, creative restaurants of the 10th and 11th, Montmartre, and so on—were the parts of Paris that were, to me at least, the parts worth knowing. And instead of recognizing that, instead of trying to enjoy them purely, as if this were my first time in Paris, I was pointlessly pursuing an impossible goal, and filling myself with an angst that masked a weird truth: I was having a great time. Down the rue Catherine in St. Germain, I'd found a postage-stamp cinema showing Humphrey Bogart movies, and (thanks to a subway ad!) I'd discovered an exhibition of body-part-themed art at the Espace Fondation EDF, and I'd been plowing through a new Haruki Murakami novel at cafés across the city. And then there were the baguettes and cold wine at sunset . . .

But there on the ground, it was hard to see that. Instead, all I could see was failure—a lazy, cheating hipster doing what he always did in Paris.

It shouldn't be this way, I kept thinking. And on other "Getting Lost" trips, it wasn't. In Las Vegas earlier that year, the adventure had unfolded so smoothly. I'd landed at the airport, picked up my rental car, and proceeded to find, by accident, with almost no conscious effort, exactly what I'd hoped to find: an old-school Mexican restaurant frequented by eye-patch-wearing locals; a revitalizing downtown with lively bars and coffee shops; the Vietnamese, Chinese, Korean, Taiwanese, and Hawaiian restaurants of Spring Mountain Road; and crazy-friendly people, like the brilliantly named Krissee Danger, who directed me to odd institutions like the Pinball Hall of Fame. One afternoon, I randomly bumped into James Oseland, the editor of *Saveur* magazine, in the lobby of the Comopolitan Hotel; we went hiking together in Red Rock Canyon the next day. And one night, Krissee and I wound up in a cocktail bar with Tony Hsieh, the founder of Zappos.com, who bought our round of drinks.

That summer, too, I'd undertaken a remarkable odyssey across the Mediterranean. Make that Odyssey, for I was retracing the voyage of Odysseus, whose epic tale of getting lost is the foundation of Western literature. Having flown into Istanbul, I made my way by bus down to the ruins of Troy, from which, emulating the great hero, I would proceed to the island of Ithaca, on the far side of the Greek mainland. Our routes, I knew, would not be identical. Odysseus had gone north from Troy, then been blown off course somewhere near Kythira, winding up in absolutely imaginary lands. (No matter what the literalists believe, those lands are mythical.) I, however, went west and south, taking ferry after ferry across the islands of the Aegean—but without knowing either the precise geography of the archipelago or the web of ferry connections among the islands. Who knew if a ferry onward would leave the next day—or the next week? Or where I could get to two or three hops down the line? Certainly not the Greeks themselves, who had only rough ideas of which islands were reachable from their own. Each step forward, then, could have led to a dead end, forcing me to backtrack, as Odysseus had through the twin horrors of Scylla and Charybdis.

Every day I boarded a new boat and landed at a new port, usually with enough free time to rent a car, drive up into the switchbacked hills, find a taverna, and sip sour wine along with a dish of braised lamb and a cucumber-tomato salad. I hiked through Cretan gorges and discussed with a Greek named Little Jim the deaths of his father (at the hands of the Nazis) and his mother (decades later, at the age of one hundred), and stayed at a whitewashed boutique hotel for a mere €40, and met a young hipster with a penny-farthing, and drank Belgian beer while watching clouds rise over a ridge on the island of Kythira, where Odysseus had lost his way.

"That one looks like a man," said a bartender.

His boss agreed: "Like the god Hermes."

My Odyssey was a fraught one, in which I alternated between a wanderer's ebullience and a writer's deadline anxiety. There was so much to discover on each overlooked island—cafés next to earthquake-ravaged churches, Greeks who'd returned from overseas to restore their grandparents' houses, tantalizing hints of the historical Homer, the looming political and economic chaos in Athens. Each hospitable Greek who offered me friendship or a free espresso was a Calypso, bent on trapping me here in these edens of olives and ouzo. And yet I had to go, to stumble forward and trust that Tyche, the Greek goddess of luck, would be with me at the port and on the seas. Nothing would be certain until I set foot once more upon a new shore.

And despite certain last-minute delays (no bus out of Neapoli after 5 p.m.!?!) and expenses (€30 for a taxi across Kefalonia!?!), I made it at last, after ten days of unsure island-hopping, to Ithaca, Odysseus's home, a camel-humped green island wreathed in morning mist, where I did nothing but rest and stroll and, for a handful of hours, attempt to process my adventures.

I could not. I never could—not there in the moment. I needed time, and distance, and a blank computer screen to make sense of what I'd gone through. That was where the epiphanies exploded, in the act not of traveling but of writing. But no, I can say now, as I write this, they happen in both places at once—the former may uncover the latter, but the latter was always there, hidden, lost. With perspective, the revelations begin to flow. I can see now, for instance, the difference between getting lost in Vegas and Greece versus elsewhere. On those trips, I'd forgotten to care about geography. Vegas was so flat and obvious I never considered the possibility of losing myself in its grid, while my odyssey was so fast-paced I could look only forward—onward! And by setting aside the prosaic practicalities of getting lost, I opened myself up to the far more important act of getting lucky.

I was, although I didn't know it until now, really traveling like an amateur again, trusting that the world would reveal its secrets to me if only I went looking for them. Though I'd honed my navigational skills over decades, it was luck that had always guided me—luck and the courage to accept its sometimes ambiguous consequences.

Luck, for instance, was with me my first day in Chongqing. Luck sent me to the no. 601 bus headed downtown, past Prada billboards and cloverleaf highways and across the snarling Yangtze River. Luck delivered me a schoolboy who directed me down an alley to a good bowl of noodle soup, crimson with chili oil, fragrant with numbing, citrusy Sichuan peppercorns, studded with bits of pork and intestine. Luck led me past the contradictions of the explosive city: the defunct revolving restaurant atop a skyscraper, the historic neighborhood where trees grew from brick walls and brass plaques championed the deeds of Communist heroes, the central People's Square where retirees warbled old songs accompanied by guitar and two-stringed erhu. (It took me a few minutes to realize this show was no tourist trap but simply how Chongqing's elders amused themselves.) All I had done was walk, and ask simple questions, and walk some more, allowing myself to be overwhelmed by the physicality of a city where everything existed on a massive scale—like San Francisco with more hills, two rivers, ten times the population, and neither building codes nor centralized urban planning—and luck had done the rest.

Until, at last, luck was done with me. As the sun went down, luck deposited me at what I thought was a tidy little hotel but turned out to be seedy, run-down, filled with all-night mahjong players and their rented girlfriends. Luck lured me down to a raucous nightlife area where every bar and club was so flashily, noisily packed that I despaired of ever meeting anyone interesting, or even audible. There were fancy hotels here, and I asked their English-speaking concierges where I might find quieter, more convivial watering holes. They looked at me quizzically and directed me back to the scrum, in which I would be helplessly alone.

This shouldn't have unnerved me the way it did. I'd managed days—weeks!—alone before, in Vietnam and on small American highways, and I'd always found my way, always found a bartender happy to discuss Thelonius Monk for an hour, or a friendly bistro owner ready to offer me a few nights' stay in her guest bedroom. I'd been other kinds of lost before, too, had been lost every which way but geographically, and I'd pushed on, ignored the language barrier, gotten lucky, survived.

But Chongqing's size and chaos were beyond me. How could I find anything human-scale and relatable in these concrete-and-steel depths? All my travel powers had fled me, it seemed, and I despaired of making any connection. By the next morning, I was ready to give up. I caught a bus back to the train station, where I'd stashed my bags, and on the way I considered fleeing not just the city but the country. Could Cathay rebook me to Hong Kong or Japan? Danielle would understand. She trusted me. This trip was an adjunct to an assignment for another magazine; it would barely cost the *Times* a thing; it would be okay. I'd written hundreds of stories already. I could live with one failure, right?

No, I couldn't. This would gnaw at me forever.

The bus rolled on. Another twenty-four hours and I'd be far away, visiting friends in Shanghai or Osaka and trying to forget this unfortunate interlude. I sweated and ground my teeth and wished I were back in Brooklyn, and I cursed these idiotic "Getting Lost" rules. Who came up with them, anyhow?

I had, I suddenly understood, and if they were my rules, and arbitrary ones at that, I could change them any time I liked. I took out my iPhone—equipped with a local 3G SIM card—and Googled "Chongqing hostel." And there it was, Tina's Hostel, a funky little warren of cheap rooms not far from where I'd been staying, in the 18 Steps, an old, hilly neighborhood almost all of whose buildings had been painted with the character "chai," meaning they were slated for demolition. Inside were a gaggle of young Chinese employees and travelers (it was hard to tell the difference), most of whom spoke decent English, all of whom were curious to explore Chongqing— from its funky underground bars to its far-flung art galleries—and happy to invite me out for a dinner of spicy Sichuan hotpot.

My room was small, my rules were broken, and I knew exactly where I was, but I felt free at last to make new friends, to ride buses to nowhere, to nibble rare chili peppers in hilltop gardens. And although I never admitted it to myself until just now, I'd discovered what happened when I finally got well and truly lost: I freaked out—and then moved on.

∾

Chapter 7

## Happy Families

### How I Faced the Ultimate Horror—
### Traveling with My Family—
### and Survived to Tell the Tale

"I scared!" screamed Sasha Raven Gross, age two years and four
months, aboard Cathay Pacific flight 472, from Hong Kong to
Taipei. "I scared! I scared! I scared! No no no no no no no!" As
the Airbus A330 taxied toward its takeoff position, she writhed in
her seat, clawing at her belt and reaching for my wife, Jean. "I scared!
I scared! I scared! I scared! I scared! I scared! I scared!"

There was nothing we could do, no matter how much we wanted
to free her from her seat or how many irate neighbors stared at us
with what the Chinese call "stinky face." Sasha was old enough now
that she couldn't sit on our laps, the flight attendants had said, but
mere size and age, we knew, were no substitute for emotional ma-
turity. Twice, the flight attendants had come by to see if they could
help, but there was nothing to be done. Sasha was scared—terrified
by the sound and action, unable to process what was going on around
her—and no matter how tightly we held her hands, no matter how
softly we cooed that everything was going to be okay, she was going
to stay scared. Worse, she knew she was scared, and had the self-
consciousness to verbalize it. This was what terror felt like: "I scared!"

This had happened on the last flight, too, the fourteen-hour nonstop from New York, but in that case the departure had taken Sasha

187

by surprise. She'd shrieked in fear then, but soon the plane was in the air, and stable, and she'd calmed down. Now, however, she knew what was going to happen, and the horror had built up early.

As the jet reached the head of the runway, a flight attendant came over one last time—carrying a parent-child belt extension. For everyone's sake, she said, we could break the rules and belt her to our laps. Just do it quickly.

We did it quickly. Sasha calmed down, but only a little. As the jet's engines roared to life, they blotted out her wailing, and I relaxed a scant degree. In less than two hours, we'd land in Taiwan, where Jean had lived until the age of eighteen, and for the next ten days we'd have her family—her parents, her brother and his wife and their daughter, her many aunts, uncles, and cousins—to help watch and entertain our Sasha. It would all be okay.

It had been okay before, too. Almost from the moment Sasha was born, in December 2008, it was determined she would be a traveler like her parents. Within a month, we'd driven her out to Provincetown, Massachusetts, for a snowy Frugal Traveler weekend on Cape Cod. (While pulling her infant carrier out of the car, I slipped on the ice, banged my knee, and dropped her. She was fine.) And just two weeks later, Jean, Sasha, and I flew off to Italy for another lengthy Frugal Traveler excursion: a week in the chill damp of Venice, and another in foggy Milan.

That Italian expedition, undertaken with not a little trepidation, was eye-opening. I mean, we hadn't chosen Italy at random—everyone we'd consulted had talked about how child-and-baby friendly Italians were—but we simply didn't expect the level of hospitality and attention we received everywhere. "*Cara!*" exclaimed Italians— female and male, old and young. "*Che meraviglia!*" Sasha became known as *la principessa,* or *la piccolina,* or even sometimes just *Sascia,* with a dramatic Italian intonation. She slept quietly in our arms at trattorias, and slept quietly, nestled in her Ergo baby carrier, at the Palazzo Grassi and the Peggy Guggenheim Collection.

Only once she did erupt into tears in a public space—inside the Palazzo Ducale, whence the doges of La Serenissima managed their sea-spanning empire—but that was because we'd accidentally broken the unspoken covenant between traveling infant and traveling parents: Keep me warm, Sasha was (preverbally) saying, keep me clean, and keep me well-fed, and I will sit, sleep, and look cute as long as you want. I don't need toys, I don't need entertainment, I don't need activities beyond the everyday dandling. But deny me any of my preferred comforts, and I will make you suffer.

In the Ducale case, we'd neglected to warm her milk bottle sufficiently—by nestling it between her body and ours in the baby carrier as we walked—and her subsequent wails echoed throughout the cold stone corridors. Quickly, though, museum employees came to our rescue, and guided us to an unused room where Jean could breastfeed.

Apart from that one failure, we kept the covenant throughout the trip, ate, drank, and shopped well while managing not to spend too much money, and ultimately convinced ourselves that, yes, we could do this. Two weeks after we returned, we were off again, to Taipei for a family visit, and then to Minneapolis on a business trip. Frankfurt for a wedding. San Francisco—just me and Sasha, not Jean—for another Frugal challenge. Cape Cod again. Taipei again. Not once did we hesitate to book a flight. We'd mastered Italy with a six-week-old, after all. This was almost becoming easy.

I can't say for certain that this is what Jean and I had hoped for when we decided to have a child, because that decision itself is shrouded in the fog of memory. What I do know is that, once upon a time, Jean and I were happy to be childless—so happy that we planned to remain that way. We were living in a sixth-floor Lower East Side tenement, making decent if not incredible money, eating out when we wanted, staying up late and sleeping late, flying to Mexico for vacation if we felt like it. While Jean was not quite as adventurous as me, she proved herself relaxed and adaptable. On one of those Mexican vacations, a road trip from Mexico City to Oaxaca and up the Pacific Coast, everything went wrong: The airline neglected to bring our luggage, so when we arrived and Jean got her period—surprise!—she had no pads, and only thong underwear, and it was Saturday night and everything was closed, and then a few days later, she lost her Taiwanese passport in Oaxaca City, and we spent a frantic few hours trying to find a phone number for Taiwan's semi-official representative office back in Mexico City, and then we survived a harrowing drive through the cold, piney mountains, where overturned trucks lay placidly in the highway and groups of men surrounded our car and forced us to stop for *"cinco minutos!"* until, from around the bend, we heard music, and a stream of children in costumes—skeletons, vampires, witches, ghouls—flooded toward and around us, accompanied by their mothers and sisters and aunts, and then they all vanished into the rearview distance, and we drove out of the hills and I got sick (*Giardia, you old so-and-so! Where ya been?*), and we kept driving and driving—a thousand miles in all— and throughout Jean remained cheerful, overjoyed just to be on the road together, even if when we got to each new hotel I'd retreat sickly to bed with a bottle of Gatorade while she went swimming in the pool and ate roadside tacos. It might not always go smoothly, but this was our life together, and it was fabulous.

Whenever anyone asked me about the future, I'd say that Jean and I planned to become the cosmopolitan aunt and uncle to our siblings' and friends' children, returning from far-off lands with exotic gifts (helicopters wrought from Coke cans, obscure Japanese electronic doodads) that would make those kids (not to mention their parents) deeply envious of our liberty. And that was, for a while, in a low-budget kind of way, how we lived.

Until I turned twenty-nine. Then, one day, out of nowhere, I wanted children. I didn't build up to it, didn't go through a series of events that taught me I was fated to be a father. No, it was like a genetic switch had been flipped, and every cell of my body wanted to procreate. If men have a biological clock, too, then this was my alarm. At best, I could claim that my omnipresent fear of death had finally collided with my fear of failure as a writer—that since I'd not yet produced any lasting words, my only hope for quasi-immortality was to preserve my DNA in a new generation of Grosses. (People have had kids for worse reasons.) Whatever its origins, and however it may have been complicated by the next few surprising years of professional travel and writing, the switch was irrevocable. Jean (who went along with the idea for her own mysterious reasons) and I would eventually have children. It was decided.

Had I known the kind of turn my life was going to take in the next couple of years, I might have reconsidered. It is commonly accepted that traveling with your children is one of the worst experiences imaginable, for parents, kids, and onlookers alike. Which doesn't quite explain why, if it's all so awful, families continue to travel together, on vacations both touristy and adventurous. I mean, obviously, in some ways, families *have to* travel together. The machinery of modern Western life—where vacations, as brief as they are, remain as inescapable a part of the calendar as work and school— doesn't shut down when people have children, or shut them out until the kids are mature enough to handle an intercontinental flight without tears. The war between traveling families and traveling non-parents, waged with unrelenting bitterness in the comments sections of travel-themed Web sites, is a will-sapping stalemate, in which neither side wants to recognize reality: that kids can be awful travelers, that kids can be great travelers, that adults are just the same, and that none of this is going to change anytime soon.

My own memories of family vacations are, as such memories tend to be, rather pleasant. We visited my grandparents in Connecticut; we drove around Scotland, France, and Italy; we took the occasional flight to California or Paris, Paul Simon's *Graceland* played in the station wagon all the way down to Florida; there were years abroad in England and Denmark. Naturally, not every trip was hitch-free—my mother was hospitalized with a bladder infection near Pisa, my father got pulled over and breathalyzed one night near Yosemite (judgment: myopia, not inebriation), I fought with my younger siblings, Steve and Nell, over the tiniest matters (he's *breathing*). But no conflict was so nasty, no failure so catastrophic, that the Gross family considered swearing off future trips. This was what we did—who we were: travelers.

And I hated them for it. Not because I didn't like the travel, or resented their company, but because I loved both too much. And as an adolescent, and then a young man, I wanted desperately to rebel, to craft an identity separate from that of my family, and yet at every turn I found myself loving and indulging in the activities my parents had established as definitively Gross. Worse, I couldn't compete on their level: My mother had done a grand tour of Europe in the sixties, my father had taught abroad in Paris; they had money and experience it would take me years to acquire, and yet to acquire those things, I knew, I'd have to rely on their finances and expertise for years to come. I never consciously wished to be free of them entirely, like one of the Grimm brothers' orphans, but one night I had a dream that has stuck with me through the years. In the dream, I'm driving away from my family's house, knowing two things: (1) everyone is at home, and (2) within moments, a bomb will blow up there, killing everyone. The most disturbing part? The tone of the dream was cheerful and calm—this was no nightmare. Afterward, I would be free, independent at last.

And independence had always seemed like my birthright. I'd been born in Concord, Massachusetts, and was therefore a child of the American Revolution; independence was in my blood. And I'd been born in Concord only because my historian father had made the town, from the Minutemen to the Transcendentalists, his life's work. I grew up with "self-reliance" and a solitary cabin in the woods near Walden Pond—I was supposed to value independence, and the American embrace of independence, and yet that value was itself a hand-me-down, as inescapable a part of growing up Gross as curried lamb meatballs for dinner and owning a passport.

Instead of murdering my family, I declared my independence by keeping secrets and going to extremes. I'd borrow the car and drive two hours north with my friends to Washington, D.C., never revealing the destination to my parents. I shunned history and studied math and shaved my head. And then I moved to Vietnam, relishing the shock the news would have on baby boomers—and yet feeling mild disappointment when, after telling my parents about the chaotic traffic and ubiquitous prostitutes, they decided against coming to visit, and asked me, please, just don't go to Cambodia, it's too dangerous. (Next stop: Phnom Penh!)

The funny thing is that my ploy worked. After surviving Vietnam, establishing myself in New York, and embarking on regular overseas trips as an adult, I became within the family the travel expert—the one who knew the best way to buy plane tickets and find neat new restaurants, who was pretty much going to be okay anywhere, without anyone's help. And when I began traveling professionally, I took the opportunity to incorporate my family members into my adventures: my mother joined me for a Frugal weekend in Santa Fe, and my Frugal road trip ended in Seattle, where Nell had settled after college. In both cases, we all got along fine. Mom even drank whiskey with me in some punk-rock basement dive bar, and she turned down my invitation to the coed naked spa out in the New Mexico hills. Perfect. Of course, we were never together all that long—no time for sparks to fly or disagreements to fester. And each little success helped me feel like I was overcoming my travel-bred resentment of my family.

Except when it came to Steve. Four years younger than me, Steve had annoyed me our entire lives—unintentionally, of course. The annoyance was all in my mind, typical first-child resentment, and I took it out on him cruelly, wrestling with him when we were young, and later, when we could really hurt each other, through psychological means. I ordered him to fetch Lego pieces for me to build rocket ships with, I sneezed on him, I ridiculed him. Once, while he and I were out with some of my friends at a Burger King, I poured an entire orange soda over his head, supposedly to impress my pals.

The idiotic thing was that, even as I did everything I could to demonstrate he was beneath me, I loved and admired Steve. He was a stellar piano player, and would soon find work as a teenage computer programmer, and he had a whole group of smart, creative, well-adjusted, school-minded pals who were utterly unlike the misfits with whom I'd surrounded myself. At times, I was jealous of Steve's circle, and proud of his accomplishments, too. He was so clearly intelligent, inventive, and kind, and I was often happy to have his innocent energy and unquestioning companionship, whether we were exploring the creek behind our house or out skateboarding the next town over.

And despite my misdeeds, we were still in the same house, forced to interact, and still brothers, which somehow still meant something to both of us. Which must be why, the summer before my senior year of high school, I let Steve in on a huge secret: I had a girlfriend— my first. Her name was Amy, she loved the Pixies, and, incredibly, she found me attractive. Please, I asked thirteen-year-old Steve, keep it to yourself. I don't know where this is going. Don't tell anyone, least of all our parents.

Steve swore he'd say nothing, and my dates and first kisses were our secret for two weeks. Until, one night at the dinner table, I decided to reveal everything to the family. I told them about Amy. My father had a smile on his face.

"We knew," he said.

Steve, it turned out, had told them almost immediately. He was smiling too.

As betrayals go, this was a minor one, but it stuck in my mind. Had Steve really been so oblivious? Was this his revenge? What was I supposed to do now?

Luckily for Steve (and for me), I did nothing. Within a month, Amy and I had split up. And within a year, I'd left for college, Vietnam, life on my own. Steve, too, would leave for school, a semester abroad in Strasbourg, jobs in New Jersey, Cleveland, Minneapolis. For years, we would see each other only at Thanksgiving or briefly during summers. We communicated little, despite the fact that we each spent our days in front of computer screens, and were absolutely fluent in the use of e-mail, IM, Skype, and Facebook. Occasionally, he'd call me up late in the afternoon and ask my cooking advice: What should he do with twenty pounds of ground beef? Did I know how to make duck confit? What about all this eggplant?

These calls were gratifying. At last, I could give older-brotherly advice on a topic we both held dear! But at the same time, I was frustrated. Shouldn't he know how to braise a rabbit by now? Had he really never grilled a steak, or eaten Sichuan peppercorns? I had figured these things out myself over years of trial and error. (Okay, I've never braised a rabbit, but I know how!) Why shouldn't he do the same?

To me, this illustrated a fundamental difference between us. I was independent, and willing to face failure as a possible outcome of my quest for knowledge and experience. Steve, as brilliant as he was, needed to have the world explained to him. He would not pick up on the unspoken expectations of life unless someone pointed them out to him. (A projection of my own anxieties? Perhaps.) Time and again, I saw my thesis proved: One January, for instance, my mother and I embarked on a speedy cross-country road trip—we were delivering Jean's Volkswagen Jetta to Nell in Seattle—and after two or three days of driving, we approached Minneapolis. I called Steve to let him know we'd arrive soon, and to make dinner plans, and he asked, "So, where are you guys staying?"

Mom flipped out. She had assumed Steve and his wife, Tara, would put us up in their new, fairly spacious two-bedroom apartment. I had, too. We were family, right?

This, however, took Steve by surprise, not because he had some fundamental objection to us staying with him (although he was worried there wouldn't be space) but because the assumption—that family stays with family—was alien to him. Maybe it had just never happened before (our family small, such random visits uncommon), but his reaction made it seem as if we came from entirely different planets.

Our mother, in a tone of unconvincingly restrained fury, told him that if we had to stay in a hotel, we should forget about having dinner together. Steve, to his credit, understood how serious this was and invited us over, and a fairly pleasant night was had in the end. But it did nothing to bring me and Steve any closer.

So it went until the fall of 2010. One evening that October, I was having drinks in Brooklyn with two old friends, Lauren and Nathan, when Nathan told us about his wife's father and his siblings—how they were all old, and had failed to maintain ties with each other, and were now facing death and regretting the distance they'd allowed to grow between them. It sounded awful, and it sounded familiar. I searched my memory for moments of happiness and cohesion, times when Steve and I had accomplished things together without rancor or manipulation, and my memory turned up blank. We had nothing whatsoever. All I could remember were the miseries I'd heaped upon him, and I felt like a truly shitty brother. I'd had a few beers by this point, but my epiphany was sobering: I needed to do something about me and Steve, this brother who, despite our decades of bickering, I loved, and wanted to share my dwindling supply of important secrets with. And what I needed to do was equally obvious—we would have to take a trip together.

"Do you want to drink coffee?" Dr. Kan-nan Liu asked me one evening in 2002. We were sitting on the couch in his living room, and the TV was on, showing the daily news. Dr. Liu's daughter, Jean, who would in a few years become my wife, was in the kitchen with her mother and the family's longtime cook, A-Mui. Jean and I had landed in Taipei only a couple of hours ago, on this, our first-ever visit to her family as a couple, and I was wiped out. I could really have used a cup of coffee. Instead, I kept silent.

This was, I think, because Jean's father had been speaking Mandarin. He'd spoken so softly (and I'd been so jetlagged) that by the time I realized he'd been addressing me, and that I did, to my surprise, understand those simple words, it was too late to respond. A few quiet minutes later, Jean came in and we went upstairs to bed, in separate rooms.

As first encounters with future in-laws go, this was not auspicious—exactly what I'd feared. At the time, Jean and I had been dating a few years and were fairly serious. We'd moved in together, to an overpriced studio on the Lower East Side, but we did it secretly, so as not to offend her traditionalist parents. Some guys, I knew, would be hurt by this need for secrecy, but not me. I understood that she needed to maintain one image with her family, and another with me. This was a basic component of Asian life: the clear distinction between one's public and private faces. In public, one strives to appear upright and honorable, but behind closed doors, one can be, well, anything one wants. The disjunction between these two identities may be the kind of thing that provokes outrage in the West, but in much of Asia, it seems more accepted. Not to say Asians (and even using the term *Asians* is a sketchy generalization) aren't outraged when some moralizing politician turns out to be a criminal; there's simply less *surprise*.

The distinctions between public and private, and the sometimes obvious contradictions between them, also allow people to feign belief in the former in order to preserve some semblance of interpersonal harmony. That is, I don't know whether or not Jean's parents knew we were living together, but because she acted as if we didn't, that became the accepted truth, even if, occasionally, when they'd call her late at night, I'd answer the phone. *Oh, he's just visiting,* she'd say. And because no one wanted a fight, that was what they chose to believe.

Jean, however, had her limits. During her year abroad in Paris, she had actually dumped me. Her mother was coming to visit for Christmas, she'd told me by phone, and she didn't want to have to lie to her about us. And so we broke up until she returned to New York the next fall.

Though she'd hate for me to remark on this, her desire to be honest with her mother was probably a sign of her Americanization. Jean had grown up in Taipei, had gone to school and learned to read and write Chinese there, but at eighteen she'd come to the United States, first to study biology at Johns Hopkins, then earning a second B.A. in fashion design at Parsons. By the time we went together to visit her family, she'd been living here a decade and had changed in subtle ways—one of which was that she was willing to date a white guy.

This should not have surprised her family. After all, they were the ones who'd sent her overseas. What did they expect? Nor were they outwardly traditional or backward bumpkins. Both her parents were doctors—her mother a general practitioner, her father a neurosurgeon—and the extended family was full of other doctors, dentists, bankers, and engineers. They lived in the center of Taipei, in an old but neon-lit neighborhood where teenagers shopped for cheap fashions and snacked on grilled fish balls and skewers of stinky tofu. Their home, four stories carved from a former hospital, was comfortably modern, if not showy. Jean's parents spoke some English— better than my Chinese, but not fluent—and they vacationed all over the globe, from Japan and Russia to Italy and South America. That they could bring their daughter up in such a worldly environment, and send her abroad for years, and still expect her to date and marry a guy from back home seemed unrealistic.

On that first visit, at least, they showed none of what was likely a growing frustration with my presence. Along with several aunts, uncles, cousins, and Jean's grandmother, we went as a family to a sparklingly new Shanghainese restaurant, where, over racks of bamboo steamers full of the best soup dumplings I'd ever eaten, they quizzed me on my own family background. That my father was a history professor and my mother an editor seemed acceptable. My great-grandparents' origins provoked brief discussion—how do you say Lithuania in Mandarin? in Taiwanese?—but it was interesting for them to learn I was Jewish. In Asia (as elsewhere), Jews have a reputation for being clever and successful.

From across the table, Jean's grandmother made an observation: "Good thing your eyes aren't too blue," she said, "otherwise it would be scary!"

Her eyesight, it should be noted, had faded with age. My eyes are large and frighteningly blue.

By the time we flew home, a week later, I could tell the trip had not gone well. There had been no catastrophes. I wasn't the guy in *The Joy Luck Club* who pours soy sauce over the delicate crab. Instead, I was an enthusiastic eater (especially when it came to the meals prepared by A-Mui, the live-in chef), and I knew my way around a pair of chopsticks. To Taiwanese, who are easily as obsessed with food as any Brooklyn blogger, this was important. Also, I was polite and deferential—I had to be, since I didn't speak the language—and I tried never to appear loud, in the way, or stereotypically American.

Once we were back in New York, however, the criticisms began to trickle through the grapevine. My Chinese wasn't very good— true (but I could learn). I was a writer, unable to support their daughter—true (but she didn't want such support). I was an American, and therefore a wasteful spendthrift; I was Jewish, and therefore wealthy and, at the wrong times, stingy. Although one of Jean's aunts was lobbying for me, I was not right for Jean. No one mentioned the first night's coffee incident, but I bet Jean's dad—with his gentle demeanor and easy smile—was thinking about it.

But Jean and I lived on the other side of the planet, so life went on much as it had before. I did my copyediting jobs, and Jean worked her way up in the fashion world. Who cared what her parents thought?

One night in the middle of 2003, after a few years of relative peace, things came to a head out of the blue. Jean's mother called up. Voices were raised, tears were shed. I tried not to listen too closely, even though they were arguing in a language I didn't understand, and when Jean finally put down the phone, she explained the situation.

Her parents, she said, thought we should break up. They wanted her to date, and eventually to marry, a Taiwanese man. (And, incidentally, not any other Asian, nor any Taiwanese whose forbears had immigrated from the Chinese mainland after 1945.) Jean, however, had held firm—I was hers. And so she and her mother had arrived at a compromise. For two years, Jean agreed not to get married—two years being the length of time, as specified by the family fortune-teller, during which it would be inauspicious for Jean to marry at all. And during those two years, Jean would agree to go on dates with Taiwanese men her family found for her in the New York area. If, at the end of two years, she hadn't found someone she liked better than me, then the family would try to accept me.*

So, I asked, all we had to do was let her date other guys for two years, and then we'd get their blessing?

That, she said, was how it was.

This . . . was . . . amazing! Instantly I realized the comic potential, and I formulated a plan of my own. Whenever she had a date, I would have to make one, too—for the same place and time, with some Jewish girl I'd find on JDate.com. That way, Jean and I could

---

*Jean now disputes this account, but the craziness of the situation fixed it in my brain. She's wrong, I'm right.

keep an eye on each other, and sneak away whenever possible to make out by the payphones. What would we do if we were caught by our dates? Could we try to hook them up instead? What if we, you know, kind of liked them? The weirdness of this relationship wouldn't just be a trial—it would be prime material for a brilliant magazine article. No, a screenplay!

"How soon can they set you up?" I wanted to ask. But I didn't. Jean had only just stopped crying. We'd get to comedy soon enough. For the night, tragedy reigned.

"You are brothers!" cried the money changer from behind the bulletproof Plexiglas window in Montreal's Chinatown. "And I would bet anything that he is the older one!"

The man, of South Asian extraction, was pointing directly at Steve, who looked at me and smiled. We'd been playing this game for several days in the frozen February streets of Montreal (average temperature: 25 degrees Fahrenheit), and it always came out the same. Steve, one inch taller than me, his hair longer but his hairline more receded, his clothing more restrained, his face clean-shaven, was the older one. I, trim-bearded and thinner (not that you could tell under my insulated outerwear), was the younger.

In the context of Montreal, this reversal was a regular amusement, but also a relief. Here, at last, our traditional roles might not define us, and we could just be ourselves, two guys in their mid-thirties sharing a love of Francophone culture and hearty, fatty, inventively delicious Québécois food. For a little over a week, staying at a rented sixteenth-floor apartment in the heart of Le Plateau, the city's hippest neighborhood, Steve and I figured we'd do little but wander the streets, eat and drink to excess, pose for the photographer from *Afar* magazine (for which I was writing about the trip), and do something vaguely highbrow, just so this wouldn't be another tale of nonstop gastro-indulgence.

There was one thing, however, I did not tell Steve about our adventure: that its true purpose was to save our relationship. This felt like too much to burden us both with—what if it didn't work out? What's more, to reveal my ulterior motive would have required me to admit, up front, why I thought the relationship was in peril, and I was definitely not ready for a confrontation so explicit. Plus, I didn't really have any idea whether Steve himself thought there was a problem. For all I knew, he thought things were great, functioning just as a brotherly relationship was supposed to function. We were each other's only brother, so why would he think it should be any better— or worse?

And so, instead of discussing these sensitive topics, we ate. Foie gras poutine and "duck in a can" at the famed Au Pied de Cochon, where we watched another table receive a whole roasted pig's head garnished with an entire lobster. Smoked-meat sandwiches at the Jewish diner Schwartz's, where the French menu lies under the heading "Sandwiches" and the English menu under "Les Sandwiches." Surprisingly good Vietnamese food in Chinatown, and incredible Portuguese roast chicken from Rôtisserie Romados, and more poutine, spiked with merguez and jalapeños, at La Banquise, a twenty-four-hour joint that was almost across the street from our apartment. In the sunny windows of Club Social, we drank well-pulled espressos, and we downed early-evening beers at a half-dozen neighborhood bars, our winter gear piled high on banquettes.

Eating worked, mostly. Put a platter of pig or duck parts in front of me and Steve, stick wineglasses in our hands, and we will grin, gobble, and moan with delight. We love this—we understand it. And we can look into each other's eyes and know that the other guy, my brother, gets it, too.

Except when we don't. That is, I couldn't help noticing that our tastes did not entirely overlap. At Schwartz's, Steve had plucked the fat from his smoked meat and laid it on his plate, never to be consumed, just as he'd done with everything from bacon to well-marbled steaks since we were children. At a dark lounge called Après le Jour, we happily ordered beers—a bitter hoppy ale for me, a Belgian-style white for him—and we were each disgusted with the other's choice. These were minor differences, I knew, and I kept quiet about them, but they annoyed me all the same. And that annoyed me even more—that I was annoyed in the first place. Why couldn't I just accept Steve for what he was? How is it that I could put up with recurrent giardiasis, survive long, lonely nights in strange lands, and subject myself to the indignities of an artificially tight budget, but I couldn't do this?

It's different, though, when you're traveling with someone. Out of your element, out in the wider world, where nobody knows you and you can do just about anything you want, you actually live in a bubble that draws you closer than you've ever been—than you've ever wanted. You want to be in sync, to enjoy (or detest) the same things the same way, because if you're not, then what are you missing that the other one gets? Or vice versa? And when that unsynched someone is family—a person you're supposed to know better than anyone else, a person you will continue to know and see and interact with long after this disastrous trip, a person whose identity has been bound up with your own since the earliest days of your lives—the failure to get along and enjoy (or hate) the journey as equal partners can be crushing. Now that I'd brought Steve into the universe of the globe-trotting writer, I desperately wanted him to see things as I did, to understand that it's the brisket fat that makes the smoked meat so incredible.

And when he didn't, all I could see was Steve being Steve—off in his own bubble, cooing over every halfway adorable dog on the street and squealing "Meester Gross!" at random moments (a tic, I'm told, he learned from our grandfather). In our apartment, Steve would belch operatically, and everywhere we went, from the Bikram yoga studio to the comic-book shop, he'd quiz people on points of French vocabulary. How, he asked the comic-shop clerk, do you say "poke"? Sadly, the clerk said, there was no such word.

"What do little kids do to annoy each other, then?" Steve asked, not entirely joking.

Listen and observe, I wanted to tell him (but didn't), that's how you learn. It's what we'd done one night at the theater. The play was *Histoires d'Hommes*, and it was highbrow indeed: Three actresses embodied a dozen different characters, all monologuing about the crazy men who'd made them crazy in turn.

Or something like that. The play wasn't just in French but in slangy, heavily accented, imitation-drunk French, with no overt narrative to link one scene to another. Only afterward—over deer carpaccio and maple-lacquered duck at the chicly rustic La Salle à Manger—did Steve and I have a chance to figure out what we'd understood. *Amour de shit?* Got it. *Se tromper,* we deduced, did not mean "to err," as it normally does, but "to cheat." Altogether, I estimated, we understood 65 percent of the play, a shared success—perhaps our first in decades—and we didn't have to ask anyone but each other for help.

The thing is, maybe Steve had the right approach. After all, his French was better than mine, so good that the owner of one antiques shop complimented him on his accent, and asked if he had any French background. (He'd lived in Strasbourg one summer, Steve stammered, switching self-consciously to English.) And during a dinner party we threw for a small group of friends and friends of friends, everyone seemed to find his questions amusing: How do you say "jailbait"? "Hooters"? "Bring it on"? "Fuck it!"?

As we went through six bottles of wine, a deli's worth of cheeses and cured meats from the Marché Jean-Talon, a couple of *frangos* from Rotisserie Romados, and some potatoes that Steve had roasted perfectly, I watched how our guests—one Francophone Montrealer, two Anglophones, and two expatriate Parisians—were interacting with Steve. He was on fire, issuing informed opinions on everything from the design of bike lanes to gas plasmification, a high-tech waste-disposal process. And they were hanging on his every word, amused at his enthusiasm and amazed by the breadth of his knowledge. As was I. I was even a bit jealous of his ability to be so happy, so un-self-consciously himself—as if, as the money-changer and countless others had suggested, he was the role-model older brother, I the younger looking up.

As he spoke, however, I also felt myself retreating from the conversation, watching and observing but speaking less and less, no longer the travel writer at home anywhere but a bit player in this drama. And as I turned inward, I wondered again: Why can't I be happy for/with him? Why does it have to be a zero-sum game?

The next morning, as we rode the elevator down to the lobby, Steve started talking about some cute puppy—a French bulldog—he'd spotted in a store the day before, and I finally blew up at him.

"You know, Steve," I said, "I really don't like dogs at all."

"Well," he said, "I'm not going to stop talking about them."

Just before the elevator stopped and its doors opened, he added, "You really have terrible relationships with living things, don't you?"


Sasha was cranky. Two-and-a-half-year-olds, you see, don't understand jetlag. They don't understand that the world is big and round, that the sun revolves around it, and that flying from one side of it to the other, in the span of twenty-odd hours in an aluminum tube, means that their sleep cycle will fall out of sync with that of everyone at their destination. We adults do what we can to game that system: We time our in-flight naps, we take melatonin supplements, we go for jogs on landing. But to a toddler, every detail of the jetlag-adjustment routine is a mystery so absolute it's not even recognized as a mystery. All Sasha knew was that she was tired, or hungry, or wide awake, and that Jean and I were not. And so Sasha was miserable and making us miserable too.

If we had anticipated the horrors of intercontinental air travel with Sasha, we might also have been prepared for what awaited us on landing in Taipei: a full-family multiday road trip to the southern tip of Taiwan. Correction: We did know that less than forty-eight hours after we arrived, nine of us would ride the high-speed train to Kaohsiung, Taiwan's second city, then climb into an enormous rented van and roam around the south for a few days. We knew all this, and there was still nothing we could have done. There was no staying home to catch up on sleep and adjust. This was a family trip, and we were family.

That Jean and I had come this far, family-wise, should, I guess, have been counted as a triumph. A few years earlier, I had been the guy Jean was supposed to give up—a non-Taiwanese non-doctor persona non grata. But Jean and I and our relationship had leapt the hurdles her family put in our way. Soon after the two-year marriage moratorium began—and one day after we moved into a new apartment together—Jean relocated for work reasons to Columbus, Ohio, which had a dearth of eligible Taiwanese men for her to date. I, meanwhile, stayed in New York, and she and I took turns visiting each other every few weeks. We were both a bit lonely, but this distance felt normal, too. My parents had occasionally spent time apart, when my father was on some teaching trip or another, and Jean and I had dated only six weeks before she'd left for France. To be in love and apart—was that really so terrible?

After a little over a year of this, I, too, decided to flee New York, and embarked on the Southeast Asia trip that would turn me into a travel writer. As I bounced between Vietnam, Cambodia, and Thailand, Jean and I wrote each other daily e-mails and even managed to rendezvous for a few days in Hong Kong, where she'd been sent on business. All the while, the clock kept ticking on the family-mandated waiting period, and Jean and I remained as emotionally close as ever.

By the time we reunited in New York, in early 2006, marriage was a foregone conclusion. I think Jean just happened to mention it to her parents over the phone one evening, and that was that. They had said they would try to accept me, and they would. Jean's brother, Louis, was himself getting married in March, and we—along with my family and a couple of my friends—would be there to celebrate it, and to announce our engagement, which in some Taiwanese families is as important as the wedding itself.

The Gross family's March expedition to Taiwan went remarkably well. Nice hotels. Several whole-family meals, during which our parents made polite, even friendly, conversation. (Steve was his usual self. "How do you say *explode* in Chinese?" he asked at one lunch. *Bao cha!*) A two-day trip to hike Taroko Gorge and eat rustic Taiwanese mountain food. Strangers offering my parents directions on the streets of Taipei. All culminating in a huge wedding, where close to four hundred people—friends, family, coworkers, parents' friends, and assorted important people—gathered in a luxury hotel's ballroom to celebrate Louis's marriage (to a sweet Taiwanese woman named Charmiko) and my and Jean's engagement. Speeches were made by the fathers (my dad was introduced by a retired judge, who recited his entire résumé), and then the four of us younger folks, plus Jean's and Charmiko's parents, went table-to-table, toasting the guests with grape juice poured from an empty French wine bottle. (With at least thirty-five tables to visit, real wine might've been a bad idea.) Finally, Louis and Charmiko cut a slice from their wedding cake—a cardboard fake, as it turned out. In Taiwan, symbolism is sometimes more important than dessert.

From there, it was a swift waltz to our own wedding, a smaller affair, on the beach in Cape Cod, six months later. But Jean's family's seeming acceptance of me had not yet alleviated my anxiety. I was still not Taiwanese, and though I'd finally found good work as a writer, I wasn't going to be making doctor-level cash anytime soon, if ever. I had mild nightmares of Jean's father, the neurosurgeon, sneaking into my bedroom at night to operate on my brain and rid me of whichever lobe made me love his daughter. There had to be, I thought, some way of making her family not only accept me, however grudgingly, but understand and embrace me as truly one of their own. But how?

A couple of days before our wedding, I stumbled on a potential solution. Our families had gathered in Truro, not far from the tip of the Cape, and Jean's relatives—her parents, brother, aunts, uncles, and assorted cousins—were staying at a pair of adjacent houses we'd rented for them. In all, they totaled fifteen people, and their first night on the Cape, they needed to be fed—a job that fell to me, and which I attacked it with relish. This, I realized, was a way to demonstrate that although I might be American, and although I'd probably never make the kind of money needed to "take care" of Jean, there were at least some situations and challenges I could handle. Dinner for fifteen? Adapting local ingredients to suit Taiwanese palates? Putting it all together in a reasonable amount of time, and in an unfamiliar, ill-equipped kitchen? That I could do.

Watched over by Jean's mother's cousin's girlfriend, I chopped and sautéed onions and garlic, grated lemon zest, seared chunks of Portuguese chouriço, cranked open cans of crushed tomatoes, and finally added to the simmering sauce several dozen well-scrubbed littleneck clams—all to be served over perfectly al dente spaghetti, alongside a simple green salad. As the family gathered to eat at two long tables, I congratulated myself: I'd found just the right dish to appeal to the Taiwanese relatives' sense of familiarity (they get red-sauce pasta) and their craving for seafood as a signifier of a special meal. And it was pretty good, too—the kind of thing I'd make at home, even if this version needed perhaps a bit more salt, maybe some clam juice. The point was, I'd gotten it done, and her parents had seen me get it done. I was not completely incompetent!

But whatever words of praise or thanks they offered were not enough for me. The wedding itself went smoothly and enjoyably—no missteps, no embarrassments, no hurt feelings—but it felt like a formality. Jean's parents had agreed to accept me months earlier, so the ceremony was really just the ratification of their decision. What

I wanted was something deeper: full acknowledgment of the effort I was making to be a part of this family.

Yes, I was insane.

At the same time, I didn't pursue it. Over the next two years, I did nothing at all, and in that time, relations between us were normal. Jean's parents even gave us a chunk of money to help buy an apartment in Brooklyn (okay, so I'm not that keen on *total* financial independence), and while they voiced some initial concerns about my name being on the mortgage as well, we told them it would be hard for a married couple to get a loan otherwise. And that was that.

Only when Jean became pregnant did I realize I had another opportunity to prove my dedication. I was, I knew, a failure in many ways. After ten years with Jean, I still spoke little Chinese, and soon I'd be bringing our daughter up in New York, far from the family and their linguistic and cultural influence. Jean would do what she could, but I wanted to participate, too. And what I could do was cook. I needed, I decided, to learn to make the dishes that Jean herself had grown up on—the soups and stir-fries that A-Mui had made for the Liu family for more than thirty years. Someone, after all, needed to carry on the family's culinary traditions, and it might as well be me.

In October 2008, two months before Jean was due, I flew to Taipei—solo. I'd been to Taiwan now more times than I could count, but this was nerve-racking. This time I'd be alone, without Jean to translate or to act as a buffer. It would be just me and her parents and our pidgin conversations—and my instructor, A-Mui, who spoke not only no English but no Mandarin either. Instead, A-Mui spoke Taiwanese, a dialect understood by more than two-thirds of the island's citizens. Today, almost everyone in Taiwan also speaks Mandarin, but A-Mui was from another era. Orphaned in the 1940s, when Taiwan went from Japanese colonial rule to briefly rejoining China to being run by the fleeing Nationalist army, A-Mui had been adopted by a farming family in central Taiwan—not a place where educating girls was foremost in anyone's mind. Taiwanese was good enough.

Instead, Jean's mother told me in a mix of English and Chinese, A-Mui learned to cook, and was engaged to marry the family's son, A-Hang. The marriage, however, was not to her liking, and after several years, sometime in the late 1970s, she fled to Taipei, where thanks to a neighbor's recommendation she connected with Jean's family. She'd been there ever since.

And now A-Mui was getting ready to retire. She was in her late sixties, shaped like a large pear, and her sense of taste was fading. A recent soup, I'd heard from the aunties, had come out comically salty. Now she was preparing to move south, where she'd bought land with her earnings. (She'd also managed to send two kids to medical school.) Hearing A-Mui's biography, I felt a weight on my shoulders. This wasn't just some experiment I was engaged in; A-Mui's legacy was in my hands.

The weight, however, evaporated when I met A-Mui each morning at 6 a.m. for our daily trip to the market, a damp concrete underworld where blowtorch-wielding men singed the hairs off pigs' feet and purple, yard-long dried squid reconstituted in plastic tubs of water. I loved it, and although A-Mui and I could barely communicate, I knew she could tell. Her scratchy voice cackled with laughter as she explained my presence to the meat and vegetable vendors she knew so well, and her eyes twinkled—yes, twinkled!—when she looked over to check on me.

By 7:30, we'd return to the Liu family home, our arms laden with plastic bags full of pork and chicken, tender bamboo shoots and leafy greens, blocks of tofu and sheaves of scallions. And then, after a quick breakfast of egg pancakes and fresh soy milk, I'd collapse back into bed—and miss out on all of A-Mui's prep work: the washing, cutting, shaping. By 11 a.m., she'd shake me awake and lead me into her kitchen, a small, hard-tiled space with two burners, one sink, and a fridge. As she assembled dish after dish—deep-fried pork chops marinated in fermented rice paste, sesame oil chicken, braised pigs' feet with peanuts—I'd take notes, amazed at her practiced efficiency. Five dishes at lunchtime came out in around twenty minutes. I'd like to see what she could do with Portuguese sausage and some clams!

In the afternoon, I'd rest, or ride the subway across town to take Chinese lessons with a private tutor. And in the evenings, I'd meet up with friends—Jean's schoolmates or the various people I'd met on Taiwan visits over the years. One frequent companion was Jean's cousin Vince, a six-foot-tall dental surgeon whose enthusiasm for food nearly matched my own. He'd tracked down a restaurant serving the most authentic udon noodles outside Japan's Sanuki Province, and he lavished geeky attention on his home espresso machine, rhapsodizing about different beans and roasts like a San Francisco barista.

Actually, he lavished almost as much attention on me. We went out regularly, for spicy, aromatic beef noodle soup, for *lu rou fan*, a classic Taiwanese dish of stewed ground pork over rice, or to wander the city's many night markets. And although he was generally my guide in this, his hometown, I never felt chaperoned, like a visitor, but rather embraced, unexpectedly. What had I done to earn Vince's kindness? We only saw each other once every couple of years, and yet our interactions had a surprising ease. Over coffee one day, I asked him why he'd chosen the English name Vince when his Chinese name, Yu-Wen, could so easily have become Ewan, like Ewan MacGregor. His reaction was exaggerated, a clownish facepalm; he'd never thought of it, he said, and besides, back then no one had ever heard of Ewan MacGregor. It was a small moment, a flash of light humor, but it was the kind of thing that had always been difficult with Steve—my question would have been read (and maybe intended) not as inquiry but as criticism. So, was this how brothers were supposed to get along?

At the same time, I saw in Vince a kind of sadness. Not that he was lonely, exactly—he had his own friends in Taipei, of course.

But I sensed something missing, a void only partially filled by coffee connoisseurship and noodle hunting. Jean pointed out that among her generation of cousins, all of whom had grown up together, he was almost the last still living in Taiwan. He'd been applying for postgraduate fellowships in the United States, but so far had no luck. And so maybe my presence meant something to him, a new tie to the world beyond the small island, and a family tie to boot—a new peer.

The thing is, I wasn't at all sure of my place within the family, and Vince's acceptance of me was unnerving. How was I supposed to react? At one of the night markets, the great one on Raohe Street, with an elaborate temple at one end and crammed with some of my favorite vendors (ooh, that pigs'-blood-and-sticky-rice popsicle!), I finally worked up the nerve to ask Vince the question I'd been dying to ask.

We were standing on line, waiting to buy *hu jiao bing*, a wheat-flour bun stuffed with sweet ground pork and lots of black pepper and baked in what looks like an Indian tandoor. The wait was long—thirty minutes, at least—but Vince looked patient and happy as we inched forward. This, I knew, was my time.

"Vince," I said, "can I ask? What does the family think of me?"

He looked down at me quizzically, as if trying to figure out if this was nonsense or a serious question. "Well," he finally said, choosing his words with care, "you're just . . . part of the family."

Part of the family? Really? I knew what Vince meant, that I was already in, that the family had accepted me, that there was nothing more to be done, and that there would be no big moment for me. No payoff, no hugs, no quiet, emotional moment at the end of this trip, during which Jean's mother, her eyes welling up, would thank me for my effort, and Jean's father would apologize for having once considered operating on my brain to make me give up on his daughter. Vince's statement was it—the only climax I'd ever hit in Taiwan. And now there was nothing left to do but sit on the steps of the temple, watched by carved stone dragons, and eat our sweet, peppery pork buns, together.

Country cold is different from city cold. City cold, at first bracing, reminds you in minutes that you're surrounded by buildings—heated buildings, draft-proof buildings, buildings where you can remove your thick gloves and fake-furred hat and armored parka and expose your tender skin to the air. City cold is manageable, but it's rarely welcome.

Country cold invigorates. When you stride across a landscape of ice and snow, sucking frosty air into your lungs, you are in a world without recourse. This is all there is, and the layers of fabric clinging to your body and wicking away moisture are your only building now. You are alive, the cold reminds you, and you must do what you can to stay that way.

That, at least, was what went through my mind as Steve and I set off on snowshoes through the Laurentian Mountains an hour or two outside Montreal. The pork and duck and beer and wine had all been fine, but this was why I'd eaten them, to insulate and energize in preparation for a long slog across the hardpacked snow of Val-David's nineteen miles of trails.

"Unabashedly happy" was how Steve described my mood, and he was right. Out there, I felt free in a way I hadn't all week, as if the city, with all its complexities and choices, had hemmed me in. In Montreal, I'd been the travel expert, who knew how to find the best restaurants and quirkiest neighborhoods, and who could be responsible for our minute-to-minute happiness. I'd been my brother's keeper. Now there were no more choices to make—right or left, perhaps, but forward by default, deeper into the pines and drifts where our shared exertion might bond us once and for all.

For a while, we shared the trails with others. Kids cavorting around a heating hut, couples glancing at maps near walls of ice. But thirty minutes in, the crowds disappeared. Splinters littered the snow around a broad tree trunk, evidence of woodpeckers. The chirp of chickadees echoed in the white-and-gray emptiness. We marched and marched, and when we began to sweat from the effort, we shed our coats and scarves and let the fresh, frozen air rush over our skin. At a picnic table, Steve and I paused for lunch: wild boar sausage, a magnificently subtle goat cheese, fresh bread from a Val-David boulangerie, and, most important of all, a bottle of good Québécois apple cider. It had taken a while to find the cider; we'd bought it the night before after a long quest that had led us through several small towns in the Laurentians, where a liquor store with a decent selection was surprisingly difficult to find. It had been puzzling—this kind of cider was a specialty, so shouldn't it be everywhere? And finally, we'd found a big wine shop, and I'd selected this bottle, and now here we were at last, the Gross brothers, with our typical feast and a fine drink to cap it with. I swigged from the bottle. Fruity but dry, with hard and tiny bubbles. Perfect.

I handed it to Steve, and he sipped politely, but that was it. It's all yours, he said. I don't really like cider.

The fury that welled up in me at that moment was nearly impossible to contain. Why? Why couldn't you have said something last night? What's wrong with you? I must have begun to sputter angrily, and an image flashed through my head—the cider bottle upended, the liquor cascading like orange soda over Steve's head—but I managed to control myself. I drank another swig and asked myself: What's wrong with *you*? Here Steve and I had the cold and the quiet and the trees and each other—and a nice picnic spread—and I could enjoy none of them, but only because I wouldn't let myself. Or rather, because I so desperately cared about how Steve felt, and what he was enjoying, and how, we were trapped. He didn't want or need such attention, and I resented feeling compelled to give it.

And so, with a deep breath of cold air and a supreme effort of will (and maybe another glug or three of cider), I changed my mind.

No longer would I care—this world was too beautiful for such pettiness—and by not caring, I'd show how much I cared.

We packed up and marched on through the woods, and I didn't care. I felt light. When Steve came across a couple with three dogs, and cooed like a schoolgirl, I let him. When he spoke French to the couple, who were clearly Anglophones, I said nothing and smiled. If he was happy, I could be, too.

We marched on, and our snowshoes crunched out a rhythm I suddenly recognized. It was a Paul Simon song from *Graceland,* the album our parents had played incessantly on road trips for years. I pointed this out to Steve, and we sang together in the quiet woods:

> *I know what I know*
> *I'll sing what I said*
> *We come and we go*
> *That's a thing that I keep*
> *In the back of my head.*

The Tropic of Cancer neatly bisects the island of Taiwan. Above it stretches a dense urban fabric—the ports, factories, homes, and businesses of Taichung and Taipei. Below it, by coincidence, the island starts to feel truly tropical, the air warm and damp, the mountains and ocean close at hand.

This part of Taiwan is not just scenic—it's where Jean's mother's family originated, generations ago, and as we drove through the region we paid visits to the relatives who still lived here. One served us bell fruit and papaya harvested from his own trees. In another village, a small side road led us to a vast mansion on a manicured lawn, the home of another, extraordinarily distant cousin, the former director-general of the Investigation Bureau of the Ministry of Justice, under Taiwan's ex-president Chen Shui-bian; like Chen, the cousin was in prison on corruption charges. Still, we walked across the neatly trimmed grass and peeked in the windows with a proprietary air. We could do this—we were family, weren't we?

In a third village, we stopped at a temple run by the Dai clan, another precursor of Jean's family. The temple was tight and unadorned, more like a two-room schoolhouse than a proper temple, and as Jean's family chatted with a caretaker, I flipped through the Dai Family Annual, a catalog (in Chinese and English) of relatives around the world, with photos and updates and contact information. These were, I realized, my relatives, too, and the enormity of the connection was overwhelming. The Gross family was tiny: I had no aunts, one childless uncle, no living grandparents, no close cousins, no bushy tree extending through the generations. Mom and Dad and Steve and Nell and I were it, and though Uncle Gary and the wives and boyfriends fleshed us out a little, the Grosses were but a tiny band.

No longer. There was, I knew, a bigger world I was now part of, and in my travels I might one day come across a Dai or Liu or Chen who could trace his or her lineage to that southern Taiwanese village as well, or back to the mainland, or to Canada, or to Brooklyn. I was, as Vince had said, family—we all were.

Which was what was so maddening. Because this family's travels around southern Taiwan made no allowance for the fact that the youngest of us, Sasha, was having a terrible time—and therefore so were Jean and I. Jetlag reigned. I could barely stay awake, or I couldn't fall asleep, and I certainly couldn't enjoy myself, even though I'd wanted for years to visit the south. We seemed to be constantly on the move, and lunch and rest stops always came too late; for a toddler accustomed to eating at noon, 1:30—when she was normally well into a two-hour nap—was pure torture, especially when she hadn't had a chance to expunge her morning's supply of energy. The final day was perhaps the worst. The van trip that morning took hours and hours, and Sasha's fidgeting, a horrific mix of hunger and restlessness, threatened to boil over entirely—*bao cha*! The only thing we could do to keep her calm was feed her lollipops and hard candy until at last we reached the city of Kaohsiung, where we stretched our legs at a riverside park and watched candy-powered Sasha run a flat half-mile nonstop.

Where, I wanted to know, was the sign of our—Sasha's and my—acceptance into the family? Where was the concern for our comfort and sanity? We'd been enthusiastically welcomed back to Taiwan, but now we were being taken for granted.

Oh. Right. This was it—this was how I knew. It's when you—your personality, your history, the fact of your presence—are finally taken for granted, even ignored, that you've truly found your place in a family. When no one notices you coming and going, when they no longer feel responsible for your happiness, when they stop asking if you need a towel or whether you'd like to drink some coffee, that is when they are treating you as their own. We were family, and we were miserable, and we were the one because of the other.

And two days later, we were back in Taipei, comfortable once more in the family home. And Sasha played eagerly with her three-year-old cousin and held her grandparents' hands without fear, and random people in the street remarked on how curly Sasha's hair was and asked if we permed it (uh, no), and A-Mui cooked amazing lunches, and Jean and I got a little sleep. Not enough, never enough, but a little, and that, I guess, was enough.

One day in Montreal, Steve and I rode the Métro to the Olympic Stadium and walked a few unlovely blocks to a bland, one-story building with mirrored windows on Rue Hochelaga. This was Les Princesses, the most famous "resto-sexy" in all of Montreal. This was a topless diner. This was our destiny.

Long before I'd planned to visit Montreal, I'd heard of its topless diners: Diners! Where you could get fried eggs! Served by topless women! I'd never been a strip-club habitué, but this seemed like such a weirdly unique Montreal institution—representative of the city's working-class tastes and its Frenchified libertine pretensions—that I had to check one out. Maybe two. But no more than three. (Okay, five.)

But when I told my Montreal friend Stacey of my plans, she revealed that the English phrase "topless diner" didn't quite, uh, cover the reality. The waitresses, she said, would be completely naked, and hardcore porn would be playing on TVs around the diner. These restos-sexy were serious.

When Steve and I mustered the courage to walk through the door of Les Princesses, we were horrified. The waitresses were . . . wearing bikinis? The TVs were showing . . . local news? Was this the wrong place? We sat down, and a pretty woman with a belly-button ring took our orders: black coffee, smoked meat, french fries. It was dreadful.

A few weeks later, I would learn what happened. In December 2009, the city had brought Les Princesses to court, arguing that it was an erotic business operating in a zone where erotic businesses were forbidden. Claiming it was a restaurant (never mind the nudity and porn), Les Princesses won the case—then lost when the city appealed. Since then, Montreal's resto-sexy waitresses have worn swimsuits, which make the restos feel even more desperate and tawdry.

Still, we were disappointed. No nudity, and bad food to boot. We walked out into the cold and headed for the subway.

After a while, Steve spoke. "I know you're my big brother and all," he said, "and you wanted to introduce me to women. But is that *it*?"

And that was it—but a different it. His comment had been so perfect, so balanced between comedy and gentle criticism that I knew then things could get better—and that I would have to tell Steve a secret. Really, the Secret, one of the very, very few details of my life I'm unwilling to reveal to the general public (including you, dear reader).

But how, and when? No moment seemed right—I certainly couldn't say anything out here, in the blasé wasteland outside Les Princesses. So I put it off, again and again, until our final night together in Montreal was upon us. I'd booked us in to Le Club Chasse et Pêche (the Hunting and Fishing Club), a lush, cozy restaurant in the old part of the city. It seemed ideal for the exchange of intimacies: private, dark, refreshingly old-school. But from the arrival of our cocktails—Sidecar for him, Negroni for me—the meal got in the way. Oysters, bison tartare, razor clams, arctic char, seared veal— each new course filled our mouths with joy, and kept me from saying what I needed to say. Because what if I failed? What if my revelation hurt Steve, and ruined dinner? And so I held my ecstatic tongue all the way through the ice cream, and then we were stumbling out again into the cold, searching for a taxi to take us downtown to Club Soda, where I'd bought tickets to see a French-Moroccan indie-pop singer.

We were too late. As we arrived at the theater, the last round of applause was dying, and the crowd began streaming past us into the street. Steve and I shrugged. Oh well. We walked back into the subzero streets once more, looking for just the right bar, not finding just the right bar, and talking about nothing in particular.

The night, we knew, was over, and so was our Montreal adventure. We flagged down another taxi, and on the way back to the hotel, almost without realizing what I was doing, I told Steve everything: that ever since he'd betrayed me to our parents, revealing the existence of my first girlfriend almost twenty years earlier, I hadn't been able to trust him, but that now I wanted to, and thought maybe I finally could. *Betrayal?* Steve, it turned out, didn't remember any of that. And why should he? He was a kid. So was I. But, with any luck, we no longer were.

And so I told him my secret.

When I'd finished, he looked at me and started to smile. Then he said, "Okay."

~

## Chapter 8

# The Touron's Lament

### On the Differences Between
### Tourists and Travelers, and Never Quite Knowing
### Whether You're One or the Other

"Hey!" said the man who walked up to my table late one night at an outdoor rotisserie-chicken stand in a suburb of Tunis. I'd been tearing crackly skinned thighs apart with my fingers and dipping the meat into a puddle of *harissa* and olive oil, and I looked up at him with shreds of chicken still in my hand. He was in his mid-forties, neatly dressed, with a ghostly silver mustache.

"We know each other," he said. "From Saudi Arabia. Ten years ago."

I didn't know how to respond. Had I been in Saudi Arabia a decade earlier? Was this a spy's coded message? And why was he addressing me in English rather than in French? At last, I answered him with another question: "Who do you think I am?"

It was a question I might as well have asked myself. To this man—Kamel, he called himself—I was Tarek, an Englishman originally named Tom, whom he'd befriended ten years earlier in Jeddah, Saudi Arabia. And for a moment, this seemed plausible. Maybe I *was* Tarek/Tom. My time in Tunisia had been so invigorating, so confusing and rushed and scattered and enjoyable, that I no longer felt like the Matt Gross who, just a few days before, had blindly boarded a plane for the middle of North Africa's Mediterranean coast.

That Matt Gross vanished soon after landing in this metropolis of four million, depositing his bags in a locker at the Tunis train station, and plunging into the medina, the beige and white morass of high-walled alleyways, crumbling arches, pocket mosques, spontaneous markets, and hidden palaces that make up the UNESCO-approved historic heart of the city. The facts of those first medina hours were sketchy: one (or three?) cold glasses of street-corner lemonade (more common, to Matt's surprise, than orange juice); an encounter with Ali, mustachioed, snaggletoothed, and vibrantly be-shirted, who attached himself to Matt as his personal guide after discovering him at a royal mausoleum; the acquisition of a cheap rented room atop a defunct museum devoted to dusty pottery and nineteenth-century caftans and connected, in some shadowy way, with Sicily.

But what's beyond doubt is that by the afternoon, Matt had become someone else—whatever other people thought him to be. How long, strangers would ask, had he been living in Tunisia? Were his studies, a taxi driver inquired, going well? Assumptions bred assumptions—Ali the guide apparently thought Mathieu would be interested in a medina alley full of prostitutes who were, as he put it, "not very expensive to fuck"—and Mathieu was often too polite to correct them (although he did stay out of that alleyway; he'd learned *something* since Cambodia). Instead, the layers piled up, and he was everything, all at once.

No, this is all wrong. I did not become "someone else," or at least not consistently enough throughout my four days in Tunisia that it makes any narrative sense to view the experience through that thematic lens—even if Tunisia's own multiple identities are worth exploring.

Three thousand years ago, Tunisia's arid nook of the Mediterranean was populated by Berbers and Touaregs, the indigenous nomads of the Maghreb, but in 800 B.C. a ship arrived from the city of Tyr, in what is now Lebanon, bearing the Phoenician queen Elissa—a.k.a. Dido—who'd fled home after her brother, the king, killed her husband, who was also her uncle. The land she secured for her people (in a tricky real-estate deal involving a cow skin cut into slivers) became the legendary city of Carthage, a haven of civilization for hundreds of years. Until, led by the General Hannibal, Carthage took on the Roman Empire and was utterly destroyed, its earth salted, its people slaughtered and enslaved and colonized. By the fourth century A.D., Carthage still existed, but in a degraded, depraved state—a "cauldron of unholy loves," as St. Augustine described it in his *Confessions.*

Later, Arabs came, and Italians of various stripes, and then the French, and for a short time the Germans, and then the Americans and the British. And since World War II, they've all left, except for the Arab-French-Berber-Touareg-Carthaginian-descended people who now get to pick and choose which of their forbears to acknowledge.

One proud, self-identified Carthaginian was Abdelaziz Belkhodja, a novelist and amateur historian I located through A Small World and met up with my first afternoon in Tunis. Curly-haired and pink-skinned, Abdelaziz was obsessed with ancient Carthage, and as we sipped coffee at the hilltop Café des Nattes, in Sidi Bou Saïd, a seaside suburb of blue-trimmed whitewashed homes, he told me how he'd mined Carthage's legends and heroes for his thrillers, apparently earning a reputation as Tunisia's Dan *"The Da Vinci Code"* Brown. Then we climbed into his Mercedes and drove past the old Punic seaports of Carthage, now a well-to-do suburb. Carthage was Abdelaziz's passion—and probably, he said, laughing, the reason he'd never married.

That day and the next, I hung out with Abdelaziz, meeting the owners of five-star boutique hotels and former national soccer heroes, drinking wine with his friends in modernist condos, and going on lunch dates with his glamorous female friends, one of whom flirtatiously asked what I, the New Yorker, thought of *les tunisiennes*. Uh, how do you say "flummoxed" in French? (And where was my brother when I needed him?)

Okay, now this seems promising: a quirky "Carthaginian" who seems to embody modern Tunisia. Where did he lead me? What strange adventures did we get up to together? Well, problem there: After a few days, the relationship with Abdelaziz fizzled. Suddenly, he was hard to get a hold of—I'd text and get no response. I wasn't sure if he was avoiding me—was my French *that* bad? should I have said something clever about *les tunisiennes?*—or if he simply had other things to do, but without a local contact I felt untethered. I e-mailed other members of A Small World, heard nothing back. I considered CouchSurfing, but felt overwhelmed by the dozens of Tunisian members. Which of them should I contact?

At a loss, I turned to Twitter, hoping to plead for suggestions or meet new friends, but Twitter was blocked. Oh, right: Tunisia, for all its beauty and ease, was also a police state, run for twenty-seven years by President Zine El Abidine Ben Ali, whose face gazed down from billboards all over Tunis.

"I bet his hair hasn't grown a bit grayer over the years," I'd said to Abdelaziz as we drove past one.

"On the contrary," he said, "it's gotten blacker!"

So, politics? If only I'd known that within six months, a vegetable seller in a small Tunisian town would set himself on fire, kicking off the region-wide revolutions (and quasi-revolutions) that became the Arab Spring, I'd have delved deeper, sought out persecuted bloggers, uncovered the nasty, honest underbelly of this vacation paradise. I'd have had something serious to discuss with Abdelaziz, who in postrevolutionary Tunisia became the head of the country's Republican Party, which was less about American-style antifederalism than about secularism and the free market. On one of our lunch dates, he and

his blond friend had counted women in headscarves on the street—
only three, but that was too many for him, and a marked change,
he said, from a few years earlier.

But with only four days here, how deep could I get into Tunisia's
complicated politics? *Afar* magazine had assigned me just one thousand words for this story—hardly enough space to describe the setting
and craft a couple of meaningful scenes, let alone discuss the plight
of Tunisia's working classes in a sagging economy, the suppression
and potential rise of Islamist factions, and the dicey position of any
nominally secular state in the greater Middle East, especially if I
couldn't always get Abdelaziz, my most politically involved contact,
to meet up with me.

Depth of any kind felt out of my reach. With no proper assignment, I felt unfocused and unsettled—in part because I was quite
literally unsettled. After spending my first night at the weird ex-
museum in Tunis proper, I'd moved to a cute little hotel in Sidi Bou
Saïd, the Bou Fares, which meant that if I wanted to go anywhere
outside the village I needed to hail a taxi or wait for the commuter
train. And I did this a lot—there always seemed to be somewhere
else I needed to be, the Carthage National Museum, or a restaurant
serving lamb's head in the Tunis medina, or an interior design boutique in another suburb.

There were pleasures in this, of course. The conversations with
taxi drivers were amusing. One was terribly disappointed when I
told him I did most of the cooking back home—a woman's job, he
said, insisting I marry a Muslim woman, or maybe four of them,
one to cook, another to keep house, another to be pregnant, and the
last to sleep with until she gets pregnant, after which they'd all rotate
duties.

"How many wives do you have?" I asked.

None, he said, then added: "All the women of Tunisia are my
wives! Except my mother and my sister. But all the rest are my
whores!"

I loved it, this weird interlude on the road from Tunis to Sidi Bou Saïd. But it was, I told myself, only an interlude—it didn't matter, it didn't count, certainly not compared with what would happen once I stepped out of the cab. Perhaps, I often wondered, I should instead have made a beeline for the desert—to have sought out Luke Skywalker's old home near Tataouine. That at least would have given me some narrative structure on which to hang my observations of Tunisian life. But here in transit—and I always seemed to be in transit—I was merely skimming the surface of things. How could I shape these random moments into a story that made sense to my editors, my readers, and myself? And if I couldn't, well, then I was nothing more than a goddamn tourist.

As far back as I can remember, I've always hated tourists. As a teenager in Williamsburg, Virginia, I saw them everywhere—driving slowly on the Colonial Parkway, wandering in poorly dressed packs up Duke of Gloucester Street (Dog Street, to us locals). They were omnipresent, always in my way, stupid as hell. We called them "tourons," a portmanteau of "tourist" and "moron." We hated them most of all because we depended on them. The town ran on tourism—Colonial Williamsburg, Busch Gardens, and Water Country USA. Tourists slept in Williamsburg's hotels and ate at Williamsburg's restaurants, from Taco Bell to Mama Steve's Pancake House to fancy-pants joints like the Trellis.

And because the town ran on tourism, the town (it seemed to us) ignored its own residents. To be a Williamsburg teenager—a teenager with time on his hands—in the 1980s and early 1990s was to be bored, and to be bored of being bored. Where could we go? What could we do? There were no coffee shops, no central parks, no teen centers, no video arcades—nothing that might suggest to the youth of the town that they were wanted in any kind of public space. Sure, we had the library and, eventually, a twenty-four-hour Denny's.

But often we'd set up camp in the little alley off Dog Street, near the Williamsburg Theater (okay, we had an art-house cinema, too), and sneer at the tourons who obliviously passed us by. What else could we do? The money they spent trickled down, in obvious and not-so-obvious ways, into the hands of our parents. Without them, there'd be no us. And so we hated them even more.

Within a few years, however, I had landed in Vietnam—on a tourist visa. Yeesh. This could not stand. I was not a tourist. I was here to go deep and long, to work my way inside Vietnamese culture, to understand and adapt and prove that I was more than just an over-flowing wallet from abroad. How I would accomplish this I didn't know, but as I surveyed the neighborhood I'd wound up calling home—the messy zone centered on Pham Ngu Lao Street—I knew what I would not become: a backpacker. Sloppily dressed, itinerant, subsisting on banana pancakes and sticking to Lonely Planet–approved routes, they were almost as bad, I could sense, as the tourons of Williamsburg. And though we might very well all hang out at Apoc-alypse Now, Bodhi Tree, and the Saigon Café, it was obvious, to me at least, that we were hardly the same class of Vietnam visitor.

One afternoon at Saigon Café, however, Dave Danielson—the American who'd given me my first real teaching job in Vietnam— brought my attention to a third kind of visitor, one I hadn't been aware of at all. Sitting up straight in his plastic chair, he adopted a mock German accent: "I have a passport and a Visa card," he said, sounding more Hans und Franz than Schwarzenegger. "I'm not a tourist—I'm a *traveler*."

It was a distinction I'd hear dozens of times over the years. A traveler, that is, was no mere tourist. A traveler was smarter and sharper, more flexible and less tied to itineraries, more willing to go off the beaten path, less concerned with having the right experience and seeing the important sights, more excited about connections with locals than about acquiring souvenirs. For travelers, life was about travel. For tourists, travel was what you did on vacation.

If the traveler-tourist dichotomy had first been presented to me differently, I might have signed right on to the traveler side. It was pretty close to how I viewed myself—mostly uninterested in bagging the famous sights, eager for weird experiences, excited to meet new people, willing to put up with more than a bit of discomfort. Unlike the tourons (and even the backpackers), the other travelers and I would come to know the world in a fuller, better, more meaningful way.

But Dave's presentation eliminated the possibility that I'd ever unquestioningly self-identify as a traveler. As he made perfectly clear, travelers were a snooty bunch who considered themselves far superior to everyone else. As much as they touted their deeper, more honest travel experiences, they also engaged in constant one-upmanship, judging each other on arbitrary scales of authenticity. They were almost worse than the tourists, because at least tourists knew their place, and probably wouldn't speak to you anyway. But a traveler— a traveler would want to know where you'd been, and if you'd found the secret noodle shop or met the mad, multilingual Buddhist monk in the mountains or done ayahuasca ("*real* ayahuasca, man") in Peru, because if you hadn't, well, then you hadn't really been there at all.

Of course, my own refusal to pick sides meant I was superior to both travelers and tourists. With no model to follow, I alone could decide what kind of, uh, traveler I was, and which, you know, tourist visas I'd get stamped into my passport.

But then what kind of traveler was I to be? What exactly did I want to do, here in Vietnam and anywhere else I might go?

I didn't know, and I doubt I ever formulated the questions in such explicit terms. Instead, I was too busy trying to find work and earn money, and those efforts, more than anything else, molded my approach to travel. As a poorly paid English teacher or a hustling writer/editor, I had relatively little time to explore Vietnam. While backpackers, tourists, and travelers alike were visiting battle sites from the French and American wars, I was riding my 70cc moped to class. While they went cruising or kayaking among the dramatic limestone islands of Ha Long Bay, I was correcting hilarious typos at the *Viet Nam News*.

My life was never all work and no play. But instead of spending Sundays at the beach resorts of Vung Tau or Phan Thiet, my friends and I would head out the highway for an afternoon of ice-skating at the city's first rink, where despite the fact that it had just opened a crew of local teens was whirling and gliding like New England prep schoolers. I may have gone to the Museum of American War Crimes and to the Cu Chi Tunnels, but I made those excursions early in my stay, and as I carved out a life for myself in Ho Chi Minh City, such "touristy" attractions held less and less attraction for me. Not because they were touristy but because I had other, more important things to do.

In the fifteen years since I left Vietnam, I've often regretted this unintentional prioritizing of my own comfortable life over the serious exploration of a new country. Yes, I can tell people I lived in Vietnam for a year, but if they ask me about the rice paddies of the Mekong Delta or the coffee-producing Central Highlands, I can only shrug. If they want to know if Sapa, a northern town famous for its colorfully dressed ethnic minorities, is worth visiting, I can explain that, from what I've read and heard from knowledgeable friends, mass tourism has changed its tribal traditions into a money-making exercise in public theater—but of course, that's only what I've read and heard. I may know my way around Hanoi's ancient 36 Streets, but I've never seen Uncle Ho's embalmed corpse, on display at his mausoleum.

More tragic was my failure to learn Vietnamese. After dropping out of the class I'd enrolled in, I ceased improving almost entirely. I picked up a few things here and there, particularly curses and profanity, but four months in I was not yet able to cope with even the simplest situations in the local tongue. Not until February, when I visited Phnom Penh to cover the Southeast Asian Film Festival, did I renew my efforts to learn Vietnamese, for it was there that I saw my good friend Douglas chat easily with hotel clerks, prostitutes, and moto-taxi drivers, who'd learned the language during Vietnam's decade-long occupation of Cambodia. When we returned to Saigon, I vowed to learn as much as I could, primarily by talking to the staff at the Lucy Hotel and asking everyone I knew for guidance and instruction. I was, by July, able to understand and answer the basic questions Vietnamese ask new acquaintances: What's your name? Where are you from? How old are you? Are you married? (And do you have children?) What's your job? What's your salary?

But that was it. I could order noodles, and direct a taxi, and cheer on my pool-playing pals ("*Hai qua!*"), but I couldn't have a proper conversation with anyone, about anything. Frustratingly, my accent was often good enough that people would assume I was more capable than I was. Then they'd pause, and wait for my reaction, and I'd stare at them blankly and, shamefully, admit I didn't understand a word.

There was so much I didn't know about this country that I loved, and yet in some ways I knew it very, very well. I knew how to cross the street safely through a flood of cars and motorbikes, and I knew how to open a bank account. I knew how to make a toast ("*Trăm phần trăm!*" means 100 percent, or Bottoms up!) and I knew how to handle things when the toasting got too intense ("*Năm mười phần trăm!*" or 50 percent!). I knew where to find good French pâté and when to eat *phở*, and when I wanted to buy a copy of the *International Herald Tribune*, I knew to ask around Pham Ngu Lao for the deaf newspaper vendor who always carried an extra copy.

Most of all, I knew how to *be* in Vietnam. You could teleport me there today, to a village I've never heard of, and I will feel at home. I will recognize the smells (old coconut, burning charcoal, exhaust, jasmine, fish sauce) and the improbably melodious cacophony of honking Hondas and synth-pop music and constant construction, and I won't worry that I don't know what to do. This may be, I'll admit, a profoundly mistaken attitude to proclaim—

presumptuous, even condescending—but I'm sure I can also deal with the consequences of that mistake.

Whether I planned it or not, my Vietnam experience became the model for all my future trips. The philosophy: eh, I'll do whatever. When I visited Jean in Paris in 1998, she and I walked around, shopped for neat clothing, and talked. True, we did spend a morning at the Louvre, but my memories of that—I remember vastly preferring the Winged Victory to the *Mona Lisa*—are nothing compared to the intensity of others: exploring the street market near Grenelle, where vendors sold heaping piles of choucroute garnie and brilliantly clean-flavored olives, *lucque super*, that I've never found since; getting rudely turned away from a wild-game restaurant where we had reservations. At the Fondation Cartier, we saw a marvelous exhibition showcasing the avant-garde work of Issey Miyake, the Japanese fashion designer, and in the museum bookstore I found portfolios by the Malian photographers Malick Sidibé and Seydou Keïta, who'd documented their country's ebullient postindependence era, and I was struck by how casually all these forces and nationalities intersected and overlapped: America, France, Japan, Taiwan, Mali; art, fashion, photography, romance. That night, I believe, we accidentally locked ourselves out of Jean's apartment and had to check into a cheap hotel down the street, and although it meant I would miss my flight the next day, I was ecstatic. Eiffel Tower? Panthéon? Pompidou? Why bother when real adventures were to be had!

I was, proudly, a bad tourist. I went to Bangkok two or three times before, at the behest of a friend of a friend, I visited the magnificent Royal Palace. (Haven't been back.) Two or three trips to Rome before I saw the Colosseum. (Incredible!) In Mexico City, Jean and I never even tried to figure out what you're supposed to see in Mexico City. Instead, we busied ourselves with a daylong exploration of the Mercado Central, which is surely on the list of things to see, but the point is we went there because *we* wanted to—we wanted to see the piles of dried chiles and sample tacos stuffed with braised bulls' balls. At least, that's what I assumed was in them, given the vendors' unrestrained amusement at Jean's hearty chomping.

There were times, of course, when proper sightseeing was inescapable. On my first trip to India, for a wedding in 2003, my friend Sandra and I stayed in New Delhi with her friend's family, in a big house next door to the Saudi Arabian embassy. It was December, and Delhi was chilly, misty, grungy, and a bit boring, and since Sandra and I had several days to kill before the multiday wedding began, we decided to explore. Luckily—sort of—the father of our host family owned a tour company (also, the exclusive rights to import Cuban cigars). All we had to do was show up, and a trip was mapped out for us. We would drive through Rajasthan, go on a tiger safari, and finally see the Taj Mahal.

Rajasthan, the arid but colorful state southwest of Delhi, was fine. Mostly, I remember visiting a lot of forts. Impressive, old, fascinating forts. Forts that seemed to mean a lot to the guides who wanted to take us to one after another after another. But had I not gone to a single fort, I know now I would not have missed them. Even though, as I said, they were just fine.

The tiger safari, however, had me and Sandra much more excited. Tigers! Early one morning, we clambered into the open back of a jeep along with twenty other tourists, a mix of Indians and Brits, and sped into Ranthambore National Park. Down the bumpy hard-packed roads we went, our guides warning us not to get our hopes up too high. With just twenty-six tigers living in 150 square miles of jungle, they couldn't guarantee a sighting. But look, there was a deer! And over there—a colorful bird!

Around this time, a British man with a drooping face, grayish complexion, and unfashionably thick glasses began to grumble quietly to himself. About the crowding here in the Jeep, about the difficulty in seeing anything the guides were pointing out, about the cold weather. Sandra and I began to speculate about him: Why was he here at all, and alone? He looked to be in his mid-fifties, and we concluded he was either a widower or divorced, and his friends back home, in an effort to cheer him up, had convinced him to take this trip to far-off India, whose exotic action would make his life vibrant again. It didn't seem to be working.

Suddenly, the Jeep slowed to a stop. Beyond a thin line of trees to our left, a vast field dotted with ponds and streams. A guide pointed into the field, and there, in the middle of it, almost hidden in the deep grasses, was a tiger! A real tiger. We held our breath. The tiger got up. It walked, lazily, as tigers do, across the field. All were silent, motionless, awestruck—except for the Brit, who muttered about how he couldn't actually see the tiger. And once he could, once he'd fixed on its position, once he'd watched it saunter majestically out of the woods and into the road two hundred yards ahead of us, he announced, in a clearer voice than before, "It's like watching paint dry."

Then the tiger disappeared into the thicker woods on the other side of the road.

It was about 10 a.m., and our guides and drivers, formerly worried we might not see a tiger, had a new problem. We'd seen a tiger, yes, but we still had four hours left on the tour, and if we were going to be honest about things, there wasn't much else to see in Ranthambore National Park except tigers. Deer and colorful birds are fine, but after you've seen a tiger, they're like Cheerios to a child who's tasted Froot Loops.

And so, with four hours to go, miles and miles of road to cover, and nothing left to see, the driver stepped on the gas. And so, for four hours, through miles and miles of forest, Sandra and I and the sad Brit and everyone else huddled in the back of the Jeep, suffering through hard incessant jouncing, shivering in the wind chill. A kind Indian woman loaned the sad Brit her silk scarf, and he'd draped it over his head and shoulders to keep warm; he looked suicidal.

Near the end of this unpleasant voyage, the Jeep pulled to a stop so that we could, incredibly, gaze upon a *second* tiger as it loped in the distance. And then, when it had gone, the Jeep zipped back to the park's entrance, and we achingly returned to our hotel—a threadbare, insect-ridden "resort" where our attempts at sleep were interrupted by the rumble of trucks on an unseen highway, like dinosaurs lowing in the distance.

Early the next morning, Sandra and I fled. We'd been scheduled for another tiger safari (in case we hadn't spotted one the first day), but that did not seem advisable. Instead we rushed to the train station, where we admired the "Rogus [*sic*] Gallery," a wall decorated with photos of known thieves and pickpockets, then turned around to watch an organized gang of monkeys rob a passerby of his bag of mangoes. At last we boarded the third-class train that would deposit us somewhere near Agra, and from there we caught a bus to the city—and the great Taj Mahal.

The Taj Mahal—built by a seventeenth-century Mughal emperor in memory of his third wife, visited by millions of awestruck visitors every year, one of the finest pieces of architecture in all of India, if not the world—is, in my humble estimation, quite symmetrical. Really, that's about all I have to say about it. The Taj Mahal is beautiful and inspiring and so on, but its perfectionism—embodied in that attention to symmetry—didn't resonate with me. I wanted flaws, I wanted quirks, I wanted a human connection. Instead, our guides emphasized its flawlessness, its precision, its holiness. To me, those attributes are boring.

What bothered me about the Taj Mahal, and much of our sightseeing in India, was the feeling of obligation that surrounded it. If you were in northern India, it felt expected, almost required, that you'd go there. Otherwise, why else would you have come to northern India, if not to see the Taj Mahal, the forts, the tigers?

Although I understood the reasoning, I still bristled at such expectations. Why should I spend my time and money on things and places I'm not interested in, especially when so many other, over-looked experiences beckon? After the Taj Mahal, Sandra and I had to figure out a way to spend the afternoon, and I had an idea. All over town, I'd seen posters—in lurid Day-Glo colors—advertising the circus. We had to go!

And we did. That night, in the company of the guides hired by our friend's father's company, we watched clowns joke in Hindi, and motorcyclists drive upside-down in mesh spheres, and poorly trained acrobats leap, tumble, and fall, then get up to do it again. After a brief moment of calm, a hippopotamus appeared from behind a curtain. Led by its trainer, it stumbled around the ring and opened its cavernous mouth, into which the trainer tossed a cabbage. Then it stumbled back behind the curtains.

Amazing! Granted, this was no Barnum & Bailey, but the circus performers were trying, with what little resources and talent they had, to put on a show, here in this city where a circus could never compete with the Taj for the public's attention. No one laughed or cheered at anything that night—not even the children in the audience. I've never understood why not. But I do know that Sandra and I cheered and laughed all the harder to make up for it, and that next time I wind up in Agra, I'm crossing my fingers the circus is in town. But that Mughal tomb? Eh. Seen one Taj, seen Mahal.

Surely, I can't be the only traveler who feels trapped, or threatened, by the necessity of sightseeing. But I at least have options—I can get myself out and go do whatever it is I feel like doing.

But not everyone realizes they can do the same thing. In 2008, Stanley Fish—one of the most renowned academics in America—published an opinion piece on the *New York Times* Web site in which he declared himself to be "a bad traveler." On recent trips to England, Ireland, and New Zealand, he explained, he'd gone to museums and abbeys and Stone Age sites and suddenly felt the weight of what he called "strategic fatigue":

Strategic fatigue sets in whenever I enter a museum (when I saw that the display case containing the Book of Kells was surrounded by other tourists I didn't have the strength to push myself forward) or when I approach an ancient site (at Clonmacnoise, the location of an ancient abbey, I retreated immediately to the coffee shop and never saw the ruin) or when the possibility of getting out of the car to enjoy a scenic view presented itself (I protested that it would take too much time, or that we needed gas, or something equally feeble).

Translation: he was bored. "I just don't care about seeing sights," he wrote.

Now that is an attitude I understand very well! But what left me perplexed about Fish's article is the question of why, if he didn't care about sightseeing, he spent all his travel time sightseeing. Why not, you know, *go do something else*—something he did care about?

If I were going to jump into the tourist-traveler debate, I'd peg this approach as the worst aspect of the classic tourist: the assumption that one travels only in order to sightsee; that there is no alternative but to accept and try vainly to enjoy what is presented; that one cannot act with independence and imagination; and finally, that one's travel life must be fundamentally different from one's home life.

Back when I was in the business of giving advice as the Frugal Traveler, I would tell readers to plan trips this way: *What do you like to do at home? Okay, now go do it somewhere else!* Whatever your hobbies are—needlepoint, running, chess, classical guitar, yo-yoing—you will find a group of like-minded enthusiasts abroad. Just Google the activity and your destination, and more often than not, you will discover them. And those people will in all likelihood be overjoyed to hear from you, a foreign devotee, and accept you into their circle. (And yes, *someone* will speak English.) And when you're all finished jogging up the waterfront or rocking the cradle, they will probably invite you out for a meal or a drink or to see some other aspect of their cities and towns that you couldn't have imagined. And then you will have a very good time indeed. Professor Fish, you will not be bored!

During my Frugal Traveler stint (and even afterward), I spent an awful lot of time wondering: what do people actually like to do when they travel? I knew what I liked, and that was fine, but since I was writing these stories for a much broader audience, I felt compelled to do more than just wander and sit around and eat and talk to people. But what else was there? Okay, a museum. Fine, a play. Some famous thing that everybody always goes to—why not?

The great thing about doing this as the Frugal Traveler was that many of the most noted attractions were beyond my budget, so I could guiltlessly write them out of the story. But I could also twist my themes to avoid them. The first time I went to Rome, for example, I quoted Mark Twain in *Innocents Abroad*:

> What is there in Rome for me to see that others have not seen before me? What is there for me to touch that others have not touched? What is there for me to feel, to learn, to hear, to know, that shall thrill me before it pass to others? What can I discover? Nothing. Nothing whatsoever.

If Twain could find nothing whatsoever to discover in the classic sights of Rome, why should I, the Frugal Traveler, even try? Instead, I wouldn't. "If I missed something big," I wrote, "well, I could always come back in a year or ten. There's a reason they call it the Eternal City." And so I based myself in Trastevere, the once-unfashionable district on the wrong side of the Tiber River, and ate at ramshackle trattorias and met people who remain good friends to this day and never gave a thought to all the great big famous things I was missing.

Money saved by not visiting the Colosseum or the Forum: €25.50. Finding literary justification for my personal predilections: priceless.

So maybe that's what really separates the so-called traveler from the stereotypical tourist—the former's sense of being unbound by expectation. Travelers go where they want because they want to, and do what they want simply because they like to. (Although we mustn't forget that they, too, are bound, by other, less obvious forces.) And so, for temporary rhetorical purposes, I suppose that's how I have to identify myself. Why else would I go to some of the places I've been?

Take Pailin, a small Cambodian province on the western border with Thailand. If you've heard of it, it's likely because for nearly twenty years it was the home base of the Khmer Rouge. Forced from power by the Vietnamese in 1979, Pol Pot, his associates, and their soldiers retreated to Pailin's jungle-covered hills, where, in desperate need of cash, they began cutting down valuable hardwood trees and mining the earth for rubies and other precious stones. That was about all I knew of Pailin when, in 2003, I decided it would make a good setting for *The Jungle Always Wins*. What did it look like in the 1950s? Who lived there? How did it operate? It didn't matter. I'd write the scenes first, then, when I had the opportunity, I'd find out firsthand.

In the spring of 2005, I found out firsthand. My forays into Cambodia's National Archives had been surprisingly successful—emphasis on surprisingly. As I read dusty, disintegrating newspapers and reports from the French colonial Resident in Pailin, I learned that the Cambodians living in Pailin were not actually primarily, you know, *Cambodian*. Instead, they were Burmese, brought to the region, it appeared, by a Thai-British mining concern to excavate rubies at the end of the nineteenth century. This would require some rewriting of the novel, but that was the point—this was what I'd come here to learn.

What I didn't find in the archives was information about what life was like in Pailin. I'd imagined something along the lines of an actual town, organized somehow, with residents trying to create lives for themselves and their children—a very American sort of place, I now understand. But I barely even had a sense of the layout of Pailin, let alone what sort of legal and social forces governed it. I had to get out there.

Getting out there was a schlep. From Phnom Penh, I took a bus several hours to Battambang, a medium-size town about fifty miles east of Pailin. For that final leg, however, I had to squeeze into a taxi—technically, an aged Toyota Camry—along with seven other people and endure a three-hour journey across roads so wrecked and rutted they barely qualified as roads at all. Not comfortable, but I guess I'd suffered worse.

As we neared Pailin, I noticed a shift in the landscape. The dense jungle that had covered the hills thinned, then disappeared; the slopes appeared naked and gray, almost alien—the result of decades of indiscriminate logging. When the taxi deposited me in the center of Pailin, my mood collapsed even further. I'd been in Cambodia long enough to know that urban planning was lacking in most towns, but even so Pailin was a shithole. Damp, muddy, broken-down, with a haphazard market in the middle and hastily assembled concrete buildings surrounding them. I checked in to the Pailin Ruby Guest House, a four-story yellowish hulk described today in an online review as "your only reasonable downtown option."

Somehow, I had arranged a guide for my visit, and that afternoon he took me around. First, he brought me to a mine—which was, again, not as I'd pictured the ruby mines of Pailin. No huge tunnel descending into the darkness, no signs of heavy industry. Basically, it looked as if some guys with a Home Depot account had rented a personal backhoe, bought a case of beer, and gone to town on the backyard—every weekend for thirty years. They would dig deep into the red earth, spray the soil with gallons of water, and then an enormous, rickety machine would suck up this slurry and sort the solid pieces, which were hand-inspected for possible gems. The owners of this particular mine hadn't found much, my guide told me, and many people worried that Pailin might have run out of stones.

As the guide took me around Pailin, I began to notice holes everywhere—in empty lots, patches of farmland, across the naked hills. Wherever there was open space, there was a hole—a crater—as if every square inch of land had been bombed. The ground beneath my feet began to feel unstable, and the prospect of sticking around Pailin for another couple of days unappealing. The guide had introduced me to a woman who claimed to be from one of the last Burmese-descended families—the Cambodians refer to them as the Kula people—and I'd wanted to learn more of their history, but when I woke up early the next morning, I decided I couldn't take it anymore. Pailin was too depressing, too awful to bear. What more could I do here? What was the point of this visit? Trying to see the Pailin of sixty years ago in the raped-and-strafed hellscape of today was impossible, insane, nauseating. I paid my hotel bill, hailed a motorbike taxi, and rode it to the Thai border—down a road as smooth and flat as any in the West, past a shiny, well-maintained casino— where I texted my guide to say I wouldn't need him again after all.

For years, Pailin served as a personal defeat, but a humorous one. Here, at last, was a place even I couldn't stand—the town where I discovered the limits of my tolerance for grittiness, poverty, and discomfort. But underneath that joke lay a worrisome fact: I had gazed into the abyss—and blinked. What did it say about me as a traveler if I couldn't handle Pailin, which despite its ugliness was not particularly dangerous or threatening?

In 2007, while driving across America, I got a chance to relive my Pailin experience. I had just passed through the Black Hills of South Dakota—on washboarded logging roads and pine-lined highways slick with rain—and I wanted to travel no further west. I was only about halfway through the summer, and the center of the country, not to mention the Southwest, needed to be explored.

There was another thing I needed to do, too. Although the premise of the adventure was "money-saving, high-living road trip," I had a separate principle guiding me as well. Roughly put, I wanted to

see how people live differently all across America. And as I descended
the Black Hills, I knew it was time to drive into the Pine Ridge
Indian Reservation, where diabetes, alcoholism, and despair collab-
orated to produce one of the poorest places in the entire country.

The sky was clear and the sun brilliant as I drove onto Oglala
Lakota Sioux land. In the town of Oglala, I visited a Jesuit-run school
and learned there were no banks on the reservation (and therefore
no business loans), and in the larger town of Pine Ridge I ate a terrible
"Indian taco," and I tried to make sense of what I saw. The towns
both looked rundown, with businesses in varying stages of collapse
and far too many trailer homes, but not necessarily worse than other
places I'd been, although the heat of the day perhaps made everything
look extra tired and slow.

On I drove, then, to Wounded Knee, where in 1890 the U.S.
cavalry killed three hundred Sioux they—mistakenly—believed were
plotting against the government. At a parking lot near a memorial
center, I stopped Vivian the Volvo to look at Wounded Knee Creek,
site of the massacre, and there I met J.T. Kills Crow, a local with a
broad face, round nose, and a blue towel hanging around his neck.
J.T. offered to show me around, and since the memorial center was
closed and I had no other plans, I agreed. For thirty minutes, we
walked through the tall grasses, and J.T. gave a convoluted explanation of the attacks, jumping back and forth so freely from the 1890
massacre to the 1973 battle between federal agents and members of
the American Indian Movement, that I didn't quite understand him
when he said he'd seen a dead body at the age of seven. More bodies,
he said, lay under the earth, hidden by slabs of rock, undiscovered
because no one wanted to relive the nightmares of the past—which
in any case were ongoing.

"The government still mistreats us," he said.

J.T. and I got along well enough, I guess, that he invited me
over to his house, a bungalow that, unlike many of its neighbors in
the little neighborhood cluster, was neither covered with graffiti

nor surrounded by chicken wire. For most of the afternoon, we sat on his stoop, drinking beer from plastic cups (officially, the reservation is dry) and watching life go by. Friends popped over to ask for money—usually for medicine or gas—and when they left, it was often in cars that seemed destined for the junkyard. "Indian cars," J.T. called them with a laugh. Myanmar, I thought, had better vehicles.

Across the way, a neighbor and his wife emerged from their house and got into their car—which, J.T. noted, didn't have a fan belt. Wherever they were going, they'd drive till the car overheated, stop to let it cool down, then carry on.

Almost as an afterthought, he added, "And he doesn't have any kidneys either!"

That was life in Wounded Knee: no money, no fan belt, no kidneys.

As the day waned, J.T. offered to let me pitch my tent in his yard, and to thank him I suggested we go into town and grab some pizzas for dinner. On the drive in, I noticed J.T. still had his cup of beer with him, and he warned me to be careful whenever we passed a police car. I could tell something was off, but not what, and after getting the pizzas we drove just over the Nebraska state line to a liquor store. Two cases of Hurricane malt liquor set me back $42 and had some interior alarm bells flashing, but with J.T. guiding me, everything seemed so normal—he did this all the time, right?—that I didn't quite understand that by bringing back the booze (which J.T. covered with a blanket) I was not only breaking reservation law but enabling a guy who later happened to mention he was an alcoholic.

In retrospect, on paper, it looks awful: I showed up in one of the poorest, saddest towns in American and helped an alcoholic Indian smuggle in booze. But on the ground, it was harder to see things in such harsh, statistical light. At the time, J.T. was the stranger who'd welcomed me into his home, whose life I was trying to understand, not influence. And J.T., far from embodying the clichés of contemporary Indian life, was a complicated figure, not a lifelong loser. He'd lived off the reservation, working as a foreman in Denver, and though he was now an out-of-work alcoholic, he'd once been a police officer himself. Likewise, his son, though overweight and with high blood pressure, had lived for a year in Sweden, of all places. This family was not just a statistic.

That night, as we ate the pizza—slathered with Sriracha sauce, which I introduced to the family—we watched MTV's *Laguna Beach*, whose blondes were discussing Mercedes SUVs. The ironies were palpable, but they weren't the whole story either. Those blondes were human beings, too. Then I went outside to my tent and crawled into my sleeping bag. Outside I could hear J.T. and his friends drinking Hurricanes through the night.

When I woke up, I was alone, and the dawn was breaking over the prairie. Pale light coasted up the sky; a breeze filtered through the grasses. The corpse of a Pontiac stood in for the bulk of a dozing bison. Inside the house was my bottle of Sriracha, and I left it there—a gift for J.T.'s family—and quietly rolled up my tent. I'd been carrying a pack of Cuban cigarillos I'd bought in Turkey, and I crushed one, letting the tobacco leaves fall to the ground—a Lakota tradition, J.T. had told me.

Then I got in my Volvo and drove away.

An hour later, as I crossed into the Badlands, my cell phone rang. It was J.T., politely asking if I could send him $25 by Western Union for gas money.

"Sorry," I told him, "I wish I could."

Again, I knew, I was fleeing—but from what, exactly? What was I supposed to do for J.T.? Support him? Save him? Had the mistakes I'd made at Wounded Knee been predictable, or avoidable? I had wanted to go deep in my travels, and my wish had been granted, and I hadn't known what to do at all—how to act with grace and responsibility.

Guilt overwhelmed me, and I thought, for neither the first nor last time, of driving Vivian off the road into the menacing rocks of the Badlands. But guilt is the ultimate province of the thinking traveler. As a citizen of a wealthy, mostly functional country, you can't see what goes on in the poorer corners, or meet people with lives truly out of their control, without in some way feeling responsible. So what do you do?

What I did was drive to Oklahoma City, where I wrote about the vibrant Vietnamese community and, in particular, about their restaurants. But I did not try to make any new immigrant friends to lead me into the community. I spent some time at the monument to the 1995 bombing of the federal building, but I did not attempt to plumb the depths of lingering antigovernment resentment in Oklahoma. And at the National Cowboy & Western Heritage Museum, I wrote that the exhibits only seemed to perpetuate the romantic myth of the cowboy without trying to understand that myth's role in contemporary culture—but that was as far into that subject as I was willing to go. In the next paragraph, it was back to food.

In short, I retreated to the surface. In Oklahoma, and then in the hill country of Texas, I became a tourist—by choice—and I tried simply to enjoy myself at institutions that had been created for the sole purpose of pleasure. I ate barbecue and went to naval museums and horse races, and I tried to write energetically about these experiences, because they, too, were worthy of my readers' time and attention.

Tourists, I could now better understand, were not some lesser species. Like all travelers, they had earned their right to travel as they wished, and if that meant organized tours and checklist sightseeing, who was I to tell them they were wrong? Travel did not always have to be hard or deep. It could even be easy and fun, and even I could do it, guiltlessly.

Besides, those of us who thought of ourselves as travelers were really just kidding ourselves. We might spend weeks in Pailin or Pine Ridge, but we could always leave, and once we left, we'd more than likely be forgotten. Apart from our ability to inject cash into new economies, we would not matter to the places we visited. We'd have no claim on them, and they none on us. As deep as we looked into the pools of other people's lives, we'd always be skating the surface. We were—we are—all tourists.

And that's okay, even if sometimes it's frustrating. When I now think of my trip to Tunisia, I still can't quite put together a coherent internal narrative of my time there. It doesn't gel. But the article I finally wrote for *Afar* does. And it does so by both embracing and stripping out the complicating factors.

The story begins with the taxi driver who declared, "All the women of Tunisia are my wives!" But instead of presenting it just as comedy, or as a way of showing how easy it was to talk to people, I focused as well on its clichéd quality—the way he was embodying the "stereotypically Muslim male chauvinist point of view." But was it what he really felt? Or just the role he took on around tourists, who might have expected exactly that kind of sentiment to come from a cab driver?

And in the course of describing this interaction, I began to realize that I, too, could choose a stereotype to lead myself through the story. And the one I chose was that old standby, my favorite crutch: gastro-tourist. Yes, I wrote about Tunisian food, and my pursuit of it from the shores of the Mediterranean to the depths of the medina. With Abdelaziz, the curly-haired *carthageois* counter-cliché, I ate *salade méchouia*—a platter of roasted peppers, hard-boiled eggs, olives, capers, shredded tuna, cucumbers, *harissa,* and more, all mixed together and scooped up with fresh baguettes—and feasted on grilled fish and delicate *brik.* I got in taxis and asked to be taken to the best roast chicken in town (which is how I met Kamel and became

Tom/Tarek). And one day, on my own, somewhere in the medina, I devoured half a roasted lamb's head, brains included, and discovered that hidden away at the base of the tongue, where you might never expect to find it, was the sweetest, most tender meat of all. It was, I wrote, "like Tunisia itself, so instantly and easily enjoyable that the clichés and counter-clichés fail to matter, and you must admit to yourself that some things are simply good."

∾

Chapter 9

## Jiggety-Jog

On Leaving Home, Coming Home,
and Seeking My Proper Place in the World

What had I done? It was the middle of August, I was sitting in a rented house in Truro, and I was going crazy. Just a few weeks earlier, I'd been in Ho Chi Minh City, immersed in stimulation—the arrhythmic bleat of mopeds, the aromas of charcoal and melting fat, the guileless interrogations of random Vietnamese people. I'd been living a life I'd never imagined, working as a journalist, coming home to close friends, learning how to navigate not just a new language and culture but a new world of my own making. I had a motorbike, I had air-conditioning, I had freedom and independence. What I didn't have was a professional future, and so I'd given up everything else. Roughly two weeks shy of the day I'd moved to Saigon, and just before my birthday—a birthday I could have spent surrounded by those wonderful new friends!— I'd boarded a Cathay Pacific flight bound for home via Hong Kong.

But now what had I done? Those first weeks back with my parents in Virginia were terrible. I had no car, no friends, nothing to do. This was a sensory deprivation tank, solitary confinement. And even when my family assembled for a week's vacation on the Cape, my mood did not improve, despite the sunshine, the clean air, the seafood, the peace. I was filled with hate. I hated this staid, boring place. I hated my parents for bringing me here. I hated America for not being Vietnam, and for barely even having Vietnamese food. I hated the prospect of spending the next nine months in Baltimore, a city I hated. And I hated myself for having made the decisions—on my own, independently—that led me to this position.

Without telling anyone, I walked out the front door and down the road to the center of south Truro. My brown leather boots clomping on the pavement, I marched past the overpriced grocery store and turned left onto the road that led underneath the highway. On I walked for I don't know how long, stewing as I went. The worst part was that I knew this fury and frustration were simple reverse culture shock, the awkward and painful re-familiarization process that many long-term travelers go through. I was a textbook case: Friends and family wanted to hear about my travels, but they couldn't really understand (it seemed) what it was like for me over there; I felt like I had no place or purpose here; and I worried that expressing my disappointment would make me seem whiny and ungrateful. I'd had this amazing experience—why couldn't that be enough?

I turned off the main road to the beach, and soon the cute shingled houses vanished, and I was in a more densely wooded area with few cars. No one was walking to the beach. No one knew where I was. I was alone. I kept going and going, and I didn't know where this would end. It didn't matter. With every step, my mind calmed. This was what I needed—this relentless momentum, the sense that I was going *somewhere*, even if I didn't know my final destination. Birds chirped and black flies buzzed my head. Sand flecked the edge of the road. Onward, the sweat beaded on my lower back. I wasn't deluded enough to imagine myself an explorer here, as if that could compensate for my stupid choices. I simply craved movement.

Midway up a hill that I would later learn led to the eminently swimmable Great Pond, I stopped. I'd come far enough. The anger had been dealt with. My family might start to wonder where I was, and I didn't want them to worry. I turned around. It was time to go home.

Everybody wants to go home. Everybody always has. From the Israelites and Odysseus to every ethnic, political, and religious group today, humans have been searching and fighting for the one place where they can finally settle down, where they belong—the place that is theirs, and theirs alone. Even modern-day nomadic communities are not true wanderers. Their homes simply span a broader swathe of earth, and their journeys are determined by regular, often seasonal constraints. No desert bedouin treks into the boreal forest or midwestern plains. Most people know where they come from, and where they hope to be.

Not me. Early on in my adult life—after I'd been asked, one too many times, "Where are you from?"—I consciously gave up on the concept of home. It was a question that maddened me. Was I from Massachusetts, and if so Concord or Amherst, and if not, then Brighton or Williamsburg or Baltimore (none of which I was ever going back to)? "Where are you from?" As casually as it was intended, it left me open-mouthed, my brain working frantically to come up with a brief but accurate answer.

And the answer was that it didn't matter. Other people, I knew, had grown up under even more itinerant circumstances—in military or diplomatic families, for instance—but even so, I'd moved enough. "You people," my mother's mother, Grandma Rosalie, whose Plymouth Acclaim I would one day inherit, said after another of my family's relocations. "You're like Gypsies!"

So, fine, we were Gypsies. I was a Gypsy. I would move and move and move, knowing who I was but not necessarily where I was from, and I would never pin my identity and my future on some fantastical, unrealizable idea of home. It would be easier this way, I thought, although I'd probably sound pretentious when I answered "nowhere" to "Where are you from?" I would simply be where I happened to be, for as long as fate decreed. "Home for now" would be the closest I ever got to "Home."

I don't doubt this attitude helped me when I began traveling overseas. Despite all the lonely and awkward days in Vietnam, I never once felt homesick, never once wished I was with old friends in Baltimore or back skateboarding in the Williamsburg bowling alley ditch. I'm not even sure I ever wished I was *elsewhere*, only that my Saigon life could be better, fuller, cheerier. Had I grown nostalgic and dreamed of Baltimore, I wouldn't have lasted as long abroad as I did.

When my travel-writer traveling commenced several years later, this lack of attachment was an unquestioned strength. My trips could be lengthy—three weeks, say, or three months—and they took me away from my wife, my friends, my things. And while I certainly missed them (Jean in particular), I did not ache for them, thanks to Facebook and Skype and the ease of buying prepaid SIM cards in every new country, and I did not regret my circumstances. How could I when I was driving across the Oregon desert or sipping tea in the Himalayas? Here was where I wanted to be, wherever here was.

Sometimes, "here" happened to be a far-flung neighborhood in New York. One day in September, soon after I'd returned from my 2007 road trip across America, Jean and I were contemplating a trip to visit friends on the Upper West Side, when Jean explained that to do so she'd first need to put herself in an Upper West Side frame of mind (whatever that was). In other words, she needed to mentally prepare herself for the geographic and cultural shift. What's more, she claimed this was how most normal people behaved. I told her I'd never found such adjustments necessary—I could just go.

"There's something wrong with your brain," she said.

That may be, but whatever was wrong with my brain rendered the constant transitioning of my life a nonissue. At the end of every Frugal summer, having been away from New York for three months, I always expected that I'd never want to leave again. With disconcerting ease I'd immerse myself in the habits of home, catching up with Jean and my friends, cooking dinner, watching TV, waking up and not immediately packing my bags. This was vacation! Infinitely more relaxing than racing across continents on a tiny budget, afraid I wouldn't learn enough or have the right experiences to craft compelling stories. Here at home, no one cared whether I could put it all into sixteen-hundred words of clever context.

But then, after a few weeks of this holiday in Bizarro World, I'd find myself eager to get moving again, almost as if I were allergic to staying put. The restlessness was a slippery phenomenon. It didn't build gradually over those weeks, nor did it come on suddenly, an epiphany over a cheap beer at the Gowanus Yacht Club. It's more that I began to realize my wanderlust was always there, and had never gone away at all. I'd been ready to depart at just about the moment I arrived.

And then I'd make plans to leave.

Every part of departure pleased me. The night before, I'd decide which clothes to bring (including, of course, a pair of pants I'd never wear), and which tools and accessories (headlamp? water-purifying tablets? portable speakers?), and what to put everything in: the rolling duffel, the hefty backpack, the black leather weekend bag, the oversized tote? I enjoyed waking up early to catch 8 a.m. flights, and riding the A train or, sometimes, if the budget allowed, a car service to La Guardia or JFK. That half-hour or so of nothingness on the streets of New York—Atlantic Avenue still asleep, the BQE my own private highway—allowed me to relax and to focus my excitement on the adventure ahead. Waiting for the AirTrain at Howard Beach in winter, I'd look out on the frosted reeds and icy pond just below the tracks, and in summer I'd watch the waterfowl dip into this overlooked patch of green. I was leaving this all behind, but leaving was the only way I'd ever see it.

The uncommon joy of the departure found its parallel in the return. Early in the morning, my flight would glide over the wetlands of Jamaica Bay, the just-risen sun casting silver pools through the inlets. At midday, my flight—its landing happily delayed—might circle Manhattan, the lines and angles of its skyscrapers stark in the clear October sun. At night New York was a field of light, the streets of Brooklyn and Queens marked in dotted lines that extended to the edge of my vision; I'd search the angles of Flatbush and Atlantic and try to pick out my own dark little corner. We'd land, and I'd endure the slow-motion hassles of passport control and baggage claim, but then I'd be in a taxi—always a taxi, I'd earned that luxury—mounting the Kosciuszko Bridge, gridded gravestones below, the skyline closer than I'd ever thought home could be. In the next month, I might see them a hundred times, but never notice them once, not until I'd put ten thousand miles between us again.

Instead of being at home at home, I was at home everywhere else. The process of arriving, setting up camp, and exploring took on a rhythm that my New York life never had. In late 2009, I followed video directions on my iPhone to a spacious apartment I'd rented in Shibuya, one of Tokyo's churning epicenters of fashion, nightlife, and foot traffic. Then I drank a coffee, had a shower and a bath in the voluminous tub, and stepped outside to look for the first of what would amount to nearly thirty bowls of ramen that week. Around me rose a forest of towers, and I could communicate with almost no one, and I could read but a handful of Japanese kanji, and even then I knew only their Chinese equivalents. I'd spent a little time here before—Japan had been my first stop after the 2007 road trip—but this was still a foreign place, unfamiliar and new.

But it didn't feel foreign. As I walked down the street toward Shibuya Station, I was as relaxed as I would have been on St. Marks Place. I was exploring, and I'd always been exploring. Back when I'd lived in Manhattan's Lower East Side, I used to take the opportunity, one weekend night every month or two, to walk almost every block and just see what was going on. New hotel? Synagogue collapsed? There was no project involved—I wanted only to see and to know, and that was what I was doing now in Tokyo. And ah! Here was a ramen shop—not on my list, but I had to start somewhere. I walked in, sat at the counter, pointed to something tasty-looking on the laminated menu, and prepared myself to slurp. Wait, "prepared"? I was born ready to slurp.

And in a similar way, my Lower East Side strolls were not preparation for my trips abroad, home-based experiences I could translate into new contexts in Playas del Coco or Ouezzane. Rather, the overseas explorations came first, and the exploratory walks in New York merely recalled that foreign behavior, allowing me to exist at home (such as it was) exactly as I had abroad: with a clearly defined purpose.

That, I think, explains how comfortable I felt in countries and cities and situations seemingly designed to discomfit a traveler: I had something to do—a cultural phenomenon to understand, a money-saving strategy to test, a difficult journey to undertake, the lay of the land to mentally map. In Osaka, a city obsessed with takoyaki—battered balls of octopus slathered in mayonnaise and other sauces—I had to find the best. And in Sadec, in Vietnam's Mekong Delta, I was tracking down traces of Marguerite Duras, who'd lived (and loved) there eighty years before.

In New York, where I had permanent lodging and access to all my possessions, I had the freedom to do whatever I chose, but that freedom bred confusion and laziness. I could do anything, but what? And why? And couldn't I do that later? I'd be back here eventually, right? Naturally, there were some constraints. I had to write my articles and pitch new ones and go shopping and cook dinner and wash clothes. But those were flabby errands, infinitely delayable, inconsequential when compared with walking from Vienna to Budapest, a 160-mile trek that left my feet shredded with blisters, my back and knees buckling, my psyche in tatters. Every step was torture, and yet I couldn't give in—this was the route taken by one of my idols, the war hero, polymath, and travel writer Sir Patrick Leigh Fermor, who'd trekked from Rotterdam to Istanbul in the 1930s. Now that was a life with purpose! And I had to measure up to his example, blisters or no blisters, in cozy pensions or under starry open skies. Every morning I'd awake knowing exactly what I had to do, whether I wanted it or not: put one foot in front of the other, again and again, until I just couldn't walk any more. What might happen along the way was yet to be determined, but the structure was there, and it told me one thing only: Onward!

"Would you like to know your name?" Regina Kopilevich asked me in a courtyard café in the old town of Vilnius, Lithuania. A pile of folders and papers on the table lay before us, promising to answer, perhaps, the mystery of my family's origins. Regina, a multilingual genealogist of Russian Jewish extraction, looked at me eagerly, her blue eyes wide.

Her question was a funny one. When you grow up with a name like Gross, you never forget it—no kid at school will let you. Early on, I'd had to learn to embrace my Grossness, to understand its many meanings—large, excessive, a dozen dozen—and to shrug off insults with a yawn. "'Matt is gross'? Seriously? That's the best you can come up with?" Gross dominated my life, just as it had edged out three other, duller grandparental names: Chadys, Goldman, Miller. Gross was all that remained.

But I had, in my twenties, started to hear rumors—via my father and his father, Samuel Gross—that our name had once been different. *Grosshüt*, they said, was what it had once been, back in the old country: "big hat." I imagined an ancestor of mine who wore his big hat so often that whenever he walked down the street, people would say, "Hey! Here comes Mr. Big Hat!" Or maybe it was a reference to the wide-brimmed hats that my Orthodox Jewish ancestors wore—although why, of all the big-hat-wearing Orthodox in their community, my ancestors got the name was unclear.

This was, historically, unsurprising. Millions of immigrants to this country had their names changed on arrival, whether by accident or intentionally, by authorities or by their own assimilationist selves. But in my family, this was surprising, as we had virtually no stories at all about life in the old country. We didn't even necessarily know which country *was* the old country. Russia, they sometimes said when I asked. Or Poland. Same difference—Russia controlled that whole area, including what would become the Baltic states. It was as if our family did not exist until the great-grandparents' generation arrived on this soil.

The only story I'd ever heard about our past was that my great-great-grandfather on my mother's side had had twelve children and had died when his beard got caught in the family's mill. His son, the one who came to America, took the last name Miller.

But on my father's side, nothing. For years we didn't even know where precisely they'd originated, not until my father dug up my great-grandfather Morris Gross's World War II draft card on Ancestry.com and saw his place of birth listed as "Marijampolė, Lithuania," a town near the Polish border. All we had beyond that was this vague allusion to a former name—a name that Regina now offered to reveal to me.

I nodded. Regina opened a folder and pulled out a piece of paper, a photocopy of a form from an ancient ledger.

"Can you read that?" she asked, pointing to a word handwritten in Cyrillic.

Remembering the Cyrillic alphabet was one thing, but making out the handwriting quite another. The first letters I could kind of understand, and I tried to pronounce them. "Gross—" was how it began, but the rest was gibberish. I looked up questioningly at Regina.

"Grosmitz," she said.

I looked more closely at the Cyrillic ending: -мус, which could be pronounced -mitz or even -mütz, a kind of cap. So, my grandfather had been right! We had been Big Hats! But how had we lost our caps? And where had the name come from? And who were the Grosmützes before they became Grosses?

Dammit. I didn't want to care about this stuff, this question of origins. For thirty-five years, the Gross past had been a mystery to me, and I hadn't cared. Okay, I had cared a little, when it came time in school to make a family tree (always frustratingly short of branches), or when Jean's family had wanted to know about my background, but maybe only because my inability to describe my past revealed the ignorance I'd been trying for so long to conceal and destroy. But the great-grandparents' generation, by their silence, had achieved their aim: The family began in the New World, and only in the New World. My father had even become a historian whose first book told the story of the birth of the American Revolution in Concord, Massachusetts, and I'd grown up acutely aware that I'd been born in Concord, too. What did the doings of my ancestors in Lithuania matter to my life in New York and my travels abroad?

At the same time, I craved this knowledge out of simple, raw curiosity. Where and how did the Gross family's story begin? So when I'd begun planning a Frugal Grand Tour of Europe in the summer of 2008, I knew that I'd have to get to Lithuania and investigate. After all, wasn't genealogical travel the kind of thing that regular travelers did? They went to Ireland and saw the potato fields their great-great-great grandparents had abandoned, and they saw the ports in Senegal where their ancestors were forced aboard slave ships. My Lithuanian detour would be no different—an exploration, you could say, of other people's desires for completion, not my own.

Even the Grosmützes, Regina explained the next day in the sunlit reading room of the Lithuanian National Archives, were once someone else. For centuries, she said, Jews in the Russian Empire did not have family names—just patronymics. But sometime in the early-nineteenth century, the czar decreed that Jews, too, would have family names, and the process of naming began. As I would later learn, it wasn't necessarily a process of self-naming. Often, imperial officials would bestow epithets on their Jewish subjects, sometimes logically, sometimes cruelly, sometimes randomly. "Big Cap" felt a bit like the latter.

Regina had reserved several ledgers for us to look through—these were the records tracking births, deaths, and marriages in the Jewish community of Marijampolė throughout the nineteenth century. And there, in an entry dated February 9, 1829, the Grosmütz family's recorded history begins. A joyous day! Mowsha, son of Berko and Freyda Grosmütz, married Dobra, daughter of Berko and Sora Braskowicz. Mazel tov! On December 15 of that same year, they had a daughter, Freyda, and over the next twenty years had many more children—Abram Itzko, Berko, Gabriel, Esther, Liba, and Jankiel Judel—not all of whom survived.

"This is a sad page," Regina said as she pointed to the 1840 deaths of seven-year-old Abram Itzko and two-year-old Esther.

Sad? I guess. Personally, I was just excited to unearth any fragments of our past at all; learning that my ancestors' kids had died was, well, ancient history. But the fact that Mowsha was a tailor, and his nephew Chaim a shoemaker—those were details that resonated more strongly.

Regina and I flipped slowly through the pages, dust coating our fingers as we neared 1885 and the birth of Moshe Grosmütz, who would leave Marijampolė at the age of sixteen and arrive as Morris Gross in Bridgeport, Connecticut.

1859: Gabriel and his wife, Golda, have a son, Abram Leib.

1864: Mowsha's son Berko marries Chana Yenta Fertynsztein.

1865: Chaim has a daughter, Mera.

1874: Mowsha's wife, Dobra, dies at the age of seventy-three.

And that was it. From there on out, until well after Moshe had left the village, the ledgers were missing—as was the vital link between myself and these Grosmützes. Were these Big Caps really my ancestors? Probably—Regina said they were the only ones in Marijampolė whose surname approximated my own—but then why had Moshe left them behind?

The easy explanation was pogroms, the violent ethnic cleansing campaigns that periodically struck Jewish communities throughout Europe. But Regina, as well as histories I read later, described the beginning of the twentieth century in that part of Poland and Lithuania as relatively pogrom-free. Regina's theory was that Moshe fled to escape conscription into the Russian army, but without further research (which I couldn't yet afford) we couldn't be certain.

Where, I also wondered, had the other Grosmützes gone? The name had disappeared from the Lithuanian archives, and while a number of Grosmitzes appeared in the online databases of Holocaust victims, they were from hundreds of miles away, in Poland. Nor did the name have much Internet presence, although the existence of Grossmutz, a German village an hour north of Berlin, hinted at a possible ancestral homeland. If other members of my clan had made it to England or America, they might have become Grosses as well—and therefore unGoogleable.

For the next few days, I pondered my family's background. I walked the streets of the Old City, so well-preserved that my great-grandfather might have felt at home among them, and I inspected the Jewish museums for clues to Jewish life in Lithuania, and Regina and I trekked out to the Paneriai, the woods where almost all of Vilnius's Jews were killed during World War II, their bodies thrown into pits. While interviewing a rabbi from Chabad, the Orthodox Jewish outreach center, I even allowed him to wrap *tefillin*, leather prayer straps, around my arm and lead me in reciting Hebrew verses I half-remembered from Sunday school twenty-five years ago.

It left me cold, all of it. To be fair, it was enlightening to learn about the history of Lithuania's Jews, but why did I really care? I considered myself as much (or more) an atheist and an American as a Jew, and the cosmopolitan Jewish world presented at the museums didn't seem to have much to do with the lowly small-town shoemakers and tailors I'd descended from. The Chabad rabbi's religiosity might actually have had more to do with the lives of the Grosmützes, but Judaism as a religion had had nothing to offer me since I was eleven. I felt no spiritual connection.

What touched me in Vilnius, by contrast, were the wild strawberries growing among the trees of the Paneriai, and the fry-up of bacon, mushrooms, potatoes, and cream I ate as a hangover cure one morning. When I wasn't with Regina, I was hanging around with a friend of a friend who'd recently, for fun, gotten licensed as a tour guide and was excited to show me around his stunning city. This was a human connection, not the fading ink of the past.

Still, I had one more duty to accomplish in Lithuania. One Saturday morning, I took a train out to Marijampolė, eighty miles west. It was a nice town of fifty thousand, quiet and well-kept, and weddings were taking place at two churches. Most traces of the town's Jewish history—in 1861, apparently, more than three thousand of Marijampolė's 3,700 residents were Jews—had been eradicated. The synagogue was now a training center for teachers, and Nazis and their sympathizers had smashed all but eleven gravestones in the Jewish cemetery. A monument near the Sesupe River commemorated the 1941 murders of between seven thousand and eight thousand

Jews, mostly by Lithuanians—"among them university and high school students who volunteered for the 'job,'" according to a town history written by a former resident.

As I sat by the river on that clear-skied Sabbath, and later in the graveyard, where the surviving stones had been arranged in a circle, I tried to figure out what I was supposed to feel. Here I was, at last, in the town we Grosses had come from, where we'd cut jackets and cobbled boots, where we'd celebrated births, bar mitzvahs, and marriages among thousands of other Jews, and where thousands of likely friends and acquaintances of the Grosmütz family had been mercilessly slaughtered. But again, I didn't feel much of anything, although I desperately wanted to. It seemed inhuman to have so little reaction, but then *my* family wasn't buried here. We'd dodged that drama and wound up in Bridgeport. There was history all around me—and fascinating history, it was, too—but it was not mine to cry over. Really, I thought, I should never have given in to such a sentimental journey in the first place. What had I expected to find here in my "homeland," anyway? Was I supposed to become as religious as my ancestors, or keep kosher for a week? Was I supposed to develop ties to this country and this town that would keep me returning year after year? Was I supposed to break down in tears and weep at the tragic forces that had altered the fortunes of my people?

What had I learned anyway? That my ancestors had been rural Jews who stitched clothing and cobbled shoes—that they were not the individuals I'd hoped to discover but stereotypes, background figures, extras. And why had I traveled thousands of miles to learn any of this when I could have accumulated the same research through e-mails, Web searches, and hours spent in libraries?

This was neither the first nor the last time I'd asked myself this fundamental question about travel: why do it at all? Travel is expensive and troublesome and uncomfortable. You plan and plan and plan, and then you show up in Urumqi, in far northwestern China, and discover you can't buy a ticket for the train to Beijing for another four days. You find yourself bored to death in Frankfurt or bedridden in Kefalonia, and your clothes are infested with chiggers from that campground in northern Georgia. Or you cross half the globe in search of clues to your heritage and come away full of knowledge, empty of revelation.

Why bother? Why bother with anything but the simplest vacations, the package tours to Paris and all-inclusive Caribbean resorts? Why not spend the money to have a travel agent pin down every variable and let idiots like me do the rough and random exploring? Who needs the friendship of a thousand foreigners when the kids, the in-laws, and the high school pals (whom you don't much like anymore, but still) are clamoring for your attention at home? Why schlep to Bangkok and risk gastric distress when another reasonably good Thai place just opened around the corner? That guy on Yelp! said it's even better than the burrito joint that was there before.

Travelers (and travel writers) like myself love to harp on about the importance of travel. We decry the low rate of passport ownership in the United States—only 35 percent! only 110 million people!—and the lingering reliance on travel agents and pre-packaged trips. We can't understand why anyone would want to go on a cruise ship, except when we go and it's awesome, and we will patiently explain to you the advantages of various frequent-flier programs and which credit cards have no overseas-transactions fees. We talk and write about how our trips have changed us, made us into better, fuller human beings, enabled us to understand people whose lives we once thought beyond comprehension.

Travel is our religion, and we are its apostles, who will always tell you that travel is, without question, good. We want you to believe us, and you've probably already taken that leap of faith. For who among us believes travel is bad? No one. So now join us. (Although we've already got our own rough itineraries sketched out, so you should develop your own.) We have canonized saints both living (Paul Theroux, Jan Morris, Pico Iyer, Bill Bryson) and dead (Bruce Chatwin, Mark Twain, Jack Kerouac). And we quote from our inspirational gospels without prompting:

"Travel is fatal to prejudice, bigotry, and narrow-mindedness." —Mark Twain.

"All journeys have secret destinations of which the traveler is unaware."—Martin Buber.

"Not all those who wander are lost."—J.R.R. Tolkien.

And my favorite: "The world is a book, and those who do not travel read but one page."

The quote is attributed, probably falsely, to St. Augustine, whose *Confessions* has guided my understanding of travel since I read it (or most of it) in college. The work is Augustine's spiritual autobiography, the tale of his evolution from a wanton, hedonistic professor of rhetoric in fourth-century Carthage to the upstanding Christian bishop of nearby Hippo Regius. The story's great drama, as far as I'm concerned, is Augustine's conversion to Christianity, and the reconciliation of Manicheanism and Christian dogma that allows him to fully embrace Christianity. That is, Manicheanism saw the world as torn by dual, separate, competing forces—good and evil— while Christianity claimed that all things were created by God, that God was good, and that his creations were therefore good, too. But how then, Augustine wondered, to account for evil, which clearly existed? How can a benevolent god be responsible for evil? Or as Augustine put it, "Whence is evil?"

The answer he came to, after much tortuous soul-searching, was supremely elegant: Evil does not exist. What we call evil is but a lesser form of good, for it allows us to see, appreciate, and desire good in its greater forms:

[I]n the parts of creation, some things, because they do not harmonize with others, are considered evil. Yet those same things harmonize with others and are good, and in themselves are good. And all these things which do not harmonize with each other still harmonize with the inferior part of creation which we call the earth, having its own cloudy and windy sky of like nature with itself. Far be it from me, then, to say, "These things should not be." For if I could see nothing but these, I should indeed desire something better—but still I ought to praise thee, if only for these created things.

This is, clearly, the Christian version of my own travel philosophy—that I have needed to experience the bad in order to understand the good, and that I have needed to accept all experiences on their own terms, without prejudice or expectation, for every corner of the world, every bite of food, every half-drunk Canadian wanderer has had something new and wondrous to show me.

And so when Augustine says (apocryphally) that the world is a book, and that one must travel to read its pages, I am tempted to believe him unquestioningly.

But you know what else is a book? A book.

Maybe it's a little perverse for a travel writer, one whose life and career have been built around unquenchable wanderlust, to suggest reading as an alternative to actual travel. But there's something to be said for the book (and journalism) as a vector of vicarious experience. I don't plan to walk from Rotterdam to Istanbul, so Patrick Leigh Fermor's erudite tales of his own journey suffice; I am not about to summit Everest or cross the Sahara, but I will devour the stories of those who have. And if I truly wanted to understand the history of the Jews of Lithuania, there are doubtless many, many books I could read.

What I mean is that there are limits to what we can learn through travel. Few of us are willing to devote months or years of our lives to a particular place, learning the language and customs so that we understand them more deeply than a native. And there is always someone who was there earlier, or longer, who picked up the tongue and married into the family, who paid the dues and paid them again and made the exotic land into a home—and wrote a book or a magazine article about that little-known world.

Sometimes, for me, the writing creates a world better than the real one. Bruce Chatwin's books are said to have as much fiction as fact in them, and yet when he crosses Patagonia or fries up steaks-and-eggs at a cabin in the Australian Outback, I don't care what he's invented. The words form their own world, one I've loved since Tolkien's books lured me into a self-contained realm of disparate peoples and cultures, strange logic and pervasive magic, new languages and ancient genealogies. I can't stand to read those books now, but I remember well how it felt to be *inside* them. It's the same feeling I get today from reading Zola; I don't know if his rendition of late-nineteenth-century France is unerring, but the precision of his language, the raging complexity of his characters, and the quantum-mechanical determinism of his plots together construct a place I can put my faith in. If it didn't exist that way then, it does now.

It's more than that, actually. Having now spent years turning my own journeys into written stories, I have a hard time distinguishing between the two. What I *wrote* about Turkey in 2006 is not exactly the same as what I *did* in Turkey in 2006, but the articles I produced have come to define my memories of that trip, and whatever details failed to make my first draft, or were cut by my editor, are slowly fading into unreality. In writing this book, I frequently had to refer to the published stories to see what I had done, and dig up earlier drafts to see what I'd done but forgotten. Eventually, the published stories may be all I remember. And they may be all that is important to remember. When you separate the wheat from the chaff, you sometimes wind up with a lot of chaff.

At the same time, the world itself feels to me less concrete—less real—than ever. Facts are slippery, geography pliant, data-based explanations untrustworthy. And my own memory? Did these things

really happen? Did a Cambodian midget in a tuxedo once usher me
into a lightless nightclub? Did Singaporean film producers drive me
for hours through Phnom Penh's back streets, only to emerge at a
slick, French-run lounge where bartenders set cocktails on fire? On
that early February morning, as our party barge drifted, half-lost,
through the reedy tributaries of the Saigon River, did I really spot
a black man—an African-American, I'm sure of it—watching us
with his Vietnamese family from a bamboo hut high on stilts above
the shore? These moments, so fixed for so long in my consciousness,
can't be as real as they feel. But now that they are written here, they
can't be questioned, and no amount of overseas investigation will
alter that.


E nough. I need to come clean. My argument for reading over traveling has another root, too, which is that in the past two or three
years I've wanted to travel less and less. I can't remember exactly
where or when it began—Slovakia or Ireland? before Sasha's birth
or well after?—but about a week into one of those ten- or twelve-
day trips, I suddenly wished I was back in Brooklyn. It's not that I
wasn't enjoying my schnapps-based tour of Austria or navigating
the complexities of the Greek ferry system. The trip, I knew at the
time, was invigorating and eye-opening. But I also wanted it to be
over. I sensed how everything would play out from that point forward, and could almost imagine writing the end of the article right
then, well before I'd circled back by long-delayed train to Surabaya
or sipped that last glass of genziana in the hills of Abruzzo. Why
stick around?

Back home, I talked to my editors and friends. I told them I was
slowing down, that I wanted to take fewer trips so I could write
longer stories. And I did. The summer-long adventures ceased; six
months away per year dwindled to two months, maybe less. I began
turning my memories into essays rather than features, so I wouldn't

have to leave home, and when I did leave home, I made sure it was to take a trip I really cared about: running in the highlands of Kenya, say, or eating my way through newly open Myanmar.

But something else had shifted, too. After nearly eight years of intense travel—months away, fifty or sixty countries bagged, hundreds of articles written—there were few places left I needed to go. Sure, there were many destinations I wanted, and still want, to visit: New Zealand is appealing, and Patagonia, and if Mali weren't collapsing into chaos at this moment, I'd love to take my family there and have our portrait shot by Bamako's renowned Malick Sidibé, the photographer whose work I'd discovered with Jean in Paris all those years before.

Desire, however, is not the same as need. Need is what brought me to Vietnam all those years ago, need is what dragged Vivian the Volvo twelve thousand miles in twelve weeks, need is what always helped me overcome jet lag just in time to set off, two weeks later, on another epic voyage. In a handful of years, I'd circled the globe, sampled backyard wines in a dozen backyards, met Darjeeling tea kingpins, Puerto Rican pot dealers, and hard-drinking Chinese Communist Party officials, mended my relationship with my brother, and learned three ways to spell my family's true name. I'd gone from a naïve, bumbling, unworldly adventurer to an experienced traveler who, while he continued to make the same mistakes and suffer the same consequences, was slightly more aware of what he was doing (and doing wrong), and comfortable enough in that identity that flying halfway around the world was now as easy and thoughtless as riding his bike to the butcher shop. After all that, what was left?

What was left was to stay put.

I figured this would be impossible. I figured the wanderlust would rise up in me within days, and I'd book a flight, or that some editor would suggest I visit Chile or return once more to Paris, or that, well, I'd run out of money and start pitching stories and my life would go on as it had for years, with me barely touching down in New York before I was back on the A train to JFK.

At the end of March 2012, I returned from the annual family trip to Taipei resolving to go nowhere for as long as I could hold out. I had some writing to do, a few checks coming in, and no new stories assigned, but still, I doubted this self-imposed period of stasis would last long. Surely something would intervene, and I'd fall back into my old habits.

But all those years of brief "vacations" at home had prepared me for this longer one. My days were boring—gorgeously boring! I helped Sasha get up and ready for preschool in the mornings, I drank my coffee, I went running three days a week in Prospect Park. I'd write in my office, near the Brooklyn waterfront, all day long, fielding e-mails and chatting with my officemates and complaining about the poor lunch options in the neighborhood, and then, at precisely 5:20 p.m., I'd hop on the F train or, if the weather was fine, ride my bike over the Manhattan Bridge and pick Sasha up from school. On the way back to Brooklyn, we'd stop in playgrounds so she could cavort with her little friends, and their parents and I would sometimes grab a beer, and I'd pick up affordably dry-aged steaks at the local butcher, or six pounds of chicken wings to marinate (Jamaican jerk or Thai, that was the perennial question), and I'd cook dinner and wrestle Sasha into bed, and give Jean, now pregnant again, a back massage, and we'd watch TV and read and fall asleep well before midnight. And on weekends it was just the same, with a longer run and no school, and maybe we'd ride the train to New Jersey to see friends who'd given up on the city, or we'd have other pals over for dinner.

I watched the seasons change. In April, the dogwoods on our block burst with pink flowers that, after a heavy rain in May, made an eerie glowing carpet upon the sidewalk. At the end of the month, I started scouting the mulberry tree in our neighborhood playground, squeezing and tasting the fruits and planning to harvest them for jam when they were good and ripe. I loved checking on the mulberry tree. It reminded me of Montenegro, where in 2006 my local friends, Dave and Tomas, after driving me around the countryside for hours, chanced upon an isolated grove of fruit trees. *Murva,* they said the fruits were called, or *dudinja.* I'd never seen them before: nubbed like blackberries, but white with tinges of green and pink. The riper ones tasted sweet, intensely so, while the immature ones were grassily tart. We ate a few, then took off, and I didn't see *dudinja* again—not until I noticed these fruits hanging over Sasha's playground.

As Memorial Day approached, I could wait no longer. Jean, Sasha, and I tramped out to the playground with a colander we'd found on the street and, standing on benches, plucked not-quite-ripe mulberries from between the leaves. But there, in the shade of the mulberry tree, mosquitoes thrived, and they dove at our legs and ankles, and we finally fled, with barely a pint to show for our itchy wounds. That pint wound up in our refrigerator, where I failed to remember to turn it into jam, and by the time the mulberries on the tree had fully ripened, I'd lost my will to harvest. Next year, though, I swore—next year I'll do it right!

And then it was August, and my birthday, and I barbecued a thirty-three-pound pig for a few dozen of our friends, and I realized it had been four months since I'd boarded an airplane. It didn't feel like that long, though; it could have been just last week that I was in Taiwan. Hell, I could be there next week, and today, this Saturday afternoon, would feel no different. I knew what was coming. The next morning, I'd go running around Prospect Park, and I'd spot that rail-thin, bearded speed walker I always saw—Luis Rios, a former marathoner with more than two hundred thousand miles under his belt—and maybe this time Luis would give me a little wave of recognition. We'd never spoken, and surely he'd seen a thousand runners indistinguishable from me, but it was something to hope for, a minuscule sign that my endeavor to stay put had lodged me not only firmly in my own rhythms and routines but in those of strangers. It would be proof that I existed in a way I never had before.

The next day, Luis did not wave at me.

But a few days later, he did, just a little half-gesture as I passed by, and there was eye contact, I'm sure of it. I may even have said hello.

And before long it had been six months since I'd boarded a plane or embarked on an ambitious journey. (A week's vacation in Cape Cod? An overnight in D.C.? Hardly counts as "travel," I'd say.) The only odd aspect of this interlude was how normal it felt. When I mentioned this to a running buddy, he responded, "Welcome to the rest of us!"

And he was right: This stable, sedentary life was the kind of trouble-free existence most people strive for—a life occupied with friends, family, fulfilling work, decent meals, and very little drama. I began looking for a full-time job. We even renovated the bathroom! In Augustinian terms, I had surrounded myself with greater good. I'd done so, moreover, the same way I'd done everything in my travel life—on my own (mostly), by trying not to try too hard, and letting events unroll as they happened to unroll. If the trick to traveling well, which I'd figured out slowly over all those years, was not to care so much—to let go of my anxieties over sickness, loneliness, and super-ficiality—then I suppose I'd now done just that to travel itself. I wasn't traveling, and I simply didn't mind. I could even go on like this, I realized, working at home, tending to my family, running and cooking and reading and living the perfect New York upper-middle-class life for as long as I wanted—another three months, another six, and then it would be a full year since I'd traveled. (A Gross family record?) Maybe by then I'd have that full-time job, and my vacation days would be vastly restricted, and that annual family trip to Taiwan would be the only one I could possibly take: two adults, two kids, rocketing in aluminum tubes across the planet for twenty hours at a shot, jet-lagged and cranky and regretting everything until the day we'd have to return, regretfully, to our gloriously boring lives back in Brooklyn.

And maybe then I would learn what I'd always sought to understand as a travel writer, but never quite could: what it's like to travel as a regular person, with all of a working civilian's restrictions and responsibilities. Maybe I would even write about that one day . . .

Still, I know something else is bubbling up within me—the absolute rejection of all this. Gloriously boring it may be to take my kids to school and work a stable office job, and fulfilling, too, but when I step back to look at it, I see more boredom than glory. Is this the life I want for myself and my family: steady, stable, with well-controlled twice-yearly adventures overseas? And how stable anyway? Journalism is in decline; layoffs are common. The New York City public school system is a mess—a mostly functional mess, but not the kind of mess I relish navigating. Give me a crumbling medina, an Asian megalopolis! Watching cable and eating in-season tomatoes are lovely, but that kind of life is vacation life, and vacations always come to an end. One of these days, I'll need to go "home."

To be perfectly clear, I'm not yet at the point of picking up and leaving. Indeed, I may not reach that point for months, or years. But if my homecoming experiences have taught me anything, it's that one of these days I will realize that I'm ready, and have been ready all this time, and that I can once again leave without regrets. It could happen tomorrow.

I don't yet know where the Grosses will go, though Asia—Tokyo? Saigon?—is a likely bet. In Taipei, for example, we'd have Jean's family close by. All I know is that I want to live somewhere I'll have to relearn everything: how to cross the street, how to order coffee, how to deal with people whose modes of thinking are utterly, intriguingly foreign to my own. I want to be uncomfortable, to be an outsider not just in my own mind but in the eyes of everyone who glances at my awkward, bumbling self. I want to figure it out all over again, to savor the small good moments, and I want those tiny triumphs (and inevitable failures) to mark my days, and I want them to add up, over the years and the miles, to a far, far larger victory—that of experience, memory, and language over the unstoppable decay of time.

This is not wanderlust. Travel is not something separate from the rest of my life, something I need to "get back to." For me, I've come to understand, travel and life are so intricately braided together that they cannot be teased apart. After all, it's been this way in my family since my family began, the day that sixteen-year-old Moshe Grosmütz left Marijampolė behind. Why did he leave? What was he fleeing—the poverty of the shtetl or the hovering threat of his Gentile neighbors? Had the czar's army come demanding his service, or did he bristle under the restrictions of Orthodoxy? I may never know the reality, and so in its absence I will fantasize: Moshe left because he could, because he had to, because the door was there and his legs were restless and the world called out to him in a language beyond words, offering him immeasurable riches if only he'd submit to its gravitational command: onward!

~

# Index